Rise
Above It

Rise Above It

Spiritual Development for College Students

Ray and Star Silverman

Rise Above It

Spiritual Development for College Students

Ray and Star Silverman

© 2018 by Ray and Star Silverman
Author website: www.riseaboveit.org

Printed in the United States of America
through Amazon Publishing, Seattle, Washington

Editor: Mark Pendleton
Cover and book design: Richard Morris

The authors are grateful to Jamie Bloomquist, www.JamieBloomquist.
com and Skyler Williams, www.touchthetop.com for permission to use
the photograph of Erik Weihenmayer on page 266.

Publisher's Cataloging-in-Publication Data
Silverman, Ray
Rise above it: spiritual development for college students /
Ray and Star Silverman
1st edition
     p. cm
     Includes bibliographical references and index
     Library of Congress Control Number: 2018909380
     International Standard Book Number: 978-1724524645

1   Religious ethics—Comparative studies.
2   Ten Commandments.
3   Spiritual Life.
I.   Silverman, Star.   II.   Title

Contents

You and I are children of one religion,
for the varied paths of religion are but the fingers
of the loving hand of the Supreme Being,
extended to all.

Kahlil Gibran

Introduction

Taste and see ....

Psalm 34:8

The good old college try

Imagine that you've just signed up for a semester-long course about cheese. It's called "Food Science 101: All About Cheese." You have always loved cheese, and you've developed a passion for learning more about this fascinating, delicious food. You even named your cat, "Cheddar."

The course promises to introduce you to the wide world of cheese. It will include lectures on the chemical make-up of various cheeses, advanced techniques for aging cheese, and detailed information about which kinds of cheese go best with wine, on pizza, in a hoagie, or with macaroni.

Excitedly, you sign up for the course, noticing that you've already begun to salivate. You arrive at the first class, take your seat, and listen to the initial lecture. It's about the history and development of cheese. The next several classes take you through various kinds of cheese. You learn about Swiss, Provolone, Brie, Mozzarella, Roquefort, Camembert, Feta, Monterey Jack, Gorgonzola, Cheddar (your favorite), Colby Jack, Cottage Cheese, and Cream Cheese.

As the weeks roll by, and the end of the semester is approaching, your professor is giving detailed instructions on how to prepare for the final exam. Here's what your professor says:

> *The essay question on the final exam will focus on the subtle but essential differences in the various cheeses we've studied in this course, with a focus on taste. You are to build a case for your favorite cheese, using historical, sociological, and chemical analyses. This question will count for 35% of your final exam grade. Are there any questions?*

You raise your hand and respectfully say, "Excuse me. I was wondering if we are ever going to *taste* these cheeses."

Surprised by your question, your professor pauses to reflect on what you've asked. Then, after giving your question thoughtful consideration, your professor says,

> *That's a good question. I've never really thought about it. After all, this is a university, and this course is about the <u>academic study</u> of cheese. It's not about <u>tasting</u> cheese. So we will not be tasting cheese in this course. Sorry.*

Disheartened, you thank your professor for the answer, but you secretly wish it could have been different. It has been a great course. You've learned a lot. But it would have been so much nicer if you could have tasted some cheese!

While this is a fictitious story, it's intended to illustrate a truth about academic life. If you sign up for a swimming class, you are required to get into the water and swim. If you sign up for a snowboarding course, you are expected to do some snowboarding. To receive credit for a course in creative writing, painting, dancing, acting, or singing, you must *do* something. To get credit in a mathematics course, you must solve problems; in a chemistry course you must do experiments. In a speech course, you must give speeches. Similarly, if you sign up for a course that is "all about cheese," you might guess, or even assume, that it would include some cheese *tasting*.

But what about religion? Could a course on religion not only teach you *about* religion, but also invite you to experiment with a diversity of religious practices? Could a course on religion give you a chance to "taste and see"? Or to put it another way, could there be a course that not only teaches you *about* spirituality, but also invites you to *be* spiritual? In a course like that, you would not only *study* religion; you would also have the opportunity to *try out* a variety of time-honored spiritual practices.[1]

You would, at least, have a chance to "give it the good old college try."

---

1   The groundbreaking "Spirituality in Higher Education" research project, funded by the Templeton Foundation and conducted through the UCLA Higher Education Research Institute, recommends that courses and programs like this be offered on college campuses. As the authors of the report put it, "Technical knowledge alone will not be adequate for dealing with some of society's most pressing problems: violence, poverty, crime, divorce, substance abuse, and the religious, national and ethnic conflicts that continue to plague our country and our world. At root, these are problems of the spirit, problems that call for greater self-awareness, self-understanding, equanimity, empathy, and concern for others." Alexander Astin, Helen Astin and Jennifer Lindholm, *Cultivating the Spirit: How College Can Enhance Students' Inner Lives* (San Francisco: Jossey-Bass, 2011), 8.

Making moral decisions

In 2000, when we first published *Rise Above It: Spiritual Development through the Ten Commandments*, we wanted to show how the major religions, regardless of their differences in doctrine and ritual, have the same goal: to help people rise above their lower nature so that they might awaken to something higher and nobler.[2] As it is taught in the world's oldest religion, Hinduism, "Truth is one; sages call it by various names" (Rig-Veda 1.164.46).

Written as a spiritual self-help book for the general public, our first edition of *Rise Above It* invited people to experience this kind of awakening for themselves by living in accordance with what many believe is one of the simplest, most complete summaries of universal truth—the Ten Commandments.

In Judaism, Moses declares that the Ten Commandments were "written with the finger of God" (Exodus 31:8). In Christianity, Jesus says, "If you want to enter into life, keep the commandments" (Matthew 19:17). In Islam, Muhammad decrees, "In the Tablets of the Law [the Ten Commandments], all matters are commanded and explained" (Qur'an 7:145; 2:28). The Buddha teaches his followers to abstain from murder, adultery, stealing, lying, and coveting (The Dhammapada: The Noble Eightfold Path*)*. And Krishna, the visible incarnation of the Godhead for Hindus, teaches adherents to rise above violence, theft, sexual impurity, lying, and covetous desire (Bhagavad Gita).[3]

With all of this in mind, we believed that a college course in which students *practice* the commandments—not just *learn* them—would provide a solid foundation for spiritual development. In other words, this course would not just be about learning religious ethics, or analyzing them, or debating them; it would be about applying them to your life. It would be *experiential* in nature; it would be "hands on." It would be like a painting class or a swimming class where you don't just learn about painting and swimming: you set up the easel and paint; you get into the water and swim. In this course, students wouldn't just *study* the major religions of the world; they would get to *practice* them as well!

We were especially excited about this approach because we believed that ethical and moral decisions are closely related to the level of one's spiritual development. We believed that if college students practiced self-awareness in the light of higher truth, their consciousness would gradually be raised above the promptings of their lower nature. They would then be able to make *spiritually informed decisions* about their own lives.

9

---

2   Ray and Star Silverman, *Rise Above It: Spiritual Development through the Ten Commandments* (Philadelphia and Phoenix: Touchstone Seminars, 2005).

3   The *Bhagavad Gita* is the classic text of Hinduism, including all the essential teachings of the faith. Similarly, the *Dhammapada* is the most popular and most often quoted collection of Buddha's sayings.

"Gets along well with others"

When we were in elementary school, the most important grades on our report cards were not in the traditional areas of reading, writing, and arithmetic. They were in the "non-academic" areas where the teacher checked things like, "Keeps self neat and clean," "Is careful with books and materials," "Makes good use of time," and "Follows directions." The "grades" in this area were simple checkmarks in one of two columns: "Satisfactory" or "Needs to Improve." As far as our parents were concerned, the single, most significant grade was "Gets along well with others." For them, as Emerson once said, "Character is higher than intellect."[4]

In one way or another, every one of the Ten Commandments touches on what it means to "get along well with others." If you're like many of our students, you'll find that the weekly practice of connecting the Ten Commandments to your life works well—especially the commandments that involve the universal principles of honoring parents, not murdering, not committing adultery, not stealing, not lying, and not coveting. Students tend to agree that these are valuable spiritual practices, not only because "Jehovah said so," or "Jesus said so," or "Allah said so," or "Buddha said so," or "Krishna said so," but because they comprise a rational, sensible code of human behavior. Quite simply, they are about "getting along well with others."

During the many years that we've taught this course, we've found that students intuitively understand the Golden Rule: "Do to others as you would have them do to you" (Matthew 7:12). If you don't like being lied to, don't lie. If you don't like being stolen from, don't steal. If you want to have a friend, be a friend; if you want people to respect you, respect them. It's a fundamental law of the universe. It's the key, not just to getting along well with others, but also to human happiness. That's why it's called the Golden Rule.

The willing suspension of disbelief

Although you might agree that the Golden Rule is universally applicable, and that a moral code is an important aspect of a well-functioning society, you might have questions about the idea of God or doubts about the existence of God. You are not alone. Many of our students begin this course with only a hazy, childhood idea of God as "an old man in the sky who will punish you if you're bad." Some see God as a "universal force that pervades the universe," or the "cosmic energy that is the essence of all life." Others wonder, "Does God exist at all?" And some assert, quite simply, "There is no God."

If you are unsure about God's existence, or if you're certain that God doesn't

---

4   Ralph Waldo Emerson, "The American Scholar." In *Selections from Ralph Waldo Emerson*, edited by Stephen E. Whicher (Boston: Houghton Mifflin, 1957), 72.

exist, the first few commandments could be a challenge for you. After all, they ask you to "have no other gods before me," to "not take the Lord's name in vain," and to "remember to keep the Sabbath day holy."

If this is a challenge for you, that's OK. We won't try to make you believe in God. Instead, we will invite you to engage in a "willing suspension of disbelief." This is a time-honored practice in which you allow for the possibility of something that you don't currently believe. In this case, a willing suspension of disbelief would mean that you allow for the possibility that God exists, or that there may be some kind of guiding force in the universe. Give it a try and see what happens.

One student who said he was "an atheist or maybe a Buddhist" wrote these words in his end-of-course self-assessment:

> At first I wasn't sure whether this class was for me, since I'm not religious. But the part that enticed me to stick with it was when the instructors explained to us the willingness to believe (even just temporarily) that there is a Higher Power out there who guides us all in a way.

> The least I could do was give it a shot. And so I took their advice and gave the first couple of readings a chance, and I was immediately convinced that this was not just another class on the Ten Commandments. It was much more than that. This was a class designed to help each and every one of us develop into a better person than we were the day we walked in. It turned out to be the best religion class I ever had.

He then explained how the class format, which invites students to share their actual experiences of practicing the commandments, impacted his learning:

> We took each commandment deeper than I had ever done in the past, which made it applicable to even more areas of my life. The coolest thing about the class was the open-minded atmosphere that everyone felt entering the class. We were encouraged to share our experiences, which allowed for the most effective means of spiritual growth, which is feedback from fellow students who may have new insights on a topic, or even have shared a similar experience, which I quickly learned was the case.

> It was good knowing that when I walked into class on Tuesday and Thursday, that I would be entering a room where we are not being corrected or scrutinized by a teacher; rather, we were being guided down a path that opened our eyes to the false gods (lust, greed, fear, laziness, etc.) that take away our ability to be the best people we can be. In this class we really did learn how to "Rise Above It."

11

Hearing "the voice of God"
....

If you already believe in God, or if you're willing to temporarily suspend disbelief, we invite you to do so relative to a God who is gently guiding you toward the greatest happiness possible.

For many people, one of the surest guides for their life is sacred scripture. Whether it's the *Hebrew Bible* (Judaism), the *New Testament* (Christianity), the *Qur'an* (Islam), the *Bhagavad Gita* (Hinduism), or the *Dhammapada* (Buddhism), sacred scripture has always had a distinct and special place in human history. While it must be acknowledged that a superficial understanding of sacred scripture has sometimes led to horrible atrocities being committed in the name of religion, a deeper, more spiritual understanding of scripture has fed hungry souls throughout the world with inspirational, life-giving truth for centuries.

This book, therefore, contains readings from the wisdom traditions of the major religions. Each chapter focuses on one of the Ten Commandments, with key teachings and perspectives from Judaism, Christianity, Islam, Hinduism, and Buddhism. While these religions are usually considered "The Big Five," it is not necessarily because they have the most adherents. Rather, it is because they have been considered sources of divine guidance for centuries, and because they have had a profound impact on the spiritual development of the human race.

But God guides people in other ways as well.

Thomas Merton once said that God speaks to us in three ways—through the sacred scriptures, in the silence of our thoughts, and through the voices of others.[5] In this course, you will spend a great deal of time reflecting on the sacred scriptures and how they apply to your life. But you will also spend considerable time reading the words of previous students who have taken this course, listening deeply to your classmates, and silently reflecting on their words.

Perhaps, as you read and reflect on the journal entries from previous students, deeply listen to the experiences of your classmates, and relate their stories to your life, you may—in your own way—hear "the voice of God."

---

5 Huston Smith, *The World's Religions* (New York: HarperCollins, 1986), 390.

The spiritual core of our lives

The excerpts included in this book have been selected from over 12,000 journal entries, collected over twenty years of teaching this course in college settings. These excerpts reflect the sincere efforts that our students have made to examine their lives in the light of the Ten Commandments. They've recorded their triumphs, their struggles, and even their failures. But most importantly, they've recorded what they've learned about themselves, and how they've grown along the way.

As we send this college edition of *Rise Above It* off to the press, we want to express our gratitude to the students who've given us permission to quote from their journals. Although we've changed a few plot details to protect anonymity, touched up minor grammatical errors, and delicately pruned longer journal entries, the words you will be reading are real, and the struggles are authentic. As Ralph Waldo Emerson once said about down-to-earth, honest writing, "Cut these words, and they would bleed."[6]

So here it is: *Rise Above It: Spiritual Development for College Students*. We hope that you will find spiritual nourishment in the sacred texts, the words of former students, your own practice, and the support of your classmates. May it be "food" for your soul and energy for your journey, as you go through the struggles and experience the joys of spiritual development. And may it help you, as Professor Harvey Cox says, "to look beneath the daily round of classes and seminars to see the spiritual core of what for many of us turns out to be the most unforgettable period in our lives."[7]

• ● •

---

6   Emerson *op. cit.*, 293. Emerson is writing about the language and writing style of Montaigne which he describes as "vascular and alive … a shower of bullets."

7   Email endorsement from Harvey Cox, PhD, Professor Emeritus, Harvard Divinity School, July 16, 2018.

Note

Each chapter will focus on one commandment, and will include the following four-part structure:

Part 1: An introductory story

Each chapter begins with an introductory story based on world history, famous literature, or current events. The story is intended to arouse your interest in learning more about the commandments in general, while encouraging you to see how the particular commandment highlighted in the story might apply to your life.

Part 2: The commandments in world scriptures

In this part of the chapter, you are led through a survey of the major religions, with a focus on how each religion contributes to a fuller and deeper understanding of a particular commandment. The goal is to help you see how the sacred scriptures of the various religions augment and complement each another, illuminating aspects of the commandments that might otherwise remain hidden. Many perspectives on the same truth reveal multiple facets of the same gem.

Part 3: The commandments in the lives of college students

Students who have taken this course before you have submitted weekly journal entries based on what they experienced while striving to keep a particular commandment. Each week, one of those journal entries was typed up as a longer "weekly report," submitted for grading, and shared with classmates. We refer to this section of each chapter as "journal entries."

Part 4: Suggestions for further reflection and practice

Because this is an "application" course, the chapter concludes with suggestions for further reflection and practice. These suggestions are designed to help you see how a particular commandment might apply to your life, prompt ideas for journal reflection, and give you ideas about how you might incorporate the commandments into your daily life as a college student.

"I think that one of the biggest false gods I am dealing with now is the false god of the internet."

Rise above false gods ~ identify false gods in your life.

I am the Lord your God.
You shall have no other gods before me.

Exodus 20:3, 5

Aim high

On February 11, 1973, the Viennese neurologist and psychiatrist, Dr. Viktor Frankl, spoke at Massey Hall, in Toronto, Canada. The 2,750 upholstered seats in the historic building were all taken, leaving "standing room only" for the 3000 people, mostly college students, who listened attentively. At the time, Dr. Frankl had become one of the most famous speakers in the world. His book, *Man's Search for Meaning*, had been translated into twenty-four languages, millions of copies had been sold, and it was considered one of the most important books of the century.

The main point of his lecture that evening was that people should see their lives as having deep meaning. He explained that we are not "naked apes" driven by the will for pleasure or power. Rather we are human beings, born to lead rich, meaningful lives filled with love, service, and the ability to choose the highest response possible in any given circumstance.

As an example, he shared his own story. From 1942 to 1945 he was a prisoner in four German concentration camps, including the most notorious of all—Auschwitz. During that time, everything that is normally considered valuable was taken away from him, including his parents, his pregnant wife, his occupation, and even his name (he was given a number).

He and the other prisoners were given little food, were required to do hard labor, and were forced to sleep in crowded huts on hard boards. In place of pillows they rested their heads on their mud-caked shoes. Nine people shared two blankets. He saw how despair, hopelessness and meaninglessness gradually eroded the life-force of his fellow prisoners, making them more susceptible to disease and death. As a self-defense mechanism, some prisoners resorted to apathy and emotional numbness. It was their way of coping with the horror of the situation. Others ended their lives in suicide.

There were some, however, who chose a different response. As he put it in the Massey Hall lecture, "As a survivor of the German concentration camps, I want to bear witness to the incredible and unexpected extent to which a man can brave the worst conditions man can ever face and still triumph over them."[1]

Frankl was one of those who chose to respond differently. Knowing that there was little he could do to change his *outer* world (the conditions in the concentration camp), Frankl decided to change his *inner* world. Instead of dwelling on his misery, he continued to believe that there was *meaning* in his current situation, that he could rise above his suffering, and that his experience in the concentration camps could someday serve a greater purpose.

He was not mistaken. His concentration camp experiences helped to confirm what he believed in his heart to be true about human beings: although hardship could reveal the worst in people, it could also bring out the best. Here is Frankl in his own words:

> We who lived in concentration camps can remember the men who walked through the huts comforting others, giving away their last piece of bread. They may have been few in number, but they offer sufficient proof that everything can be taken from a man but one thing: the last of the human freedoms—to choose one's attitude in any given set of circumstances, to choose one's own way. ... Even one such example is sufficient proof that man's inner strength may raise him above his outward fate.[2]

The idea that people can not only rise above their circumstances but also find a way to see meaning in every situation—even the most dire—sustained and inspired Frankl. He noticed that those who suffered the most in the concentration camps were those who gave up hope, resigning themselves to the belief that nothing could be done, that they were doomed, that life was senseless, and that everything was pointless.

Frankl chose not to look at it that way. He saw his situation not only as a challenge, but also as an opportunity. Two years after his release from Auschwitz, he wrote a small book about his experience in the concentration

---

1   Quoted by Tom Harpur, religion editor of *The Toronto Star* newspaper. "Psychiatrist links violence to philosophy of 'naked ape.'" *The Toronto Star* (February 12, 1973), 1. This information is courtesy of an email from Ashley D'Andrea, associate archivist at Massey Hall, received on November 13, 2017. The email included an attachment with a PDF containing the story from *The Toronto Star*.

2 Viktor Frankl, *Man's Search for Meaning* (New York: Washington Square Press, 1984), 86.

18

camps. In it he explains how keeping hope alive was an absolute necessity for his physical, emotional and spiritual survival. In the following example he recalls a time that he was on a forced march through the bitter cold:

> *Almost in tears from pain (I had terrible sores on my feet from wearing torn shoes), I limped a few kilometers with our long column of men from the camp to our work site. Very cold, bitter winds struck us. I kept thinking of the endless little problems of our miserable life. What would there be to eat tonight? If a piece of sausage came as extra ration, should I exchange it for a piece of bread? Should I trade my last cigarette, which was left from a bonus I received a fortnight ago, for a bowl of soup? How could I get a piece of wire to replace the fragment which served as one of my shoelaces?*

When Frankl became aware that his mind was absorbed in trivialities, he decided to lift his thoughts to higher things:

> *I became disgusted with the state of affairs which compelled me, daily and hourly, to think of only such trivial things. I forced my thoughts to turn to another subject. Suddenly I saw myself standing on the platform of a well-lit, warm and pleasant lecture room. In front of me sat an attentive audience on comfortable upholstered seats. I was giving a lecture on the psychology of the concentration camp! All that oppressed me at that moment became objective, seen and described from the remote viewpoint of science. By this method I succeeded somehow in rising above the situation, above the sufferings of the moment, and I observed them as if they were already of the past.[3]*

Upon his release from Auschwitz in 1945, he returned to Vienna where he practiced neurology and psychiatry. He also taught at the University of Vienna, and then at several American universities, rapidly becoming one the most sought-after lecturers in the world. Indeed, people would come from far and wide to hear him speak on his specialty: "the psychology of the concentration camp." Often, they would be sitting "on comfortable upholstered seats."

Frankl's vision on a cold and bitter day in Auschwitz had become a reality.

In the Massey Hall lecture, Frankl spoke about the importance of maintaining a higher "aim" in life, especially when the crosswinds of circumstance make the going difficult. After commenting on the need for an aim that is higher than "making money" or "living comfortably," he offered the following analogy:

> *I started taking flying lessons recently. You know what my flying instructor told me? If you are starting here [he goes to the blackboard and makes a mark on the left side about half way up], and you wish*

19

---

3   Ibid., 94-95.

to get here, heading east [he makes a mark on the right side of the blackboard about half way up], and you have a crosswind, you will drift, and you will land here [he makes a mark on the right side of the blackboard, towards the bottom]. So, you will have to head north of the airfield [he makes a mark on the right side of the blackboard, above the previous mark]. If you head <u>above</u> the airfield, you will land on it. But if you head here [he points <u>at</u> the airfield, you will land here [he makes a mark on the blackboard, below the airfield]

This holds also for man, I would say. If you take man as he really is, we make him worse [laughter]. But if we overestimate him [laughter and loud applause] ... and see him here, above [he points to the mark above the airfield], we promote him to what he really can be.[4]

At the time of his death in 1997, Frankl was still working on a final manuscript which would later be published as, *Man's Search for **Ultimate** Meaning* (emphasis added). It had a decidedly more religious tone. In the preface, he wrote, "There is in fact a religious sense deeply rooted in each and every man's unconscious depths."[5]

It is this "religious sense," says Frankl, that is sometimes touched during difficult times. Deprived of the false gods of materialism, reputation and comfort, prisoners either went into despair or turned to a deeper source to find meaning and hope in an otherwise bleak situation. Frankl puts it this way: "Often it is just such an exceptionally difficult external situation which gives man the opportunity to grow spiritually beyond himself ... turning life into an inner triumph."[6]

On the closing page of *Man's Search for Meaning*, Frankl again touches on the spiritual theme that is subtly apparent in all of his work. According to Frankl, neither heredity nor environment ultimately determines who we are and who we may become; instead our humanity is determined by the decisions we freely make. We can choose to bow down to the false gods of fear, anger, resentment, and self-pity. Or we can decide to aim higher and reach higher, standing tall, remaining calm, and showing unflinching faith, even in the midst of the most difficult circumstances. Frankl puts it like this:

---

4   Dr. Frankl's lecture was given on February 11, 1973. The front page of *The Toronto Star* (February 12, 1973) notes that Frankl spoke to "a standing room crowd of 3,000 at Massey Hall last night." In his book, *When Life Calls Out to Us: The Love and Lifework of Viktor and Elly Frankl* (New York: Doubleday, 2001), Haddon Klingberg notes that on that evening there was "a large audience of university students . . . mainly young people who packed the house" (p. 285). Excerpts from the lecture are contained in *When Life Calls Out to Us* (285-290). The four-minute video excerpt (quoted above) was accessed on November 11, 2017 @ www.youtube.com/watch?v=fD1512_XJEw

5   Viktor Frankl, *Man's Search for Ultimate Meaning* (Cambridge, MA: Perseus Publishing, 2000), 14.

6   *Man's Search for Meaning*, op.cit., 93.

In the concentration camps ... we watched and witnessed some of our comrades behave like swine and others like saints. Man has both potentialities within himself; which one is actualized depends on decisions but not on conditions.... After all, man is that being who invented the gas chambers at Auschwitz; however, he is also that being who entered those gas chambers upright, with the Lord's Prayer or the Shema Yisrael on his lips.[7]

• • •

Throughout this course, you will be invited to remain in touch with your Higher Nature; it is the part of you that can remain at peace, even in midst of difficult circumstances; it is the part of you that is considerate and respectful of others, regardless of how they treat you; it is the part of you that serves selflessly, without thinking about reward, honor or praise. Above all, it is the part of you where you are capable of rising above all false gods so that you can experience the blessings of being your true self.

But in order to achieve your highest potential as a human being, and become the person you were born to be, you need to make choices. That's what every commandment is about, especially the commandment that calls you to focus on the God who "brought you out of the land of Egypt, out of the house of bondage" (Exodus 20:2).

You might be thinking, *I have never been in Egypt, and I have never been in bondage.* Literally speaking, you are probably correct. Perhaps you have never been in Egypt, perhaps you have never been in prison, and perhaps you have never served as a slave. But in sacred scripture these words have a deeper meaning. They refer to a state of spiritual captivity in which you have been in bondage to false gods. These so-called "false gods" can include *obsessions* (perhaps a video game or a romantic interest), *addictions* (perhaps alcohol or nicotine), *attachments* (perhaps money or fame), and *negative emotions* (perhaps anger or self-pity).

This is just a tiny sampling of false gods. However, if you don't realize or even acknowledge that these false gods have been controlling you, you can never be free of them. In other words, you can't get out of prison until you realize you are in prison!

So, this beginning commandment is also an ideal place to begin a course on spiritual development. You begin by simply identifying those things, whether they be obsessions, addictions, attachments, or negative emotions, that draw you away from being your best self. The experience of Viktor Frankl can remind you that your life can be as trivial, empty, and enslaved as the false gods you serve, or as meaningful, deep, and free as the highest aims you seek to reach. The choice is always yours.

---

7 Ibid., 157. The *Shema Yisrael* is the most sacred Jewish Prayer. It begins with the words, "Hear" (*Shema*) "O, Israel" (*Yisrael*). The full prayer can be found in Deuteronomy 6:4.

The commandments in world scriptures

Prefatory note: Throughout history, the numbering of the commandments has been a matter of interpretation. In the Roman Catholic and Lutheran traditions, as well as in Judaism, the prohibition against the worship of "other gods, idols and graven images" is considered one commandment. However, Baptist, Methodist, Presbyterian and other Christian denominations treat "no other gods" separately from "idols and graven images."

While there are good reasons for the distinctive numbering systems, the focus of this book will be on keeping the commandments (living according to them) rather than on numbering them. Therefore, instead of referring to the commandments by number, we will be referring to them by name. For example, we will speak about "the Sabbath commandment," "the commandment against stealing," "the commandment that calls us to honor father and mother," etc. We will begin with the commandment forbidding the worship of other gods, as it appears in the major religions of the world.

Judaism (1200 BCE) [8]

In the Hebrew scriptures, the Ten Commandments begin with the words, "I am the Lord your God, who brought you out of the land of Egypt, out of the house of bondage" (Exodus 20:1-3). From this point of view, the focus on *one God who delivers you from captivity* is the first and most essential thing to be known about God.

Here's the back story: The ancient Israelites, had once been free, but when a famine in the land arose they went down to Egypt. At first, all went well, but when they became too productive, they became a threat to the new ruler of Egypt. Therefore, he issued a decree that the Israelites be made slaves. At the time that the Ten Commandments were given, they had been slaves in Egypt for 400 years (Genesis 15:13). After 400 years of slavery, God came to

---

8 These dates are not exact but are rounded off for easy memory. Here they are from oldest to most recent: Hinduism **6000 BCE**; Judaism **1200 BCE**; Buddhism **600 BCE**; Christianity **1 CE**; Islam **600 CE**. The abbreviations "BCE" and "CE" refer to "Before the Common Era" (BCE) and "Common Era" (CE). Using these abbreviations replaces "Before Christ" (BC) and "Anno Domini" (AD). While this is a loss to the Christian community, it is also a sign of respect for other world religions.

their rescue, leading them out of bondage and towards Mount Sinai, where they would receive the Ten Commandments. From that point forward, if they trusted in the Lord alone and kept his commandments, God would lead them into the Promised Land—a place of freedom. They would never be slaves again.

The important thing was to keep their focus on the One True God. No more bowing down to idols, no more worshipping the sun or the moon. All of that had to stop. Their focus was to be on the One True God, *the one who brought them out of bondage and into freedom.* And he would continue to do so as long as they continued to trust in him and keep his commandments. As it is written,

> *If you walk in my statutes and observe my commandments and do them, then I will give you your rains in their season, and the land shall yield its increase, and the trees of the field shall yield their fruit. ... And I will walk among you and will be your God, and you shall be my people. I am the Lord your God, who brought you out of the land of Egypt, that you should not be their slaves." (Leviticus 26:1;12-13)*

For forty years the ancient Israelites followed Moses through the wilderness, finally coming to the border of the Promised Land. Just before they were ready to cross over into the Promised Land, Moses called them together, read to them the Ten Commandments and said,

> *These are the commands, decrees and laws the Lord your God directed me to teach you to observe in the land you are crossing the Jordan to possess .... Hear, O, Israel and obey so that it may go well with you and that you may increase greatly in a land flowing with milk and honey.*

He then gives them the *Shema*—the prayer that has become the center of Jewish religious life for 3,000 years:

> *Hear, O Israel: The Lord your God, the Lord is one. And you shall love the Lord your God with all your heart and with all your soul and with all your might." (Deuteronomy 6:4-5)*

With these words on their lips and in their hearts, they crossed over into the Promised Land.

Christianity (CE 1)

As we have seen, in Judaism the opening commandment focuses on the worship of one God. "You shall love the Lord your God with all your heart with all your soul and *with all your might.*" When Jesus was asked, "What is the greatest commandment," he was clear that it was about the worship of the One True God. So, he said, "You shall love the Lord your God with all your heart and with all your soul and with *all your mind.*" And he added, "This is

23

the first and greatest commandment" (Matthew 22:36-38).

Jesus, who was born and raised in the Jewish tradition, knew the greatest commandment well. It is interesting, though, that he inserted the additional phrase "with all your mind." By making this slight, almost imperceptible addition, Jesus shows that you must strive "with all your mind" to love the Lord. This means that you must rise above every evil desire and false thought that enters your mind, countering with truth from God's Word. This you must do, not only with all your heart, soul and strength, but also *with all your mind*.[9]

In one story, evil desire, personified as "the devil," tempts Jesus, offering him "all the kingdoms of the world and their glory." There is only one condition: "All this I will give you," promises the devil, "if you will bow down and worship me." This, of course, is another version of the age-old lie, which goes like this: "If you follow the promptings of your lower nature ("the devil"), you will have all the material possessions you desire ("the kingdoms of the world"), and all the fame you want" ("their glory"). Jesus, however, is not fooled. He rejects the devil's alluring, yet false promise with words that bring to mind the first and greatest commandment: "Away from me, Satan! For it is written, *'You shall worship the Lord, your God, and him only shall you serve'*" (Matthew 4:8-10; emphasis added).

In Christianity, "false gods" are more than statues or graven images. They are anything that can allure you away from a life of devotion to God. Urging the people in Philippi to press on "toward the upward goal of God in Christ Jesus," the apostle Paul speaks about those who focus on earthly rather than heavenly things. Rather than "aim high," aspiring to develop their spiritual nature, they aim low. As Paul puts it, "Their end is destruction, *their god is their belly*, and they glory in their shame, with minds set on earthly things" (Philippians 3:19; emphasis added).

Islam (600 CE)

The Arabic word "Islam" means "surrender" or "submission." In the context of the religion called "Islam," it refers to the voluntary surrender to the will of God. The Arabic word "muslim" also means "surrender" or "submission," but refers specifically to someone who surrenders to the will of Allah.

In Islam, the will of Allah is revealed in the *Qur'an*, a book written through the prophet Muhammad, and considered to be a continuous recitation given to him from the archangel Gabriel. The term "Qur'an" means "continuous

24

---

9   The phrase "with all your mind" is repeated in both the *Gospel of Mark* and the *Gospel of Luke*: "Jesus replied, 'You shall love the Lord your God with all your heart, with all your soul, *with all your mind*, and with all your strength'" (Mark 12:29). "So he answered and said, 'You shall love the Lord your God with all your heart, with all your soul, with all your strength, and *with all your mind*'" (Luke 10:27).

recitation." While recited by Gabriel, and written down by Muhammad, every word of the *Qur'an* is considered to be a direct and final revelation from Allah—the God of the Islamic faith.

The *Qur'an*, then, is the holy book that Allah gave to the world through his prophet, Muhammad. In it we read the equivalent of the commandment forbidding the worship of other gods: "There is no God but Allah—the Living, the Self-Subsisting Eternal. It is He who sent down to thee ... the Law [of Moses] and the Gospel [of Jesus] prior to this book [the *Qur'an*] as a guide for all people" (Qur'an 3:2-6).[10]

The God of the *Qur'an*, like the God of the Hebrew Bible, urges his people to have no other gods before him. He is the One True God—the one and only God: "He is Allah, the One and Only – the Eternal, the Absolute. (Qur'an 112:1). There is help in no other place except in Allah: "And those whom you call upon besides Allah cannot help you, nor can they help themselves." (Qur'an 7:197). Nothing in the entire universe is comparable to Allah: "And there is none like unto him" (Qur'an 112:4).

This idea, that "there is none like him," powerfully affects Islamic thought. This is the reason behind the strict prohibition against making anything in his "likeness," for that which is spiritual must not be made into that which is material. This begins with making idols and graven images that pretend to portray Allah, and extends to making images of anything directly connected with the *Qur'an*, including his prophet Muhammad. While the making of idols and graven images *with the intent to worship them* is expressly forbidden in Islam, there is debate about how far this extends. The fundamental idea, however, is that the worship of any object or person (including one's self) instead of Allah, is forbidden. The Creator of the universe must be worshipped—not the creation.

As an example of idolatry, the *Qur'an* records what happened during the time that Moses was on the mountain receiving the Ten Commandments from God. During his forty-day absence, the people grew tired of awaiting his return. So, they erected a golden calf and worshipped it. In the *Qur'an*, Allah speaks to them about their impatience, ingratitude and idolatry; he reminds them of their slavery in Egypt and how he led them out of bondage, through the Red Sea, and then to Mount Sinai where he gave Moses the Ten Commandments: "We appointed forty nights for Moses, and in his absence you took a calf and worshipped it. ... Moses said, 'O my people, you have indeed wronged yourselves by the worship of a calf'" (Qur'an 2:51; 54).[11]

25

---

10 This translation is from *The Holy Qur'an, Text, Translation and Commentary* by 'Abdullah Yusuf 'Ali (Brentwood Maryland: Amana Corporation, 1989). In the original language the phrases "Law of Moses" and "Gospel of Jesus" are simply (Torah) and (Evangel). Accessed on July 5, 2017 @ www.quran.com/3/3?translations=85

11 For the significance of the golden calf in Islam, see "Islam from the Inside." Accessed on November 10, 2017 @ www.islamfrominside.com/Pages/Tafsir/Tafsir(7-152).html

In Islam the prohibition against idolatry extends beyond the worship of statues and images. It also includes the worship of anything that might take the place of God in a person's life. This commandment is given not only for those who have turned away from God, but also for those who believe they can find God in anything other than the Divine itself. As it is written, "Anyone who idolizes any idol beside Allah has strayed far away from the right path" (Qur'an 4:116). This could include the worship of other humans, property and possessions, dead prophets and saints, even one's self: "Alas, men ruled by selfish impulse are worse than brute beasts" (Qur'an: Introduction to Surah 25, verses 21-44). When speaking of those who mock Allah and his teachings, it is written that "such a one takes for his god his own passion" (Qur'an 25:43).

It is clear, then, that Islam forbids the worship of anything that distracts from one's devotion to Allah, whether it be an idol, a graven image, or a selfish impulse. One's faith should be in Allah alone who revealed his will in the two tablets of the Ten Commandments: "And Moses took up the Tablets. The writing upon them was Guidance and Mercy for all who stood in awe of the Lord" (Qur'an 7:154).

Hinduism (6000 BCE)

The Hindu scriptures, like the Judeo-Christian and Islamic scriptures, urge adherents to reject false gods and worship the One True God. Krishna, who is called "the Supreme Lord" in the Hindu scriptures, says, "Fill your mind with me; serve me; worship me always. Seeking me with all your heart, you will at last be united with me" (Bhagavad Gita 9:34).

The Hindu scriptures are quite clear that false gods, whether they be material possessions, personal power, or the desire for earthly fame, cannot bring lasting happiness. Those who focus on the Supreme Lord are "free from false ego, false strength, false pride, lust, anger, and the desire to possess things and control people ... united with the Lord, ever joyful, beyond the reach of self-will and sorrow, they are at peace within themselves and with others" (Bhagavad Gita 18:53-54). "Every action and every thought is an offering to the Lord, and they serve the Lord in every living creature" (Bhagavad Gita 18:57).

If you ever have a chance to visit a Hindu temple, you will notice that it is filled with so-called "idols"—elaborate statues of Hindu gods and goddesses. Some of the most popular are Shiva, Brahma, Vishnu, Ganesh, Ram, Krishna and Hanuman. While all resemble the human form in some way, one has the trunk of an elephant (Ganesh) and another has the face and tail of a monkey (Hanuman). All of this is, however, deep symbolism. Every idol, when properly understood, suggests aspects of the invisible, unmanifest God that cannot be grasped without a concrete idea. The many "idols," then, serve to bring to mind the many aspects of the One True God who permeates the universe.

In the *Bhagavad Gita*, one of the most sacred books of the Hindu scriptures, the Lord Krishna answers a question about whether it is better to worship an impersonal (abstract) God, or a personal one that can be visualized. He says that it is *preferable* to worship a visible God. Here is how Krishna puts it: "Those ever-steadfast devotees who, with steadfast devotion, fix their minds on me as a personal God, I consider to be the best of yogis" (Bhagavad Gita 12:2). However, those who prefer to bypass idols, images and incarnations are not excluded from the blessings of God: "Those who worship the imperishable, the undefinable ... restraining all the senses, even-minded in all circumstances, engaged in the welfare of all creatures, they too will come to me" (Bhagavad Gita 12:3).

For Hindus, then, idols *bring to mind* aspects of the One True God. Therefore, they are not false gods. In the end, though, regardless of whether people avail themselves of idols and graven images, or not, the key is to remain focused on the One True God. Here is how Krishna puts it: "Still your mind in me. Still yourself in me. And without doubt, you will be united with me, Lord of Love, dwelling in your heart" (Bhagavad Gita 12:8).

Buddhism (600 BCE)

In a work titled *Amitâbha*, King Kanishka is asked, "What would the Buddha have taught about God?" He replies:

> *We mean God as goodness, as truth, as righteousness, as love .... God in this sense is the good law that shapes existence, leading life step by step onward and upward toward its highest goal—enlightenment.*[12]

When asked directly about God and eternal life, the Buddha preferred to refocus people's attention on the present moment, especially the awareness of one's own thoughts and feelings:

> *The Tathâgata [a name for the Buddha] is free from all theories. But this he does know: the nature of form, and how form arises and perishes; the nature of sensation, and how sensation arises and perishes; the nature of perception, and how perception arises and perishes; the nature of the predispositions, and how the predispositions arise and perish; the nature of consciousness, and how consciousness arises and perishes.*[13]

"God" for the Buddha is equivalent to the "Good Law," the infinite light that shines into our inmost being revealing who we are, who we may become, and how we should conduct ourselves along the way. The Buddha taught his followers to see themselves in the light of the "Good Law," and to grow

---

12 Paul Carus, *Amitâbha: A Story of Buddhist Theology* (Chicago: Open Court Publishing, 1906), 73.
13 *Majjhima-Nikaya*, sermon 2, p.135. Accessed on June 18, 2017 @ http://www.sacred-texts.com/bud/bits/bits013.htm

in their ability to notice how thoughts arise and perish within them. He said that if they did this in the light of the Good Law, they would gradually learn which thoughts to ignore and which ones to embrace.

Awareness in the light of higher truth, especially awareness of how thoughts arise and perish within you, is fundamental to Buddha's teaching. This kind of awareness is the main use of your intellect. According to the Buddha, any other use of your intellect—especially theorizing about abstract religious concepts—distracts you from the path of inner awareness, the path that calls you to lead a life of compassion, wisdom and purity in the here and now. This is the "Path of Virtue" (Dhammapada), also called the "True Law," the "Good Path," and the "Good Law."[14]

• ● •

The opening statement of the Ten Commandments, "I am the Lord your God. You shall have no other gods before me," is the first of those "Good Laws." It is an acknowledgement that there is *Something* or *Someone* higher, *Something* or *Someone* who can lift you out of the slavery of serving false gods, *Something* or *Someone* who can set you free.

Every major religion (in some way or other) gives testimony to this first and foremost law proclaiming that there is something "Higher," something "Supreme," something worthy of your unfailing devotion. In other words, there is a "Supreme Force," a "Higher Principle," or a "Good Law," that pervades the universe, filling it with goodness, truth, and the ability to live a meaningful life. Whoever or whatever its name may be, it assures you that your life has meaning, and that you can connect with something greater than yourself.

The mere fact that you cannot see this "Supreme Something or Someone" with your physical eyes, does not mean that it does not exist. In the famous French story, *The Little Prince*, the main character says, "What is essential is invisible to the eye."[15] And as Parker Palmer and Arthur Zajonc put it in their book, *The Heart of Higher Education*, "Spirituality is the eternal human yearning to be connected with something larger than one's own ego."[16]

---

14 The "Good Law" is also referred to as "The Lotus of the Good Law" and "The Wheel of the Good Law." The person who remains open to receive (symbolized by "the beggar") regards the study and keeping of the "Good Law" as the chief pleasure in life. Such a person "delights in the law, meditates on the law, and follows the law. Such a person does not fall way from the Good Path" (Dhammapada 25:3).

15 Antoine de Saint-Exupery, *The Little Prince,* translated by Katherine Woods (New York: Harcourt, Brace & World, 1943), 53.

16 Parker Palmer and Arthur Zajonc, *The Heart of Higher Education: A Call to Renewal* (San Francisco: Jossey-Bass, 2010), 48.

The commandments in the lives of college students

You shall have no other gods before me.

This was my first journal entry. It was also the first time I looked inside myself and saw how many false gods I serve on a daily basis.

Journal excerpt from a college junior

Addictions as false gods

This commandment is quite clear. You should not worship idols, or bow down to them, or expect blessings from them. As it is written, "You shall have no other gods before me." Today, most people understand that "idols," whether they be statues of Catholic saints or statues of Hindu gods and goddesses, are just that—statues.

But it is also understood that symbolic artifacts (statues, crosses, beads, framed pictures, etc.) can serve to bring to remembrance divine qualities and attributes. So there is nothing wrong with a little statue of Buddha on one's desk, if it serves to bring to mind the importance of inner peace; there is nothing wrong with a framed picture of Mahatma Gandhi on the wall, if it helps someone stay focused on the idea, "You must be the change you wish to see in the world;" there is nothing wrong with a tiny wooden replica of St. Francis of Assisi, with a bird on his shoulder, if it heightens awareness of what it means to be "a channel of God's peace."

None of this, spiritually speaking, is what is meant by "worshipping idols." However, when we take a deeper look at this commandment (as we will do for each of the commandments), it is not difficult to see that "false gods" are all around us.

Alcohol, for example, can become a false god when it takes over a person's life. While it is fine to enjoy a glass of wine or a can of beer with friends, the tendency to drink to excess can become an increasing burden. Shy students who need a drink or two to "loosen up" may discover that it takes increasing amounts of the so-called "social lubricant" to overcome social anxiety. For them, college parties no longer seem to be very much fun, unless alcohol is involved; it is no longer a pleasant addition to life, or an innocuous way of feeling more comfortable in

29

social situations. Rather, alcohol becomes an absolute necessity. In order to "have fun," overindulgence becomes the norm. And alcohol, when abused, becomes the "false god" they "worship."

In the 1990s, this course was taught to a group of maximum security prisoners who were working on their college degrees while incarcerated. In his journal, one of the inmates identified "Alcohol" as his false god:

> 66 While on the streets, my god was Alcohol. I did everything for that god and loved it with all my heart, soul, and mind. I went to work to make money to give to my god, and I did give generously. When I had problems in my life, or felt angry about someone or something, I'd go directly to my god for comfort. When something good happened in my life, it was time to celebrate with my god. It was the center of my life. It was my life! I'd worship my god and do whatever it wanted me to do, because it was in total control of me. 99

That was more than twenty years ago, and in a prison setting. But some things don't change. And whether it is in a barren prison building, or on a beautiful college campus, people deal with similar issues. In the following journal entry, a student identifies her love for alcohol as her false god. Like the inmate who identified alcohol as his false god, this student admits that she, too, "worships" it:

> 66 This week I called my mom to ask her about any bad habits I might have (as was suggested in class), and she was honest with me. She said, "When anything goes wrong in your life, you always reach for alcohol."
>
> I had to admit that she was right. I worship alcohol. Jesus said, "Where your treasure is, there your heart will be also," and the truth is that I treasure alcohol.
>
> This is a big problem for me, because the same problems I try to fix by drinking alcohol were brought on in the first place by drinking alcohol! Now that I have identified this false god, I can work on distancing myself from the "demons" in the bottle. 99

The parenthetical comment, "as was suggested in class," refers to the day we invited students to take out their cell phones and either call or text someone who knew them well and who might be willing to help them identify a "false god"— any annoying or destructive habit that they might not be aware of. They were amazed that we invited them to do it right then, during class time. Even more amazing, most of them took us up on our offer. It was an exhilarating experience. Many students shared exactly what friends and relatives told them—even when it was not flattering!

As an example, a student who sent his father a text was brought face to face with a nicotine addiction he had been denying:

> 66 Dad was right. He knew I would get hooked—but I denied it, and have been denying it all along. Here's the back story: When I grew up and saw the

older kids smoking cigarettes, I told myself that I would never be like them, and I reassured my dad that I would never be a smoker. I was wrong. For the past three years, I have been a slave to this habit. I have given myself plenty of excuses and justifications, so that I would feel better about serving my false god. I said that when I feel nicotine running through my body, I can calm down and feel at peace. But the truth is that the peace I feel is a temporary freedom from my addiction. And that sense of peace never lasts long, because, pretty soon I am feeling anxious again and in need of another cigarette to calm down, and another, and another.

He acknowledges that although he thought he could control this habit, the habit eventually gained control over him:

I always thought that I could control cigarettes. I didn't believe that one day this habit would control me. Even when I wake up, my first thought is to have a cigarette. It's like I am worshipping at the altar of Nicotine, and sending up my prayers of devotion in clouds of smoke. 🙂🙂

Stimulants and drugs come masquerading as helpful friends, but when abused, they can become ugly masters. In the following journal entry, a sophomore talks about her addiction to cocaine:

66 Back in the day, cocaine was my god. It gave me power, it gave me strength, it healed me—or so I thought. In fact, this drug hurt me terribly, made me sick, and robbed me of time that I could have used doing something more productive. It wasn't until I came to college that I first began to realize that this drug was not helpful, and neither were any of the other drugs I was relying on. They were all "false gods."

Each different drug I did "gave" me another emotion, another talent. Coke made me feel invincible. Weed made me feel peaceful. Mushrooms made me fun-loving. LSD made me able to imagine. But these feelings were short-lived. And after the drug lost its effect, I would go back to feeling depressed. In fact, I felt worse than ever. In pretending to give me life, these drugs were slowly taking it away from me. 🙂🙂

As these students came to realize, drugs and stimulants did not bring about lasting peace or true happiness. Rather, as dependency increased, addiction to these substances led to deeper and deeper states of physiological and psychological captivity. Remedies that at first seemed to promote freedom eventually led to slavery.

Which false god is named most often?

When we begin the study of this commandment, we often include a brainstorming exercise. In this activity, you will be invited to call out the names of various false gods that might arise in a person's life—those thoughts, feelings, attitudes and habits that get in the way of becoming the people we want to be.

31

Can you guess which false god is mentioned most often?

Alcohol? Nope.

Drugs? Nope.

Sex? Nope.

Anger? Nope.

Here it is, Public Enemy #1 … *drum roll* … Procrastination! This false god has held first place among college students in this course for over 18 straight years! A student who is frantically trying to complete his assignment for the next *Rise Above It* class puts it like this:

> 66 Here I am, half an hour before class, writing in my journal. As usual, it has taken until the last minute to ward off my false god, so that I can get my homework done. The effects of being in this kind of captivity are beginning to take their toll on me. My false god seems very friendly, and I have known him for so long that he feels like a part of me. He sweeps into my life on a magical wind of spontaneity and whispers, "Be free, have fun, go where you want, escape these foolish challenges."
>
> He comes to me clothed in a cape of adventure and unending horizons, and he carries a flashy bag of distractions. Always, without failure, his message goes something like this: "Obviously, you aren't getting anywhere with what you are supposed to be doing. Come worship me. You can escape, feel good, feel free, not be challenged, not care about anything."
>
> Wow! How often I have received that message and believed it! How often I have allowed this false god to rule over me and enslave me. This false god of Procrastination is excellent at arriving just when I begin to feel overwhelmed by the task at hand. 99

Another student, also struggling to finish an assignment, finds himself in a familiar collegiate quandary: to study or to party? He writes:

> 66 The other day it was my roommate's birthday. I had to finish an assignment, but I wanted to go out with the guys to a bar and celebrate with a few drinks. It was very tempting, and I wanted to go badly, especially because my roommate had partied with me on my birthday.
>
> At my previous university this was never a problem. I always chose to party, whether or not I had a paper due or an assignment for the next day. This was a continuing cycle that led to declining grades and a less than impressive lifestyle. I suppose you could say my false god was procrastination, or maybe a love of partying. But when I think about this more deeply, I think that my false god is my desire to escape from problems. Rather than stress about my homework, I would rather ignore it and go out with friends.
>
> The truth is that simply ignoring my problems and avoiding responsibility did

not make it go away. In fact, it created more stress. The teaching from the Buddha that we read in class really helped me. I realized that in giving up a lower happiness I could achieve a higher happiness. So, I decided to finish my work. As a result, I feel relaxed and at peace. 🙶🙶

In rising above the desire to run away from responsibility through procrastination, he experienced a new level of happiness in the form of inner peace, a peace that can last for moments, hours, even longer. The passage from the Buddha that he refers to is a fundamental theme of the course:

> In giving up a lesser happiness, the wise person beholds a greater one. Therefore, let the wise person give up the lesser happiness, so that the greater happiness might be attained. (Dhammapada 21:1)

Perfectionism

Closely related to procrastination is perfectionism. Some procrastinators (let's face it) are simply lazy; they just don't want to work, so they put it off as long as possible. Others are so focused on doing a perfect job that they seldom get anything done on time. They revise, re-read, second-guess and overthink until they run out of time.

Another kind of perfectionist strives to *always* get things done on time and to do everything right. Are you the kind of student who not only gets work done on time, but also obsesses about getting it right? Are you the kind of student who would rather work alone rather than do a group project, because that way the work will be done well? Are you the kind of student who feels bad for days, weeks, or even months if you don't get an "A" on a test or in a course? Are you the kind of student who feels that "satisfactory" is an insult?

If you answered "yes" to any or all of the above questions, your false god might be 'Perfectionism'—also known as "overachievement. If this is your false god, good enough is never good enough; second place is for losers; and less than perfect is unacceptable. Somewhere along the line, you may have gotten the message, "If you can't do it right, don't do it at all."

Detecting this false god can be tricky, especially because it doesn't appear to be a false god; rather, it conceals itself as a healthy desire to excel. But problems arise when this normally healthy desire (persistence, dedication, determination) begins to rule over your life.

In the following journal entry, a student wrestles with this issue. She writes:

🙶🙶 The false god that I want to focus on tonight is "Perfectionism." It makes me push myself until I am physically, emotionally, and spiritually burnt out. I have loved this false god for motivating me to work harder and to be a better person. As long as I had control over this god, it guided me along a right path.

However, I am coming to see that I have loved and served it too much, and

33

that's why it has become my master. Like the Israelites who worshipped a golden calf as god, I have been worshipping achievement as my god. But I now realize that there is a way back to true happiness. And it is a simple one. I need to let go of my relentless pursuit of perfection and focus more on being satisfied with who I am and what I have. 🙶🙶

Another student, dealing with a similar problem, writes about her struggle to maintain good grades:

🙶🙶 Throughout my schooling, I have always worked hard on all of my homework assignments because I could rely on getting a good grade when the assignment was returned. The truth is, though, that I began to value my grades more than the education itself. This obsession with getting good grades would give me some happiness, but it also left me terribly stressed out.

This was especially the case when I didn't have enough time to complete an assignment perfectly or if I was unclear about the assignment. Often, I would stay up so late working on a project that I wouldn't be able to enjoy the next two days of school, because I was so tired. I can see now that this urge to do well academically, though potentially a useful and healthy habit, can also be a false god.

She then gives a specific example:

An incident occurred this week that helped me realize how destructive this god is in my life. After finishing up my calculus homework, I went out to the student parking lot to get my car and drive to work. When I got there, the rear tire on my car was flat. Until that point, I felt that I had been in perfect control of my day. I knew that I didn't have time for this. I didn't have time to wait around for the tire to be changed. I needed to be driving to work. I just stood there letting the feelings of defeat overwhelm me.

It was then that I realized I was breaking the first commandment. I was serving the false god of perfectionism. This god demands that I control everything, that I stay on top of everything, that I get good grades on everything, and that everything in my life be perfect. This god has no tolerance for low grades or flat tires. According to this false god, "It's a sin to be late for class; it's a sin to be late for work; and it's a deadly sin to be anything less than perfect!" I took a deep breath and said to myself, "OK, I am not perfect." I no longer felt defeated or (like my tire) deflated. 🙶🙶

The Rumpelstiltskin effect

In a familiar fairy tale, a young woman is threatened with the loss of her first-born child. The only way she can save her child is by discovering the name of the person who wants to take her child away. Through a series of coincidences, she discovers the man's name, and says to him, "Your name is Rumpelstiltskin!" As soon as the man hears his name, he stomps the ground furiously, runs away and never returns.

The fairy tale contains an important truth. Sometimes, just naming the false god can diminish its power. We call this the "Rumpelstiltskin effect." For example, one student named her false god, "Scorn." She saw it not merely as one of her many false gods, but rather as the ruler of all the others:

> 66 The first time I read the long list of biblical laws in the Book of Leviticus, I marveled at all the laws about sacrifice. I was shocked at the carnage but impressed by the devotion to certain rituals. Now I realize that my sacrifices to the false god of Scorn are even more brutal, and far more serious. I don't sacrifice innocent animals like they did in biblical times. Instead, I sacrifice people through what I say and what I think.

She then gives specific examples of these "daily sacrifices":

> My false god demands a full and varied diet. I sacrifice people I don't know, and people I'm close to. I find myself sacrificing all kinds of people: dumb people, super-smart people, pretty people, ugly people, weak people, tough people, people who don't write well, overachievers, underachievers—you name it, and I feed it to my god. It's hard to escape my altar of sacrifice.

> The problem with this god is that he is like my fish: the more I feed him, the hungrier he gets. He's also very devious. The reason he's so good at controlling me, and getting me to worship him, is that he twists my good qualities into scornfulness. He knows that I am smart, and that I do well in school. Instead of simply letting me be grateful for my talents, and letting me use them to serve others, he twists them around and makes me think I am better than other people. When people get things wrong in class, I smirk at them. I think meanly of people whose minds don't work as fast as mine, and I get irritated when I have to slow down and explain things to people.

She then focuses on the "ultimate sacrifice"—herself:

> When I get tired of sacrificing other people, I sacrifice myself. If I don't understand things in class, I get angry and scornful of myself instead of being patient and trying to figure things out. And then, when I catch myself being scornful, I get scornful of the fact that I am so scornful!

> Trying to get free of this false god has been a fierce battle, but this naming exercise is helping me. I know that with the God's help I will overcome this false god of Scorn. 99

This student had been vaguely aware of an unpleasant attitude and the unhappiness it brought into her life, but she had never really dealt with it in a major way until she named it. By naming her false god she took her first step toward diminishing its power over her.

Another student comes to an important realization when she names her false god, "Expectations." In her journal entry, she talks about the misery she creates for herself by expecting circumstances to go the way she imagines they should

35

go. She also shows how "Expectations" can be a gateway false god, opening the way for the arrival of other, more dangerous ones:

> 66 I often find myself imagining how certain interactions will play out throughout the course of each day. I am calling these kinds of expectations my false god, because I invest too much in them, and often wind up feeling disappointed.
>
> For example, I was planning to ask my mom to help me with my homework. This is one of those times when we have a really good time together. It's very bonding. But when I got home and suggested that we could do my homework, she said, "Sorry, honey. Not now. I'm feeling a little overwhelmed."
>
> I was disappointed. Instead of understanding her situation and helping with chores, I found myself dwelling on the fact that she was not present for me. This, of course, is a set-up for the entrance of another false god that I call, "Poor Me."

She then describes how the false god of "Expectations" creeps into her relationship with her boyfriend:

> I was looking forward to cuddling with my boyfriend tonight and having a thoughtful conversation. It didn't happen. Instead, he had an "important" meeting with the other basketball players. Of course, it was totally irrational, but my false god of expectations was telling me that he loves basketball more than he loves me, and he thinks that basketball is more important than I am.
>
> I wish I could learn to be happy spending time with the people I love without building expectations about what is supposed to happen, or how our time should be spent. If I could be freed from this false god, I would be able to focus instead on enjoying the present moment. 99

Anger as a false god [17]

Right up there, at the top of the list of false gods (along with addictions, procrastination, perfectionism, and expectations) is "Anger." In the following journal entry, a student talks about the difficulty he has controlling his temper:

> 66 I have a short temper and it is often my first response when anyone says anything to me that could be taken—even slightly—as negative. As soon as I feel cornered or insulted, I turn to this god. In a way, I "pray" to my god of Anger to give me strength and ideas so that I can win arguments. Anger controls me. It's an instantaneous reaction, and my "go to" response. It's like

---

17 When we speak about "anger as a false god" *we are speaking about the anger that flares up whenever the ego is threatened or thwarted in some way.* We are not referring to "good anger"—the God-given zeal which arises to protect what is precious, to defend those who are innocent, and to liberate those who are oppressed. Anger as a false god is always mixed with the selfish concerns of the ego.

a survival instinct that comes up even before I have a chance to think about it.

For example, my girlfriend was telling me that what I was doing was bothering her. Instead of apologizing and stopping, I immediately got angry and defensive, as though I were being attacked.

Here's the strange part. Even while I was getting angry with my girlfriend for criticizing me, I knew I was being a jerk. But I couldn't admit it. My ego would not give in; "it" would not apologize. I could see that the false god of Anger was still controlling me, and that I was out of control. 〟〟

This is a crucial insight. He says, "My ego would not give in, and would not apologize." That's just the nature of the lower self. It always wants to be right—even when it's dead wrong! That's because it is wired to instinctively defend itself.

Social scientists tell us that this is a vestige of an evolutionary instinct, dating back to the ancient time when we lived in the wilderness and were constantly in danger of being eaten by a saber-toothed tiger or attacked by a neighboring tribe. We had to be constantly on guard, vigilant, on the lookout for danger behind every bush. As a result, we developed lightning-fast defensive reactions. It was simply a matter of survival.

Today, even though there are no longer saber-toothed tigers behind every bush eager to pounce on us, or neighboring tribes over the hill who might be planning to destroy our family, we are still hard-wired to be defensive. And why not? After all, we are the direct descendants of those who survived those difficult times, the ones with the lightning-fast defense mechanisms, the ones who could instinctively defend themselves without even thinking about it. Every one of us is a living example of evolutionary survival and victory.[18]

Our lower nature, then, is hard-wired to defend itself. It therefore refuses to give in, believing that an admission of wrong is deadly. It manifests as an inordinate need to be right. Consider, for example, the case of the student who titled his journal entry, "Why Do I Always Have to be Right?"

66 The biggest false god for me is anger. To be more specific, I have a big problem whenever it comes to admitting to someone that I am wrong. Even if I am wrong, I try to prove my point anyway. And the more I try to prove my point, the angrier I get.

I know that this must be super annoying to people. This afternoon my

---

18 I am indebted to Rick Hanson for these insights. For a thorough treatment of this subject, see his book, *Buddha's Brain: The Practical Neuroscience of Happiness, Love and Wisdom* (Oakland CA: New Harbinger Publications, 2009), especially the chapter on "The Evolution of Suffering," 23-48. We will return to this subject in the chapter on "False Witness," when we talk about the cognitive distortions that arise when we overreact to circumstances and interpret reality falsely. Accessed on July 26, 2017 @ www.rickhanson.net/take-in-the-good/

girlfriend and I were having an argument. I kept pushing and pushing, trying to get her to say that I am right. I kept thinking, "I am right, and she just has to see it my way." As I continued to push my point, I felt myself getting louder and louder, angrier and angrier.

I guess you could call this bowing down to the false god of Anger.

Whenever this happens, I become obsessive about being right. I get angry and irritated. It gets to the point where I become a bulldog that won't let go. I know it's a form of being a bully and that it hurts our relationship, but I just can't stop it from controlling me. It feels like I am in the "house of bondage."

This student has recognized that he has been "in bondage" to a false god. This self-awareness will become an important first step in his spiritual growth. The next is recognizing how destructive it has been to him and to his relationships. When this happens, there arises a desire to be set free. As he continues his journal entry, he talks about freeing himself from the slavery of needing to be right:

Why can't I let go? Why do I always need to be right? How can I ever free myself from this slavery? Well, I've started working on it with my girlfriend, and I'm learning that I need to step back and realize that it's OK if someone else has a totally different opinion because that person might have a totally different life experience from mine. And so what? I mean just because someone has a different viewpoint, it doesn't mean that I have to get angry or defensive. Why can't I just let go? If I could learn to do that, I wouldn't need to be right. I could let go of the false god of Anger. It would be heaven on earth. 🙶

Before leaving the subject of anger as a false god, it's important to note that anger can sometimes be a warning that something needs attention. Rather than simply "stuff it" and let it fester, we can use anger as an opportunity to look within and determine the origin of the anger. In doing this, we can learn a lot about ourselves; in Buddha-like fashion, we can observe the "arising and perishing" of anger in us, without getting attached. In the previous journal entry, for example, the student realized that his anger was related to the obsessive need of his ego to "be right." As he puts it, *As I continued to push my point, I felt myself getting louder and louder, angrier and angrier.* In other words, he noticed anger "arising." He also realizes that it if he could let it go, *it would be heaven on earth.* He would observe anger "perishing."

Facebook, cell phones, and the false gods of technology

In recent years, the false god of Technology has emerged as a major contender for a top position on the list of false gods. While technology is a useful part of life, it can gradually take over one's whole life. It can become a master rather than a servant. For example, in the following journal entry, a student recognizes that what seemed to be a harmless diversion has become an all-consuming addiction. His journal entry is titled "Facegod":

> I think that one of the biggest false gods I am dealing with now is the false god of the internet. I have three websites that I find myself on way too much, and I find myself checking them all day long.
>
> I look at Facebook for hours, and unlike many people, I don't comment, upload or write status updates. I just sit there and wait for people to load new pictures and write new statuses. As soon as they write them, I give some witty little response in my mind and move on.
>
> NHL.com is my homepage. It changes throughout the day. They will add new stories and pictures, and update injuries. I check it about thirteen to seventeen times a day. I just logon and see how my teams are doing, maybe read an article or three, and then move on with my day. And when I say, "move on with my day," I mean go to my final destination: yahoo.com/fantasyhockey.
>
> I belong to a fantasy hockey league. I have a roster of players in the NHL that I "drafted." Every night when they play and do things like score goals and get assists, I get points. It wouldn't be bad if I just checked this after the game, or maybe once during the game, but I check it incessantly.
>
> I have this insatiable need to know what's going on with my friends and with my hockey teams. I wish I could stop feeding this addiction.[19]

Closely related to internet obsession is cellphone addiction. Whether it is set on ring or vibrate, the urge to answer can be powerful. Here's how one student puts it:

> I have named my false god as Technology—to be more specific, my cell phone. For example, I am a person who really enjoys church. However, sometimes, no matter how into it I am, if my cell phone goes off, I can't help but answer. The same thing is true when I am in class. No matter how important the lecture, or how interesting the discussion, the moment I feel my cell phone vibrating, I have to see who it is and what they want. I should be able to at least wait until after church or after class, but, for some reason, I can't do this. I guess I am in bondage to a false god who is coming between me and my education, and me and my True God.

One student describes her addiction to Netflix as "the ultimate time consumer."

---

19 Marc Potenza, professor of psychiatry at Yale University estimates that 10% of college students have an internet addiction comparable to alcohol addiction. "Expert Opinion: Internet Addiction" by Marc Potenza PhD, MD, published on the internet site *Yale News* (November 2015). Accessed on July 10, 2017 @ www.news.yale.edu/videos/expert-opinion-internet-addiction See also "The Science Behind Internet Addiction" by Jess McCuan and Carlos Folgar, published on the internet site *Quid* (January 1, 2017). Accessed on July 10, 2017 @ www.quid.com/feed/the-latest-science-behind-internet-addiction

She writes:

> 66 I have been looking at different aspects of my life and discovering many false gods. But it wasn't until I did the reading for this week that I discovered one that should be stopped now before it becomes too great. This false god takes the form of Netflix, a website that provides a seemingly never-ending supply of movies and television shows.
>
> Last year, when I made the switch from high school to college, I discovered that I had more time on my hands, especially between classes. I started filling that time by watching shows on Netflix—not just between classes, but late into the night. It got to the point where I would wake up for an 8 AM class, still tired and feeling miserable. But I would tell myself, "As soon as the class is over, I can come back to my dorm room and watch Netflix." I started staying up later and later because as soon as one episode was over, the next one was only a click away.
>
> I know that this is becoming a false god, because it is taking over my life. Instead of living my life, the only thing I am doing is watching other people pretending to live theirs. I need to exert control over this Netflix god, and stop it from controlling me. 99

One of the most seductive aspects of the internet is easy access to porn sites. In a journal entry titled, "Lust: A Quenchless Addiction," one student describes his unsuccessful attempts to deal with this false god:

> 66 I have been working on getting rid of the false god of lust for a long time now, but with little success. I have reached the relatively mild point where my "go to" poison is looking up actresses on Google images and searching for the most nude. Even though I know this is wrong, I still bow down to this false god.
>
> Yesterday afternoon, after a long day at school, I was tired, and my inner resolve was weak. For whatever reason, the image of a popular actress came into my head. "Huh, I haven't seen her in a movie for a while. I wonder what she looks like now?"
>
> So, I decided to look her up—just out of curiosity, of course. I knew this was dangerous, but I told myself that it would be fine. "I'm not going to look at anything inappropriate this time." I did not want to think about it clearly. I just knew that looking at pictures of beautiful women makes me feel good. I started the googling process, innocently enough at first, but then I discovered a "gold mine" of pictures that could feed my lust. My conscience acted up. "Don't look at those. That's feeding a false god." But I decided I didn't care. So, I very quickly switched from looking at her beauty to looking at her body, and spent the next five minutes trying to quench a quenchless lust.

As this student continues to journal about his experience, he describes the terrific battle that goes on within him as he struggles to overcome his porn addiction. "Once I start bowing down to the false god of lust," he says, "I couldn't stop until I got my fill." He then came to a new realization:

> I began to realize that I had been fooling myself. Sure, I wasn't going to the hard-core porn sights, and was "only" looking up actresses. But whether I was feeding my lust in "socially acceptable" ways or not, I was still bowing down to this false god. I realized that, for me, there was no in-between. I had to focus on the One True God with all my heart, and with all my soul, and with all my strength.
>
> I closed the laptop. It felt good. For the first time, I stopped before I had my fill. I felt fully alive—far more alive than I ever felt while bowing down to my false god. I was reminded of Moses' words to the children of Israel: "I have set before you life and death, blessing and cursing; therefore, choose life" (Deuteronomy 30:19).
>
> God is life; therefore, I choose to worship him. ”

The commandment that prohibits the worship of other gods, then, invites you to identify and rise above any thought, feeling, habit, or attitude that would keep you enslaved to lower desires (false gods). In Western religious thought (Judaism, Christianity, Islam, etc.), this is a choice between life and death, blessing and cursing, heaven and hell.

In Eastern religious thought (Hinduism, Buddhism, etc.) this is a choice between the "downward path" (allowing yourself to be driven by survival instincts and ego concerns) and the "upward path"—seeing yourself as you really are: a spiritual being, gifted with freedom, reason, and the ability to rise above the false gods that would keep you in spiritual bondage.

In the work of spiritual development, effort is never wasted; even the slightest impulse to rise above false gods is a sacred gift that needs to be honored. In describing her efforts to rise above the effects of a childhood illness that left her blind, deaf and unable to speak clearly, Helen Keller says, "One can never consent to creep when one feels an impulse to soar."[20]

20 Address to the American Association to Promote the Teaching of Speech to the Deaf at Mt. Airy, Philadelphia, Pennsylvania (8 July 1896). Accessed on June 4, 2018 @ www.en.wikiquote.org/wiki/Helen_Keller

The mark to aim at

Each week, you will be given a specific assignment based on both the literal and the spiritual meaning of each commandment. This assignment is referred to as "the mark to aim at." We use this terminology because the original Greek word *hamartia* (ἁμαρτία) which has been translated as "sin," is also an archery term which means that one has "missed the mark" or is "off the mark." It, therefore, carries different connotations than the word "sin." If one misses the mark, the archer can learn from the error, readjust, and take aim again. Notice that each of these "marks to aim at" is a *spiritual* aim. It's not about improving athletic skills, academic capabilities, or artistic talent (horizontal plane); it's about the vertical, upwards plane—the path of inner spiritual development.[21]

Here is your "mark to aim at" for the commandment about false gods:

Identify false gods in your life: name them

This commandment is an essential first step. It asks you to examine your life carefully in terms of anything that might block you from becoming the best version of yourself. As you can see from the examples in this chapter, it could be anything from a dependence on drugs to watching Netflix. What prevents you from being your best self? What prevents you from doing those things that would be of the greatest benefit to you and to others? Worry? Greed? Laziness? Lust? Perfectionism? Anger? *Your aim for this week is to name it, and identify it as a false god* that you have been worshipping (paying too much attention to). In your journal, record your experience of practicing this commandment.

---

21 For a full treatment of the subject see *The Mark*, by Maurice Nicoll (London: Watkins and Dulverton, 1981), 123, 141, 151, 189-190, 201-202.

Suggestions for further reflection and practice

You shall have no other gods before me.

The following exercises contain additional information about this commandment. Read through all of them, and then focus on one or two that spark your interest.

1 Journal reflection: what kind of person do you want to be?

When you were younger, and someone asked you what you wanted to be when you grew up, what did you say? Well, now you are older, and the question is a little different: What *kind of* person do you want to be? (Write your answer in your journal.) What personality traits and habits would you need to give up in order to be that kind of person? This could include any behaviors, patterns of thinking, and deeply entrenched attitudes that might be preventing you from stepping into that description of yourself. Perhaps it is impatience, or a quick temper, or a stubborn attitude, or an inordinate desire to please, or the inability to follow through, or an addiction to a particular substance. This exercise will help you identify and name one or more false gods you've been serving. (Write your answer in your journal.)

43

2 Activity: get feedback

Talk to, call, or text a trusted friend or family member, asking for honest feedback on your weaknesses and what you need to work on. We are often unaware of some of our most annoying habits, and good friends might not feel comfortable telling us—unless we ask. So ask. The truth is, we're often blind to our faults, and unconscious of how we may be inadvertently hurting or annoying others. This exercise may help you uncover one or two false gods that have been secretly ruling over you. Or it may will help you to be honest with yourself about ones that you have been denying. It could be as simple as a desire to gossip, an inclination towards moodiness, or a tendency to monopolize conversations. Remember: the evil that you don't acknowledge is the one that will harm you.

3 **Activity:** identify the false god of self-absorption

Self-absorption can cause you to be so focused on your own life and your own issues that you have little interest in others and little time for anyone except yourself. Minor issues in your life loom large, and big issues in the lives of others seem to have little or no significance. This kind of self-absorption manifests in little ways, such as not bothering to hold doors for people, not smiling in a friendly way when in a check-out line, and not acknowledging family members or saying "hello" to people in your dormitory or classroom. When you are being ruled by the false god of self-absorption, you tend to be oblivious to those around you—except when you might benefit from them in some way. How does the false god of self-absorption manifest itself in your life? How might it be causing you to ignore, or minimize, the needs of others?

4 **Reflection:** playing Whack-A-Mole

Have you ever played the old-fashioned arcade game, "Whack-a-Mole"? Whenever a little mole pops its head out of a hole, your job is to whack it back down with a rubber mallet. The goal is to keep whacking down these little moles until they stop popping up. The tricky part of the game is that every time you whack one down, another mole—or the same mole—pops up again somewhere else!

Notice if something similar goes on in your mental and emotional world. For example, a recurring resentment or disappointing experience keeps popping up in your consciousness, and no matter how hard you try to ignore it or "whack" it down, it keeps popping up again and again. What are one or two of the mental and emotional "Whack-a-Moles" in your life? To what extent are you still hammering away at thoughts, feelings, and attitudes that you want to be rid of? What are one or two ways that God or a Higher Power could help you end the repetitive rounds of Whack-a-Mole in your head?

5 **Reflection:** "in the house of bondage"

The Ten Commandments begin with the words, "I am the Lord your God who brought you out of the land of Egypt, *out of the house of bondage*" (Exodus 20: 2). Spiritually speaking, you are in "bondage" whenever you are controlled by the pressing urges and incessant demands of your lower nature. The more obvious forms of bondage are those physical addictions (drugs, alcohol. etc.) that begin as a seemingly harmless recreation and gradually become physical and psychological necessities. As the addiction slowly tightens its grip, you become a powerless slave who does your master's bidding—that is, the bidding of your addiction.

It is also possible to be addicted to things like anger, self-pity, and greed. Even an excessive need for praise, admiration, and success can become an addiction. These lower emotions can take hold of you and make you do whatever they command. You might say, "I will not get angry," but you do. You might think, "I will not succumb to self-pity," but it happens. You might promise yourself, "I'm going to get along well with my family during this vacation," but you find yourself in another quarrel. You resolve to get up early and do homework, but when the alarm sounds, you shut it off and go back to sleep. To the extent that you are ruled by these lower emotions (anger, self-pity, the need to be right, laziness, etc.) you are in spiritual bondage. Through the Ten Commandments, God promises to lead you *out of the house of bondage*. But God cannot lead you *out of bondage* until you first recognize that you are *in bondage*. What are one or two ways that you, at times, find yourself "in the house of bondage"?

6 Reflection: "out of the house of bondage"

This chapter began with the story of Viktor Frankl and his realization about the importance of having a deeper purpose in life—a sense of meaning. As a college student there might be times when you feel undirected and aimless. As a result, you might find it difficult to put energy into your studies. This lack of focus and meaning can leave you with the feeling that you are simply "marking time," thinking *What's the use? Why bother going to class?* If this applies to you (at least, at times), keep in mind that wherever you are in life, and however vague your external goals might be, you can always have a spiritual goal—a meaningful inner direction and purpose: becoming the finest person you can be.

Reflect on having a *spiritual purpose* as a possible *meaning* for your life. In what way might a spiritual direction for your life lead you "out of the house of bondage" and into the greatest joy you will ever know? If you wish, you can include this passage of scripture in your reflection: "Seek first the kingdom of God and his righteousness, and all these things shall be added unto you" (Matthew 6:33). Or maybe this passage from the Buddha might be the one that works for you: "In giving up a lesser happiness, the wise person beholds a greater one. Therefore, let the wise person give up the lesser happiness, so that the greater happiness might be attained" (Dhammapada 21:1).

45

"Whenever I call on the name of Jesus I get a sense of peace and a feeling that I can face anything that I am dealing with at the time."

Rise above your lower nature ~ access your spiritual gifts.

You shall not take the name of the Lord your God in vain.

Exodus 20:7

What's in a name?

In Shakespeare's play, *Romeo and Juliet*, two Italian lovers are not allowed to be together because they belong to rival families. Romeo's last name is Montague; Juliet's last name is Capulet. The Montagues and Capulets have been feuding for some time, and the ancient grudge makes anyone named "Montague" an instant enemy of the Capulets, and vice versa.

Romeo and Juliet refuse to take sides in what seems to them a trivial matter compared to the depth of their love for each other. Under the cover of night, Romeo finds himself drawn to Juliet's home, and sees her on the balcony. Because it is dark, Juliet doesn't see him. This enables Romeo to secretly listen from below while Juliet gives voice to her grief. She's lamenting the fact that they are separated by their names: "What's in a name?" she says. "That which we call a rose / By any other word would smell as sweet." [1]

There is, of course, a great deal of truth in what Juliet says. A mere name should not define who we are. And yet names are significant.

Take for example the case of a famous Native American whose parents named him "Goyathly," an Apache name which means, "One Who Yawns." Not very inspiring.

During the time that his people were being rounded up and sent to live on reservations, Goyathly became known as a brave and fearless leader who

---

1   William Shakespeare, *The Tragedy of Romeo and Juliet*, Act 2, scene 2, lines 43-44.

refused to surrender. He fought back with a vengeance born of an ardent love for his family and a fierce desire to defend the Apache nation. As his reputation grew, he became something of a legend. He came to be known as "Geronimo," especially by the enemy soldiers who both feared and respected him. It was said that he could heal the sick, dodge bullets, and even predict the future.

Mostly, however, the name "Geronimo" became synonymous with a refusal to surrender, even in the midst of overwhelming opposition. In fact, Geronimo was the very last Native American to surrender to the United States government forces. He was admired for his unflinching bravery in the face of danger, and for courage that rose above fear. In brief, he was a man who would not back down.

In 1939, Paramount Pictures produced a movie titled, "Geronimo." The movie depicted Geronimo as a true hero who feared nothing. In 1940, at the start of World War II, American paratroopers saw the film, and were so taken by it that they began to shout "Geronimo" as they summoned the courage to jump out of planes.

The concept of shouting "Geronimo" before attempting a courageous act has been a part of world culture ever since. In 2014, the Australian pop-rock band, Sheppard, produced a song they called "Geronimo." Described as an "unstoppable sing-along anthem," the song quickly went to the top of the charts in countries around the world. When interviewed about the inspiration behind the song, the band members said, "It's about taking a leap of faith and doing something that may not work, but having the courage to give it a try anyway."[2] *"Take the leap,"* they sing. *"Cry, 'Geronimo!'"*

It could be that Melissa Glover was thinking along similar lines when she named her youngest son "Geronimo." As a single mom, raising two boys in a crime-ridden neighborhood southeast of Tampa, Florida, she wanted to give her son a fighting chance to "rise above the drugs and gang violence."[3]

It worked. In a 2016 news release titled, "Geronimo Allison Living up to His Name," sports writer Ryan Wood says, "His mother couldn't have known how Geronimo's name would define him. She didn't see the challenges he'd overcome. From the brink of life spiraling out of control, he rose above. In hindsight, Geronimo knows, it's fitting that he was named after a fighter."[4]

During his early years in elementary school, Geronimo had been a good student. But things changed during his freshman year in high school. He started "hanging with the wrong people"; he got involved with drugs and

---

2 Accessed on November 12, 2017 @ www.idolator.com/7570487/sheppard-geronimo-cracking-america-next-single-interview

3 Accessed on November 17, 2017 @ www.packersnews.com/story/sports/nfl/packers/2016/08/17/geronimo-allison-living-up-his-name/88890842/

4 Ibid.

gangs; and he forgot about school. Although he wanted to play sports, especially football, his 1.75 grade point average made him ineligible.

Then he met "Miss Anne," the wife of the high school football coach. With her talent as a professional tutor, and his coach's encouragement, Geronimo dedicated himself to studies, started to get A's, and was able to play football his senior year. From there he went on to junior college where he maintained a 3.0 grade point average, and then on to the University of Illinois—the "Fighting Illini"—where he was not only a starter on the football team, but also a captain. In his senior year he received the University of Illinois "Service Above Self" award.

Geronimo had indeed fought back. But he wasn't done. Although he was one of the best wide receivers in the Big Ten Conference, when draft day came, he received no bids to the National Football League. That did not stop Geronimo. Living up to his name, he refused to surrender. In that same year he showed up for the Green Bay Packers spring training camp as an undrafted free agent. On May 6, 2016, he was selected as a member of the practice squad, and when the fall season began, he was promoted to the active roster.

When asked about his future plans, Geronimo said that he would like to go back to school and get a master's degree. He'd like to coach. And he'd like to help people the way Miss Anne helped him.

What's in a name? A lot! Even more so when we consider the Lord's name ....

The commandments in world scriptures

Judaism

The commandment, "You shall not take the Lord's name in vain," contains an additional warning: "for the Lord will not hold him guiltless who takes his name in vain" (Exodus 20:7).

This warning has led some people to believe that taking the Lord's name in vain is "the unpardonable sin." In fact, the prohibition against the inappropriate use of the Lord's name was so strong that the ancient Israelites avoided speaking it and writing it altogether. Instead the word *Adonai* (Lord) was used, or the tetragrammaton YHWH—a four-letter abbreviation for the sacred name "YAHWEH," sometimes pronounced, "Jehovah."

It's no wonder that the early Israelites were so cautious about any frivolous, irreverent or empty use of the Lord's name. The punishment for using the Lord's name in vain was death by stoning: "Anyone who blasphemes the name of the Lord must be put to death. The entire assembly must stone him. Whether an alien or native-born, when he blasphemes the Name, he must be put to death" (Leviticus 24:16).

Many volumes have been written about what constitutes "taking the name of the Lord in vain" and what constitutes blasphemy. But one thing is clear: this is a serious commandment—one that is not to be taken lightly.

On the other hand, while the Lord's name is not to be taken lightly, it most definitely should be used:

> The Lord's name should be used during times of joy, celebration and thanksgiving: "Sing praise to the Lord, you saints of his, and give thanks to the remembrance of his holy name" (Psalm 30:4).

> The Lord's name should be used for courage, protection, and victory. When David took on Goliath, the mighty champion of the Philistines, David said to him, "You come to me with a sword, a spear, and a javelin, but I come to you in the name of the Lord" (1 Samuel 17:45).

> The Lord's name should be used in prayer. When Elijah challenged the worshippers of the false god, Baal, he said to them, "You call on the name of your god, and I will call on the name of the Lord, and the God who answers by fire, He is God" (1 Kings 18:24).

The Lord's name should be used by all who hope to be saved. "And it shall come to pass that all who call upon the name of the Lord shall be saved" (Joel 2:32).

The Lord's name, then, in Judaism should be used with the greatest reverence because it is the source of life's greatest blessings. No wonder people were strongly warned not to take the Lord's name in vain.

Christianity

When Jesus spoke about "the name of the Lord," he used it in positive ways. "Whatever you ask *in my name*," he said, "that I will do" (John 14:13). In the early days of Christianity, believers reassured one another with the words, "Whoever calls upon *the name of the Lord* shall be saved" (Romans 10:13). And they reminded each other that they should do everything in the Lord's name: "And *whatever* you do in word or deed, do all in *the name of the Lord Jesus*" (Colossians 3:17).

Jesus frequently speaks about the power that resides in his name: "And whatever you ask *in my name*, that I will do, that the Father may be glorified in the Son" (John 14:13-14). "Whatever you ask of the Father *in my name*, he will give it to you" (John 15:16). "Hitherto, you have asked nothing *in my name*; ask, and you shall receive, that your joy may be full" (John 16:24). He even gives the power to cast out demons in his name: "The seventy-two returned with joy and said, 'Lord, even the demons submit to us *in your name*'" (Luke 10:17).

Throughout the New Testament the phrases "in his name" and "in my name" recur with consistency, reminding the reader that God's presence is invoked through his name. As Jesus puts it, "Where two or three are gathered together *in my name*, there I am in the midst of them" (Matthew 18:20). When Jesus rode into Jerusalem on a donkey, the people shouted with joy, "Blessed is he who comes *in the name* of the Lord!" (Mark 11:9).

When the disciples asked Jesus how to pray, he gave his disciples a model prayer which mirrors, in a positive way, the initial commandments:

The Ten Commandments	The Lord's Prayer
You shall have no other gods before me.	*Our Father in heaven.*
You shall not take the Lord's name in vain.	*Hallowed be your name.*

Islam

In Islam any attempt to mistreat or mock the name of Allah, his messenger, or the *Holy Qur'an*, is a serious offense. Even expressing doubt about Allah's existence, or reservations about anything Muhammad said, could be construed as blasphemy. Depictions of Allah or Muhammad in pictures, books and movies is also considered blasphemy, and some believe that naming stuffed animals and pets after the name of the prophet is blasphemous. Much of this, however, is subject to debate because the *Qur'an* does not give specific details. It does say, however, that "those who wage war against Allah," are subject to severe punishments, including exile, and even execution (Qur'an 5:33).

Indeed, "heavy punishments" in this world and in the next are in store for those who "wage war against Allah," but there is mercy for those who repent, "for Allah is Oft-Forgiving, Most merciful" (Qur'an 5:34).

Those two qualities, "Oft-Forgiving, Most Merciful", appear throughout the *Qur'an*. In fact, every chapter of the *Qur'an* begins with the words, "In the name of Allah, Most Gracious, Most Merciful." Many Muslim scholars agree that these two qualities, "*Gracious*" and "*Merciful*", sum up the entire *Qur'an* and the essence of Allah. They are "the name of God"—the very qualities that sincere Muslims should frequently bring to remembrance whenever they pray, or whenever they praise the name of Allah: "The most beautiful names belong to Allah, so call on him by them; but shun all those who profane his name" (Qur'an 7:180).

Writing in the Sufi tradition, the mystical branch of Islam, M. R. Bawa Muhaiyaddeen speaks about "The ninety-nine beautiful names of Allah"— the divine qualities of Allah which can be found in everyone's heart. These qualities are "the ninety-nine powers of Allah," the divine attributes which can be received by every person and brought into one's life. The person who does this will have no enemies, for "patience, contentment, and trust in God … will fill his innermost heart with unity, humility and harmony."[5] There is no end to the meaning of these names: "Even if all the water in the seas were made into ink and the wood from all the forests in the world were made into pens to write with, we could not finish writing the explanations of these beautiful attributes of God … they are His qualities." [6]

To sum up, "God is he, and there is no other god. The Sovereign, the Holy One, the Source of Peace, the Guardian of Faith, the Preserver of Safety, the Exalted in Might, the Irresistible, the Supreme … to him belong the Most Beautiful Names" (Qur'an 19:23-24). "It is all the same whether you call him God or the Beneficent. All the good names belong to him" (Qur'an 17:110).

---

5 Shaikh Muhammad Raheem Bawa Muhaiyaddeen, *Islam and World Peace: Explanations of a Sufi* (Philadelphia: The Fellowship Press, 2004), 127-128.

6 Shaikh Muhammad Raheem Bawa Muhaiyaddeen, *The 99 Beautiful Names of Allah* (Philadelphia: The Fellowship Press, 2004), Introduction.

Hinduism

Whereas Muslims recite "The 99 beautiful names of Allah," Hindus recite "the thousand names of the Lord." The thousand names begin with "Salutations to the one who is the all or the whole manifested universe"; next comes "Salutations to the one who pervades everything"; then, when we come to the last two names, name 999 reads "Salutations to the one who is unshakable." Finally, name 1000 reads "Salutations to the one who has weapons that act against evil."[7]

The idea that there are a thousand names of the Lord suggests that there is really no end to the qualities of the Ultimate Reality—the reality that is present in everyone and everything. Eknath Easwaran, the author and translator of the *Bhagavad Gita for Daily Living,* adds that "The thousand names of the Lord," are not merely old Sanskrit terms, but rather "marvelous concepts which throw light on how to live."[8]

For example, the Sanskrit word *Shanti* means Peace. So, God is called *Shanti-Da,* the Giver of Peace. Keeping that in mind, you can remember that a state of peace is always available to you, regardless of external circumstances. To take another example, the Sanskrit word *Vishnu* means "the One who is everywhere." When you realize this, you can know that the Divine is present in every situation, in every created thing, and in every person. When you catch a glimpse of someone being patient, or courageous, or generous, you can say to yourself, "I am seeing God (*Vishnu*) in that person." And even when someone is not being particularly patient, or courageous, or generous, you can say to yourself, "I know that God (*Vishnu*)—the One who is everywhere—is also here, even though I cannot see a quality of God at this moment."

All of this is summed up beautifully in chapter ten of the *Bhagavad Gita,* when Krishna says, "My seed can be found in every creature, Arjuna, for without me nothing can exist. ... There is no end to my divine attributes. ... Wherever you find strength, or beauty, or spiritual power, there I am. These qualities have sprung from me" (Bhagavad Gita 10:39-41).

Buddhism

As we have seen in Islam, the phrase "name of the Lord" can refer to anything that is considered sacred or holy. Therefore, it can refer not only to God's qualities, but also to all sacred writings (the Bible and the *Qur'an* for example), and to the sacred laws about how you are to conduct your life. This is especially clear in Buddhism. If you were to say, "I am a follower of the Buddha" or "I am a Buddhist," without also living according to Buddha's

53

---

7   Accessed on July 23, 2017 @ www.saranaagathi.files.wordpress.com/2008/03/vishnu_sahasra_namavali.pdf
8   Eknath Easwaran, *The Constant Companion: Inspiration for Daily Living from the Thousand Names of the Lord* (Tomales, CA: Nilgiri Press, 2001), 293.

teachings, you would be "taking Buddha's name in vain." As Buddha says, "Even if he recites a large number of scriptural texts but, being slothful, does not act accordingly, he is like a cowherd counting the cows of others, he is not living a holy life" (Dhammapada 1:19).

On one occasion, the Buddha was approached by the citizens of a village who had heard the teachings of various teachers. They were confused, because the different teachers said contradictory and confusing things. Why then should they accept the Buddha's teachings? The Buddha gave them this answer:

> Do not accept anything on mere hearsay. Do not accept anything by mere tradition. Do not accept anything based on mere rumor. Do not accept anything just because it accords with your scriptures. ... Do not accept anything because it agrees with your preconceived notions... But when you know for yourself that these things are moral, these things are blameless, that these things are praised by the wise, that these things, when performed and undertaken conduce to well-being and happiness—then live and act accordingly.[9]

Legend has it that Buddha's last words to his disciple, Ananda, were the following: "All those who see the truth, all those who live within the law, they are the ones that pay the Buddha supreme honor. Therefore, you must live according to the law, Ananda, and even in the most trivial matters, you must follow the sacred path of truth."[10]

• ● •

9 Narada Mahathera, *The Buddha and His Teachings* (Mumbai: Jaico Publishing House, 2006), 183-184.

10 Andre Ferdinand Herold, *The Life of the Buddha* (New York: Scholar's Choice, 2015), 212.

Putting it all together

In his poem, "The Divine Image," the English poet William Blake provides a beautiful description of a connection between "the Lord's name" and the highest human qualities—those qualities that come from God, are "God with us," and therefore should not be taken lightly. Here is the poem:

The Divine Image
To Mercy, Pity, Peace, and Love
All pray in their distress;
And to these virtues of delight
Return their thankfulness.

For Mercy, Pity, Peace, and Love
Is God, our father dear,
And Mercy, Pity, Peace, and Love
Is Man, his child and care.

For Mercy has a human heart,
Pity a human face,
And Love, the human form divine,
And Peace, the human dress.

Then every man, of every clime,
That prays in his distress,
Prays to the human form divine,
Love, Mercy, Pity, Peace.

And all must love the human form,
In heathen, Turk, or Jew;
Where Mercy, Love, and Pity dwell
There God is dwelling too.

The poem suggests that God's "name" is Love, Mercy, Pity, and Peace. These qualities are the "name of God"—the God we all call on in our distress. As you rise above the merely natural dimension of your life, receiving the divine qualities that flow in, you will no longer be "taking the Lord's name in vain." Instead you will be using those qualities to enhance, enrich, and bless not only your own life, but also the lives of others.

The commandments in the lives of college students

You shall not take the name of the Lord your God in vain.

A simple missed shot will overshadow my entire thought process and ruin a night's sleep, as the memory is left on replay in my brain. I know I need to call upon the name of the Lord.

Journal excerpt from a college basketball player

Taking the Lord's name in vain

What comes to mind when you hear the commandment, "You shall not take the name of the Lord your God in vain"? Perhaps you have been taught that it's about not swearing. If so, your experience might be similar to this one, written by a college junior:

> 66 As a kid, I thought that taking the Lord's name in vain meant that you shouldn't use swear words. But I didn't think it was a big deal because everybody swears all the time anyway. "If swearing is a sin," I thought, "it couldn't be a very serious one." So I did it all the time. Whenever I did, my dad would tell me to stop swearing. But there was no punishment. I always thought that it was funny that I could say a "real" swear word and get away with it, with just a "Hey, watch it!" But when I actually used the Lord's name in an inappropriate way, my dad would get much angrier. At the time I never understood why.

After reflecting on the deeper meaning of the commandment, this student had an interesting realization about his relationship with God:

> Recently, I have begun to question my beliefs. And in so doing I have begun to doubt the existence of God. The more I begin to doubt that God exists, the easier it is to take his name in vain. I say to myself, "Well, it doesn't really matter because he might not even exist." But, whenever I think this way, I notice that it has a direct effect on my faith in God. The more I take his name in vain, the more I disrespect the name of God; and the more I disrespect

the name of God, the less I believe in him. As a result, I don't take my faith seriously.

Look at it this way. If you don't respect a class you are in, you don't take the material seriously. You will rush through the homework and zone out during class. Whenever I do this, I learn almost nothing. So, if I don't take God seriously, then how am I supposed to learn about him? I'm still skeptical that he even exists, but that does not mean I should treat him like nothing. I think, at the very least, it's a good idea to avoid taking his name in vain. 99

This student makes a good point. While he is still not sure about the existence of God, he has resolved "at the very least" not to take God's name in vain. Although he is not *using* the Lord's name, at least he is not *abusing* it.

At the most literal level, then, the Lord's name is given to be used—but not abused. We knew a couple who didn't use their expensive wedding china for fear that they might break it. Ten years into their marriage, the china was still in the original box, unopened. Similarly, we knew some people who chipped in to buy their mother a fur coat—something she had always wanted. She was thrilled to have the new coat, but she never wore it, for fear that someone might steal it. There could be many more examples, but the point is that a gift is given so that it may be used. If we do not use it, we "take it in vain."

Jesus tells a parable about workers who were given different amounts of money (silver "talents") and told to make use of what they had received. Those who invested the money wisely, using it to produce more income, were praised for their efforts. Others, who hid the money rather than use it, were rebuked. The lesson, which is called "the parable of the talents," teaches many things. Most importantly, it teaches that each of us is given talents and abilities which should be *used*. If they are hidden away or not used in service to others, they are "taken in vain." [11]

Calling upon the name of God

While the emphasis of this commandment appears to be on *not* taking the Lord's name in vain, it is useful to look at this commandment the other way around. What are the uses of the Lord's name? In what ways can "the Lord's name," when used appropriately, defend us from evil and fill our lives with greater joy? One student, a devout Christian, talks about the power of *using* God's name whenever she is feeling anxious:

66 I titled this journal entry, "Just Call Me and I'll Be There." That's because it says in the scriptures, "Whoever calls upon the name of the Lord shall be saved." Until now, I always took this to mean salvation from sin, but now I see that it has a broader meaning. It could be as simple as calling on the name of

57

11 See Matthew 25:14-30. Because the talents were made of "silver," they symbolize the divine truth which should be put to use in our lives—not hidden away.

Jesus when I am feeling anxious about the struggles of life. Whenever I do this I get a sense of peace and a feeling that I can face anything that I am dealing with at the time. I no longer worry about tomorrow or stress about homework, because if I just call on the name of the Lord, he will be there. An answer will come—maybe not words, but at least an inner feeling of peace. 🙶

For this student, the actual *use* of the name, "Jesus," is a transformative experience. She testifies to an experience of feeling "saved" by calling upon the name of her God. In this case, she uses the name of Jesus to lift herself out of anxiety and into a higher state of peace. In Eastern religions also, the name of God can have a transformative effect. The following journal entry, written by a student who sees value in all religions, talks about the usefulness of having many names for God:

🙶 I have always struggled with the idea of the "name" of God because, to me, God transcends such mundane attributes as "a name." Identifying him with one particular word seems to limit him and make him too human. There are, however, two experiences in which the name of God became important to me.

The first experience was when I began to think of Christ not merely as ransom FOR the Father, but rather Christ as BEING the Father who came down and exposed himself to the merciless harshness of the people. This realization struck me with incredible power. So the name Jesus Christ began to mean a lot to me. Now, when I say "Jesus," or think of this Holy Name, it calls to mind everything God did—and does—for me. For that reason, I do not use his name lightly, or take it in vain.

The second experience came when I began to seriously study Eastern religions, especially when I started to practice mantra meditation. In Eastern thought, there exists the notion that the mere uttering of the name of God can be both incredibly powerful and divinely invigorating. Chanting the maha-mantram on a regular basis gave me a way to focus on God without deep theological thinking. Merely coming into God's presence by speaking one of his names has been an intense spiritual experience. To me, it does not really matter which of the names I use. Jehovah, Adonai, Allah, Christ, or Krishna are all names that I associate with the one true God. They are human names, bound by human language. But they are deeply connected in my consciousness with the essence of who God is. 🙶

These journal excerpts, from two students, are quite different. One focuses exclusively on the name *Jesus*. The other takes a more ecumenical view, suggesting that, for him, calling on the name of *Jehovah, Adonai, Allah, Christ* or *Krishna* are all equally valuable. And yet, both acknowledge that there is something powerful about the name of God. They are in essential agreement that the name of God can be *used* for good, worthwhile, serious purposes; it can be *relied on* as a source of peace, strength, and encouragement. But it is not to be used lightly; it is not to be used in empty, meaningless, worthless ways. It is not to be taken in vain.

Going deeper

When we begin our study of this commandment, we will invite you to brainstorm about the "names of God." Previous students have identified a wide assortment of names. Some of the most common are God, Allah, Jesus, Krishna, Savior, Lord, Father, and Creator. This is just the short list; there are many names for God.

Every name, however, means something slightly different. Addressing God as "Creator," for example, suggests that God has created all things. Using the name "Savior" or "Redeemer" suggests that God not only creates, but also saves and preserves that which has been created. It is evident that every name for God can have a different meaning.

After brainstorming about the many names of God, we will ask you to consider your own name, and what it might mean to you to have "a good name" in the community. We will ask you about the meaning of your name, and the qualities you associate with your name. For example, most people have strong associations with the name "Mahatma Gandhi" (courage), "Abraham Lincoln" (honesty), and "Mother Teresa" (compassion). What associations do you have with your name?

If you are not sure, you may want to ask your parents why they gave you your name. What associations did they have for your name? Parents often give their children names that represent certain qualities. We have known people named "Hope," "Patience," and "Charity." When we taught this course in South Africa among the Zulus, the names of some of our students were "Welcome," "Goodwill," and "Peacemaker." They named us "Thandazani" (one who prays) and "Thandanani" (one who loves). And when our daughter taught this course in Ghana, they gave her the Twi name, "Akomapa" (good-hearted).

In reflecting on the meaning of her name, and the qualities associated with it, one student titled her report, "Jah Soleil." It was her given name, and it held great significance for her. She writes:

> 66 When I was younger my Dad said to me, "Jah Soleil, you should know that your name is God-given. It means, 'Light of God.'" My father is a devout Rastafarian, and he gave me that name. He said that it came to him in a dream, and I loved that. He said, "No matter what, you will always be the light that the Lord has sent into the world." I took this to mean that I should always live up to my divine duty to fight through any battle and overcome any obstacle. As long as I did that, I would never be taking my God-given name in vain.
>
> The truth is, though, that I have taken my given name in vain, and in that sense, I have also taken the Lord's name in vain. This is because I have not always lived up to my divine duty, and have not always lived as though I am Jah Soleil —the Light of God. But this commandment is helping me to get back on the path, to remember my name, and to continue to remember that I want

59

to live up to my name. I want to bring light to others, not darkness. When I say or hear my name called, I want to remember that I am here for a purpose, and that is to glorify God's name. **99**

Another student, who had grown up feeling ashamed of her name, had a remarkable turn-around. She writes:

66 This week, for the first time, I realized the significance and power of my own name. My name is Bernice, and I used to be ashamed of it because so few people have that name. I think I was also ashamed of my name because I was ashamed of who I was. But now I want to change all that. My name means, "Bringer of Victory." I love knowing what my name means, and I want to be proud of who I am: "Bernice—Bringer of Victory."

I know that this quality comes from the Lord, and that I can be victorious in many aspects of my life, while helping others to be victorious as well. Yes, I can be a "Bringer of Victory." This past week, whenever I was confronted with a difficult situation, I simply remembered my name knowing that the Lord would give me the strength to be victorious. I made a difficult telephone call and apologized for the way I had been acting. The result? A friendship was not only saved but deepened. I am Bernice—Bringer of Victory. I love my name, and I love the God-given quality it represents. **99**

Hallowed be thy name

When we speak of God as the "Creator of the universe," or "Savior," or "Redeemer," many wonderful ideas come to mind. Often, however, these are fairly general ideas. If we get more specific, we begin to realize that God's "name" represents every holy quality we could ever think of. For example, God's name is "Mercy," "Love," "Forgiveness," "Patience," and "Peace." When we look at it this way, the name of God can take on much more meaning. It's not just about God's *name*; it's about God's *qualities*—all of his qualities. And that awareness can change everything. It can help us realize why God's name is holy, and why Jesus, in the second verse of the Lord's Prayer says, "Hallowed be thy name." In other words, Jesus is saying that God's name should be treated in a *holy*, reverent manner.

Here are some ways that you can make this practical:

- From now on, whenever you feel grateful, and feelings of spontaneous love for a parent, sibling, or friend, arise in you, you can say, "*That's God's love working through me.*" In that moment, God's name is "Love."

- From now on, whenever you feel an impulse to be charitable, and an ocean swell of generosity arises in you, you can say, "*That's God's generosity working through me.*" In that moment, God's name is "Generosity."

- From now on, whenever you feel touched when hearing another person's story, and compassion arises in you, you can say, "*That's God's compassion working through me.*" In that moment, God's name is "Compassion."

- From now on, whenever you feel patient with other people's annoying behaviors and forgiveness arises in you, you can say "*That's God patience and forgiveness working through me.*" In that moment, God's name is "Patience" and "Forgiveness."

While these God-given qualities may feel like your own, they are not. Like the sun that fills the flower with warmth and light, but can never be the flower, the many qualities that flow in from God—"the thousand names of the Lord" as they are called in Hinduism—are, in spiritual reality, God with you and in you.

If you forget this, it can allow the ego to take over, and you may think, "I am so loving, generous, compassionate, forgiving, etc." As soon as this happens, the wonderful flow of divine energy that arises from within is blocked and stifled. It's like a clogged water pipe that is unable to let fresh water flow through. The water entering the pipe is good, but the channel is clogged. The ego becomes like sludge in the pipe, the muck that prevents you from experiencing the free flow of all the beautiful qualities that are associated with "the name of God."

This commandment, therefore, invites you to call on a Power that is greater than self, greater than your ego. It calls you to rise above the sludge of self-reliance and rely on "the name of God," those higher, spiritual qualities that you can embrace with your whole being and never "take in vain."

61

Accessing God's arsenal
....

Once you understand that the "*name* of God" refers to God's *qualities*, a new question may arise: "If I am to make use of God's qualities—not take them in vain—how do I access those qualities?" A senior, who titled her journal entry "Accessing God's Arsenal," uses the imagery of warfare to answer this question:

> 66 Last week we were asked to recognize any false gods that are actively present in our lives. But recognizing false gods is only the first step. There are still many battles ahead. So this next commandment is about building up my arsenal in order to hold my ground in this fight. It is easy to fall under the impression that I do not have the numbers or the fire power on my side. I have felt this way before. I have felt that there is little hope. But then I realize that there is more help available than I realized.
>
> There are two sides in every war. This week I sat down to write out a list of the false gods that are in my life (one side of the battle). Then I wrote down another list of the qualities from God ("the names of God") that I need to access in order to overcome these false gods (the other side of the battle).
>
> The battle seems to be an evenly matched one, and I never know which side will win. But I keep forgetting that I don't have to fight all my battles alone. God makes himself present through friends, family, and the situations I

experience. I may be thinking I am leading the struggle against the demons of my lower nature, but in reality, I am only a fraction of the front line. Often, it is the people who love me who are the reinforcements, the ones who fill in the gaps in my army. Of course, all of this comes from God.

This student beautifully describes the battle, the two sides within her, and her need for God's help, which she calls "God's arsenal." As she continues her journal entry, she talks about her own experience of accessing that arsenal:

One of my favorite quotes is, "Ask and it shall be given to you; seek and you shall find; knock and it shall be opened to you. For everyone who asks, receives; and whoever seeks shall find; and to those who knock, it shall be opened" (Matthew 7:7-8). My true arsenal is the Lord. The qualities of God and the inflow of continuous love from God have the strength to overcome false gods—but only if I want it, only if I ask.

And that means that one of the main ways I can access this ultimate arsenal is through prayer.

When I decide to pray, I am admitting to myself and to God that I need his help, support, and guidance. Opening myself up to receive the qualities of God is the most important military maneuver I can make in my personal war against false gods. Only then can I say, with full confidence, "I will fight this battle in the name of the Lord." 99

This journal entry suggests that every spiritual battle can be won if it is fought "in the name of the Lord"—that is, by calling on the Lord. As this student observes, prayer is one of the main ways that you can "access" the divine arsenal—an inexhaustible armory that is always available to you. It is there for everyone, always, just a prayer away.

In order to help you in this "holy war," we will pass out sticky notes, and ask you to write down some God-given qualities you might need to access in the coming week. For example, if you need to work on curbing your spending habit, you might put a sticky note in your wallet or purse with the reminder, "Pray for restraint." If you have a problem with getting distracted, you might put a note on your computer that says, "Pray for focus." If you have a problem with making harsh judgments, you might put a note on the doorway that leads out of your room that says, "Pray for kindness."

The content of the note and the decision about where to place it is up to you. The point is that the sticky note is your reminder to access a power greater than yourself. In the following journal entry, a student accesses God's arsenal in a battle against her old enemies "Anger" and "Impatience." She acknowledges that when things do not go her way, she loses patience quickly and gets angry. She knows she needs to have more patience. So she takes advantage of our suggestion to use sticky notes as reminders to pray for God's qualities. She has put up notes everywhere—on the walls of her dorm room, on her computer, even on the back of her phone, reminding her to pray for patience. Her journal entry is titled, "Call on His Name":

> ❝ I often ask the Lord, "Why me?" especially when I'm going through hard times. I often feel like God is punishing me, and when I call on him I picture him with negative qualities. But now I am beginning to realize that I need to see God in a different way. I need to see God as having nothing but positive qualities. I need to remember that whenever I call on the Lord, there will be an answer.
>
> So this week I put up sticky notes all over my room and in some of the common areas as a reminder to call upon the name of the Lord, even for the little things, and to ask God to fill me with good qualities that are associated with his name. The one quality that I need most is "Patience." That's because last week I named "Impatience" as my false god. I found that for me impatience leads to anger, which is another one of my false gods.

As she continues this journal entry, this is precisely what she does. She demonstrates how she called on "the name of the Lord" when she found herself in a frustrating situation:

> I had a volleyball game last week, and I really wanted my mother, sister, and boyfriend to be there. It was our second game of the season, and they had missed the first one. When the day of the second game came, I was imagining how great it would be to see my family and my boyfriend there watching me play for my college volleyball team. I knew it was going to be a great day.
>
> It was getting close to game time, and no one had arrived yet, but I was still hopeful. Then, while I was suiting up for the game, I got a text from my sister. It said, "Hey, sorry we couldn't make it, promise we'll make it next time."
>
> I didn't see a "next time." I was so angry. My boyfriend hadn't shown up either, and didn't even text me! I was really bummed. In my head I could picture the argument we would be having when I saw him again.
>
> The game ended without any of my family showing up. As I was walking back to the dorm with my friends, still feeling bummed, I heard someone calling my name. I turned around and it was my boyfriend, pulling up behind us in his car.

This is a critical moment—a "moment of truth." She is already upset and disappointed. Her family and boyfriend had promised to be there, but they have not shown up. She is already picturing a big argument with her boyfriend. But this time—maybe for the first time—she handles the situation differently:

> I don't know why, but at the moment I glanced at the sticky note that I had placed on the back of my phone. It said, "Pray." I knew that meant that I should pray for Patience and Understanding. I should not take the name of the Lord in vain. I should ask for the divine qualities of patience and understanding to come into my life. And so I did. I asked.

I know that God does not always answer prayers instantly. But this time he did. I found myself smiling and running up to give my boyfriend a big hug, even though he didn't make it to my game. He started explaining that he had driven all the way up from Virginia, got stuck in traffic, and when he got to campus he couldn't find the fieldhouse. When he finished apologizing, I thanked him. I felt flooded with understanding, and told him how much I appreciated his driving up to see me. I gave him an A+ for effort (and silently thanked God for coming into my life). **99**

When this student called on "the name of the Lord," it was a specific prayer for Patience and Understanding, qualities that would be necessary to help her overcome the false gods of impatience and anger. *If she had held onto her upset, she would have missed the opportunity to grow closer to her boyfriend.* Instead, by naming her false gods (the "Rumpelstiltskin effect"), she was able to access the specific qualities that she needed in this situation: patience and understanding.

Praying for gratitude

Sometimes, however, the struggle can be more subtle, and the quality that is sought can be harder to identify. For example, in the following journal entry a student doesn't know exactly what to pray for. He is feeling a little gloomy, like how it can feel on an overcast day, but nothing major is troubling him. So he decides to simply pray for gratitude. Here's what happens:

66 Initially, I had forgotten to put up the post-it notes that were passed out in class. Over the weekend, when I was looking to see what I had to do for homework, I found them shoved into my notebook. At first, I thought I wasn't going to get that much out of having sticky notes placed everywhere. I mentioned this in class, and said, "I think I'm just going to get used to seeing them around and forget to pray."

When I first put the sticky notes up, and started noticing them, I didn't really know what to pray for. So I decided to just thank God for what I have in my life. No big deal—or so I thought. As time went on, it became easier and easier to find things that I could thank him for. I started realizing that maybe, just maybe, I needed the quality of gratitude in my life.

During the week, as I began to ask for gratitude, I noticed my mood gradually go up and up. I started noticing when people would hold the door for me, and I felt grateful. I noticed when someone let me borrow a pencil, and I felt grateful. I noticed when someone gave me a ride to get a late-night snack, and I felt grateful. I normally would notice these things, but I never felt like I truly appreciated them until I started thanking God multiple times a day. It felt like, everywhere I turned, I was getting a daily dose of God.

As this journal entry continues, the writer compares his previous "ho-hum" mood to rainy weather conditions in Pennsylvania, and then compares his new state of mind to what happened a few years earlier after he boarded an airplane for a flight home:

> This whole thing kind of reminded me of an epiphany I had a few years ago. I remember I was on an airplane from Pennsylvania to Florida and the weather at the time of departure was really bad. It was raining and just miserable. When we lifted off, though, I remember that we very quickly rose above the storm. The sun was shining! It was so beautiful to see the sun shining in the clear blue sky. I remember thinking that it is interesting that even during a storm, the sun is still shining, we just can't see it—or we choose not to see it. But for me, during this week, the more I started making an effort to see God, the more he seemed to appear, and the easier it became to notice him. His name is Gratitude. 99

Earlier in this chapter, in a journal entry titled "Accessing God's Arsenal," a student talked about the scriptural passage, "Ask and it shall be given to you; seek and you shall find; knock and it shall be opened to you" (Matthew 7:7). Could it be that accessing gratitude through prayer has the power to lift you above any "rainy and miserable" state you may be in? Could it be that there is a power in the universe, greater than yourself, that can lift you to a place where the sun is always shining? You'll never know until you try. You'll never know until you take a "leap of faith."

65

The mark to aim at

Do not take the name of God in vain: call upon the name of the Lord

....

In the first commandment your aim was to examine your life in terms of anything that might block you from being the best version of yourself, and to name it as a "false god." In this next commandment, your aim is to *use that experience to access the opposite quality.* For example, in place of hopelessness, you can pray for optimism; in place of fearfulness, you could pray for courage; in place of resentment, you could pray for forgiveness; in place of feeling entitled, you could pray for gratitude. In fact, any false god that arises, often in the form of a negative thought or feeling, can be used to your advantage. It can show you by "the law of opposites" what quality you need to access and pray for. If the idea of "God" is a problem for you, you might think of "God" as a power greater than yourself, or a place where the sun is always shining. It's a place where you can access peace, love, tranquility, compassion, gratitude, forgiveness, joy, etc. In your journal, record your experience of practicing this commandment.

Suggestions for further reflection and practice

You shall not take the name of the Lord your God in vain.

The following exercises contain additional information about this commandment. Read through all of them, and then focus on one or two that spark your interest.

1 Journal reflection: misusing the name of God

A student once asked, "What does the 'H' stand for in Jesus' middle name?" At first, we were confused—until he told us that when his father was upset, he often said, "Jesus H. Christ!". While there are numerous theories about the origin of the "H," the most convincing one is that it is simply thrown in when people are upset—clearly a case of "taking the Lord's name in vain." The student's question is a reminder that it's good to be aware of what is happening within us when we hit our thumb with a hammer and shout an expletive that includes a sacred name. At such times, it can be useful to ask ourselves, "Is this a holy prayer for help in the midst of misfortune, or is it a worthless, empty, even profane use of God's name?" Take a moment to reflect on how you use God's name in your daily life—especially when you are disappointed or upset.

2 Journal reflection: protecting your "good name"

What does your name mean? (What did it mean to your parents when they named you? What does it mean to you today?) For example, the name "David" in the original Hebrew means "beloved"; "Emma" is a Germanic word that means "universal"; and "Erika" is a Norse word meaning "eternal ruler." What *qualities* would you like people to think of when your name is spoken? What are one or two things you can do to develop and protect your "good name" among your friends, at your college, and in your community? How can you "have a good name" or "make a good name" for yourself? What will come to mind for people when they hear your name?

3 Journal reflection: prayer in your life

This chapter focuses on accessing the good qualities you would like to develop in order to become the person you want to be. For many people this is done through prayer. What was your experience of prayer as a child? Over time, in what ways has your understanding of prayer changed, and how did that come about? What is your experience of prayer now? For example, an experience of an unanswered prayer may have caused you to stop believing in the power of prayer. On the other hand, an experience of answered prayer may have deepened your faith. Or maybe you have never taken the whole subject of prayer very seriously. If you do not currently pray, what method or methods do you use to access God or a power greater than yourself? How does this work for you? If it works well, fine. If not, why not give prayer a try?

4 Activity: put up sticky notes

For this activity place sticky notes in key places in your environment. These notes should be strategically placed to remind you to access God, engage your Higher Power, or tap into a certain quality. Put the notes in those places where you are likely to see them, and where you need to be reminded to "call upon the name of the Lord." In the past, students have put them on their phones, on their computers, on their textbooks, in their wallets, on the bathroom mirror, on the doorway going out of their dorm room, etc. Choose the places that are most strategic for you. If sticky notes aren't available, you can use paper and tape instead.

5 Activity: try a "do-over"

We are accustomed to the "instant replay" where we get to see the same play repeatedly. This can be especially embarrassing for athletes who have made an error, or fumbled the ball, or missed an easy shot. They don't get an opportunity for a "do-over." But you can have this opportunity every time you "mess up," especially in a relationship. Just apologize, say you're sorry, ask for forgiveness, and acknowledge that you were reacting from your lower nature. Then ask for a "do-over"—an opportunity to do it over again. But this time you will do it deliberately and prayerfully—consciously operating from your higher nature. If you believe in God, ask God to give you the qualities you need; if you don't believe in God, but believe in a Higher Power, tap into the divine qualities of Love, Forgiveness, Patience, or Mercy—whichever one you need—all of which are abundantly available to you.

6 Activity: rise above likes (attractions) and dislikes (aversions)

If you are like most people, you do not like to be forced, compelled or disciplined against your will. You know, in a deep way, that freedom is your birthright. At the same time, *you can use your freedom to compel yourself* to do things that you know are in alignment with your highest spiritual aspirations. This is called "self-discipline." Rather than being ruled by the forces of your lower nature ("false gods"), you can take control of your own life, doing what you know is best for you. At this level of spiritual development, it's not about whether you "like" doing something, or "dislike" doing something. You simply know what is the right thing to do, and you do it.

As a practical example, choose an area of your life where you aspire to improve. It could be as simple as cutting down on junk food or showing up to class on time. Notice the thoughts and emotions (attractions and aversions) that have been preventing you from being your best self, and identify them as false gods. It could be the false god of gluttony (compelling you to eat junk food) or the false god of sloth (compelling you to miss classes). Whatever it may be, here are three simple steps: (1) identify this attraction or aversion as a false god; (2) tap into the quality you will need to overcome the false god that has been ruling you ("call upon the *name* of the Lord"); (3) then rise above the attraction or aversion that has been keeping you in bondage.

It may help to keep this teaching from the Hebrew scriptures in mind: "He who rules his spirit is mightier than he who takes a city" (Proverbs 16:32). Or if Eastern religion is more to your liking, here's a teaching from the Buddha: "If one man conquers in battle a thousand times a thousand men, and if another conquers himself, the one who conquers himself is the greatest of conquerors" (Dhammapada 8:4). And here's a teaching from Lord Krishna in the Hindu scriptures: "Do not be ruled by likes (attractions) and dislikes (aversions); they are obstacles in your path" (Bhagavad Gita 3:34).

7 Activity: cry "Geronimo!"

We introduced this commandment with a story about the Apache warrior, Geronimo, and how his name has become synonymous with the courage required to take a leap of faith. In the spirit of crying "Geronimo," take a leap of faith. There are two ways:

1   If you are still hesitating about the willing suspension of disbelief,

    act as if inner change depends on God,

    while acknowledging that you still must give 100% effort. Cry "Geronimo!" and take a leap of faith.

2   If you are a believer,

    act as if inner change depends on you,

    while acknowledging that God is providing 100% of the power. Cry "Geronimo!" and take a leap of faith.

69

"The first thing I would do would be to finish all of my homework on Friday night. That way I would have nothing to worry about on Sunday, and could just keep my mind focused on God."

Rise above self-effort ~ let the Divine work through you.

Remember the Sabbath day, to keep it holy.
Six days you shall labor and do all your work.
But the seventh day is the Sabbath of the Lord
your God. In it, you shall do no work.

Exodus 20:8-10

71

Unplugging

A few years ago, a certain college professor was attending the regional meeting of the American Academy of Religion in New Jersey. Around that same time the college where he taught was competing in the national ice hockey quarter-finals in Columbus, Ohio. If his college won that game, the team would advance to the national semi-finals. He would have loved to attend the game in person, but he was already committed to giving a paper at the conference in New Jersey. He knew, though, that he would be able to follow the game on his cell phone, even while attending the conference. Unfortunately, the game was scheduled to take place at the same time as an important lecture he wanted to attend. *Should I just skip the lecture and watch the game on my phone?* he thought. *Or should I attend the lecture and sneak a peek at my phone every now and then?*

He decided to attend the lecture and occasionally check his phone. But it wasn't easy. He felt like a hypocrite. As his conscience began to get the best of him, he thought *How can I be so strict with my students about cell phones, and here I am doing exactly what I tell them not to do!* He felt like a college student,, torn between checking his cell phone and being present for the lecture.

He decided that he would sit in the back of the lecture hall so that he could both listen to the presenter's speech and discretely check his phone to see how the team was doing. It was an exciting game. His college won, and the team advanced to the "Frozen Four."

As might be expected, he didn't remember much about the lecture. ☺

• ● •

When we first started teaching *Rise Above It* in a college setting, our 1990's syllabus contained the usual instructions: "Be on time for class," "Thoroughly prepare for each class," and "Come to class ready to share what you learned." Gradually, though, as cell phones became increasingly popular, we added an additional instruction: "Cell phones, Facebook, texting, etc. are not allowed during class."

The syllabus for the course now contains a whole paragraph that explains the reasoning behind our ban on cell phones in class:

> *Giving your full attention to others is an important spiritual discipline; it's not compatible with multi-tasking. Moreover, cultivating the ability to concentrate fully, without distractions, will significantly enhance your education. If you need to check your phone for an emergency, let us know before class. For example: "My mom's in the hospital and I'd like to check to see if the operation was successful." Otherwise, power off your phones, and power on your ability to fully listen and engage.*

What we hadn't realized, however, was that the words, *power off your phones, and power on your ability to fully listen and engage,* are central to a counter-culture movement that is currently gaining traction, not just in academia, but across the country and even around the world. For example, an organization called Reboot sponsors a "National Day of Unplugging." On this day, people are encouraged to unplug themselves from all technology for 24 hours. One participant in the Reboot program wrote:

> *I'm so addicted to my dumb phone. It's just the worst. I check my email in the middle of the night. … What's wrong with me? Sometimes I wonder if it's an epidemic, if the whole of the past roughly 6,000 years civilization has just been a sick joke, that all of our ancestors' intrepid pioneering and sacrifice was all just a prelude to this one sad fact: That at the end of the day, all any of us want to do is sit on a chair in a dark room alone, the light from our phone on our face, watching memes of cats and braiding tutorials on YouTube. God, so depressing.* [1]

72

---

1 A "meme" is a video or picture that goes viral on the internet.

She goes on to express her gratitude for the National Day of Unplugging:

> *It is an adaptation of our ancestors' ritual of carving out one day per week to unwind, unplug, relax, reflect, get outdoors, and connect with loved ones. In other words: A 24-hour digital detox, people! Join me and others ... as we toss our phones, computers, iPads, and everything else electronic in the back of our underwear drawers and get back to the basics ... if we even remember what they are.[2]*

She not only recommends what we should *not do*. She also suggests seven things that we *can do*—instead of immersing ourselves in technology. Her list includes cooking, napping, reading, walking, meditating, hanging out with loved ones, and volunteering to help others who are less fortunate than ourselves.

It could also include "resting in God," which is what the Sabbath day is all about.

---

2   Molly Guy, "7 Tech Free Things to Do on the National Day of Unplugging" (March 7, 2017). Accessed on October 6, 2017 @ www.vogue.com/article/national-day-unplugging-digital-detox-tips.

The commandments in world scriptures

Judaism

Unplugging from worldly concerns in order to "plug in" to what really matters, is not just a good idea—it's also a religious principle. In the Hebrew Bible it is written, "Remember the Sabbath day to keep it holy. Six days you shall labor and do all your work. But the seventh day is the Sabbath of the Lord your God. In it, you shall do no work" (Exodus 20:8-10). Of course, nothing is said explicitly about unplugging from technology, but the idea is similar. The Sabbath is a time to rest. It's a time to "unplug" from busy lives, relax, and take some time "to smell the roses." In fact, in the original Hebrew, the word for Sabbath (*Shabbat*) means "rest."

In Judaism the Sabbath is recognized as a time to rest *in* God and reconnect *with* God. The idea of "reconnection" is an important one. The word "religion" means, quite simply, "to reconnect." Its etymology can be traced back to the Latin word *ligare* which means "to bind together, connect, or unite."[3] Just as ligaments (from the Latin word *ligamentum*) connect bone to bone, religion (*re-ligare*) is designed to help people reconnect with God and with each other. It's also about reconnecting with life itself—seeing meaning and purpose, seeing how all things are connected in a wonderful way.

The famous story about how God caused a heap of dry, scattered bones to reconnect and come alive is a symbol of what the Sabbath can do for people. As the story goes, the ancient Israelites were feeling spiritually dead because they were disconnected with God, and from a sense of meaning in their lives. Comparing themselves to a heap of dry bones, scattered about in a valley, they cried out, "Our bones are dry; our hope is lost, and we ourselves are cut off."

God heard their cry and said, "O dry bones, hear the word of the Lord .... I will put sinews on you, and bring flesh upon you." Indeed, God caused breath to enter the dry bones, and they stood on their feet, "an exceedingly great army." The story ends with God making this promise to the Israelites: "I will put my spirit within you, and you shall live" (see Ezekiel 37:1-14).

God, of course, is always willing to revive our spirit, but we must do our part. That's what the Sabbath is for. This becomes clear in the sixteenth chapter of Exodus. Moses has been leading the Israelites through the wilderness

---

3   Julius Pokorny, *Indogermanisches Etymologisches Woerterbuch* (Bern und Muenchen: Francke Verlag, 1959), 668.

towards the Promised Land, but they feel that the journey has been too long. They have lost hope. The long trek now seems meaningless. In reality, it's only been about six weeks since they left Egypt. Nevertheless, they tell Moses, "Oh, that we had died in Egypt ... for you have brought us out into the wilderness to kill this whole assembly with hunger" (Exodus 16:3).

When God heard their murmurings, he gave them "bread from heaven"—quail in the evening and manna in the morning. The manna was a delicate, honey-flavored wafer that could be collected every morning, but it had to be eaten that same day. If it were stored up overnight, it would breed worms. The only exception was the day before the Sabbath. On that day, a double portion of manna could be stored up, to be enjoyed on the Sabbath. As it is written, "Tomorrow is a Sabbath rest, a holy Sabbath to the Lord. Bake what you will bake today, and boil what you will boil, and lay up for yourself all that remains, to be kept until morning .... So they laid it up till morning, and there were no worms in it .... So the people rested on the seventh day" (Exodus 16:23, 24, 30).

For the next forty years, right up until the moment they were ready to cross into the Promised Land, the Israelites continued to be fed with this miraculous "bread from heaven"—a spiritual symbol of the deeper nourishment continually available to everyone who "rests in God."

Christianity

Jesus, who was raised under Mosaic law, had great respect for the Sabbath, but he understood it differently. While he still considered the Sabbath a holy day, he also taught that "the Sabbath was made for man, not man for the Sabbath" (Mark 2:27). In other words, for Jesus the Sabbath was not so much about resting from physical labor but rather, resting in God—that is, allowing God to "do the work" through us. He therefore appeared to be lax about strictly observing the prohibition against any kind of physical work.

The religious leaders, as we can imagine, were not pleased with what they considered Jesus' flagrant disregard for Sabbath law. On one occasion, when Jesus and his disciples were going through the grain fields, the hungry disciples picked some heads of grain and ate them. When the religious leaders saw this, they were outraged, saying, "Look! Your disciples are doing what is unlawful on the Sabbath" (Matthew 12:1-2).

Undeterred by the complaints of the religious leaders, Jesus pointed to God's own words when he said, "I desire mercy, not sacrifice." To illustrate what he meant, Jesus went directly into a synagogue and healed a man who had a withered hand. Again, he was criticized for healing on the Sabbath. But Jesus said, "If any of you has a sheep and it falls into a pit on the Sabbath, will you not take hold of it and lift it out? How much more valuable is a man than a sheep! Therefore, it is lawful to do good on the Sabbath" (Matthew 12:12).

75

In fact, Jesus went one step further, declaring that everyone who came to *him* would find rest: "Come to me all you who labor and are heavy laden, and I will give you rest" (Matthew 11:28). He wasn't just talking about physical rest: "Take my yoke upon you and learn from me, for I am gentle and lowly in heart, and you will find rest *for your souls*" (Matthew 11:29). Whenever God is working *through* you, you will not only find rest for your soul, you will also bear fruit. In this regard Jesus compares himself to the vine which works through the branches: "I am the vine, you are the branches; abide in me and you shall bear much fruit" (John 15:5).

Islam

In Islam, as in Judaism, the Sabbath is a time for doing no work: "O ye who believe! When the call is heard for prayer on the Day of Congregation, haste unto remembrance of Allah and leave your trading" (Qur'an 62:9). Sports and other amusements should be left behind as well: "If others see some bargain or amusement and chase after it, let them go. But say to them 'The blessing from the Presence of Allah is better than any amusement or bargain.' For worshipping Allah is best, and Allah provides for all need" (Qur'an 62:11).[4]

The idea that Allah provides for all one's needs is beautifully expressed in chapter nineteen of the *Qur'an*. There it is written that the blessings of inner peace come to all who place complete faith in Allah. They are like the prophets of old, from Adam, to Noah, to Abraham "who would fall down in prostrate adoration and in tears" acknowledging that everything they have is from Allah. And when they come into the "Gardens of Eternity" they will hear "salutations of peace, and they will have therein their sustenance morning and evening" (Qur'an 19:58, 61, 62).

In other words, those who fully trust in Allah, resting in Allah alone, discover that their innermost needs are fully met. Because they are at peace, they offer "salutations of peace" to one another, and this peace which is both offered and received becomes food for their soul, "their sustenance morning and evening." The word for peace in the Arabic is *salām*, a term that has become a formal greeting throughout the Muslim world. When understood in the context of this passage from the *Qur'an*, however, it can be seen as a blessing which comes to all those who are "constant and patient in the worship of Allah" (Qur'an 16:65).

For the faithful Muslim, true rest—the Sabbath state—can only be found in Allah: "Only in the remembrance of Allah will your heart find rest" (Qur'an 13:28).

---

4 It should be noted, however, that those who purposefully transgress the Sabbath commandment are regarded as less than human: "And well ye knew those amongst you who transgressed in the matter of the Sabbath: We said to them: 'Be ye apes, despised and rejected'" (Qur'an 2:65).

Hinduism

Although there is not a specific "Sabbath day" in Hinduism, the concept of "stilling the mind in God" is of supreme significance. Not only is this the Hindu equivalent of the first commandment ("You shall have no other gods before me"), it is also the Hindu equivalent of the Sabbath. We quote once more, "Still your mind in me, still yourself in me, and without doubt, you will be united with me, Lord of Love, dwelling in your heart" (Bhagavad Gita 12:8).

It could be said that the whole of Hinduism rests on the idea that the mind should be brought into a deeply still, meditative state, with an unshakeable focus on God. When one comes into this state of one-pointed focus, the mind "sits in evenness" undisturbed by outward events. As Krishna says to Arjuna, "Such a person is incapable of ill-will, and returns love for hatred. Such a person lives beyond the reach of 'I' and 'mine,' and is even-minded in pleasure and pain. Such a person is full of mercy and always content. That person's heart and mind dwell upon me" (Bhagavad Gita 12:13-14).

Krishna is here describing that state of inner peace known as śāntiḥ, a Sanskrit word for peace or calmness of mind. The words *Shanti, Shanti, Shanti* (Peace, Peace, Peace) are often chanted at the end of Hindu prayers, along with the sacred syllable, *Aum* (or *Om*). All of this is intended to bring the devotee into that state of perfect union with God, a state of inner peace whose chief characteristic is "evenness." The closest English synonyms are inner peace, spiritual rest, and pure tranquility. The surface of a clear lake on a windless day would give an accurate image of this state, because a perfectly still lake would clearly reflect the world around it without distortion. In the context of this commandment, it could also be called a "Sabbath state."

For those who cannot still their mind in God, the practice of meditation is prescribed: "If you cannot still your mind in me, learn to do so through the practice of meditation" (Bhagavad Gita 12:9). And if that doesn't work, selfless service is prescribed: "If you lack the will for such self-discipline, engage yourself in selfless service of all around you, for selfless service can lead you at last to me" (Bhagavad Gita 12:10).

Finally, if one is unable to do this, Krishna says, "Surrender yourself to me in love, receiving success and failure with equal calmness as granted by me ... there follows immediate peace" (Bhagavad Gita 12:11-12). For many people, especially in a hurry-up world where success becomes a false god, this final practice becomes imminently practical. The intent of this practice is to divert people's attention from attachment to outcomes, and get them to focus on the task at hand—leaving results to God. Krishna puts it like this: "Perform work in this world, Arjuna, without attachment [to results], handling both success and defeat in perfect evenness of mind" (Bhagavad Gita 2:48).[5]

---

5   While this is a combination of several translations, it is primarily based on the work of Eknath Easwaran.

Buddhism

As we have just noted, Hindus practice "stilling the mind" in Krishna and his teachings. It is quite similar in Buddhism, except that Buddhists practice "calming the mind" in "the Good Law"—the teachings of the Buddha. While the scriptural texts differ, as does the idea of God, the "mark to aim at" for both Hindus and Buddhists is the same: a tranquil mind.

And so, the image of a tranquil lake, which describes the mind of a practicing Hindu, also describes the mind of a devout Buddhist: "Even as a deep lake is clear and calm, so also wise people become tranquil after they have listened to the laws" (Dhammapada 6:7). That tranquility becomes a beacon of steady light for others: "The wise person, though young, who lives according to the doctrine of the Buddha, illumines the world like the moon freed from cloud" (Dhammapada 25:23).

In regard to a particular Sabbath "day," or "day of rest," the Buddha is silent. Instead, he places emphasis on freeing oneself from all cravings, and every excessive attachment to that which is fleeting and ephemeral. In so far as they are able to do this, Buddhists find "rest" from every anxious thought and covetous desire—a spiritual "Sabbath" state.

In the teaching of the Buddha this is described as "emptying oneself" of everything that prevents a person from becoming truly human. As the Buddha puts it: "Empty yourself of greed, hatred, folly, pride, and false teachings. One who has *risen above* these five selfish attachments will cross the river of life" (Dhammapada 25:11; emphasis added).

• ● •

This then, is a brief survey of the Sabbath, both as a day for reconnecting with God, and as a state of mind that you can achieve—an inner tranquility in which you can experience the deepest peace. It is perhaps the peace that Buddha was referring to when he spoke about the importance of the "Good Law": "Better than a hundred verses composed of meaningless words, is one line of the Law that brings peace" (Dhammapada 8:3).

It could also be the peace that Isaiah described when he spoke about the Lawgiver himself: "Thou will keep him in perfect peace, whose mind is stayed on thee" (Isaiah 26:3).

The Sabbath, then, is not only a chance to "unplug." It is also a day to "reboot"—a time to renew your dreams and rejuvenate your spirit, through reconnecting with God, others, and the purpose of your life.

The commandments in the lives of college students

*Remember the Sabbath day to keep it holy.
Six days you shall labor and do all your work.
But the seventh day is the Sabbath of the Lord
your God. In it, you shall do no work.*

My mother is constantly telling me, "Relax. Let your mind get
some rest." Well, that's a lot easier said than done. Whenever
I try to relax, I think of all the productive things I could be
doing instead of resting.

Journal excerpt from a college sophomore

Is it OK to do homework on the Sabbath?

As a college student, the Sabbath commandment can pose interesting
challenges for you—especially because this commandment says that no "work"
is to be done on the Sabbath. "Six days shall you labor and do all your work, but
the seventh day is the Sabbath of the Lord your God. In it, you shall do no work"
(Exodus 20:9-10).

At the same time, there is something called "home*work*," a familiar term for any
college student. And many students like to use the weekend to catch up on
assignments. In his journal entry titled "Sundays are for Homework," one student
writes:

> 66 When I first got the assignment to try and keep the Sabbath day holy,
> I must say that I was a little intimidated by the challenge. I had not been
> to a church service since high school, and I was already a junior in college.
> Sundays at college are homework days for me and seemingly for many other
> students. They are days when nothing much really happens. You sleep in; you
> talk to friends; you complain about the rough week ahead. You do homework.
> That is what defined Sunday for me for almost three years of my life. So
> imagine how I felt getting handed this assignment all of a sudden. (Not that I
> didn't expect it, of course.)

This student knew that honoring the Sabbath was going to be one of the commandments, and that it would be turned into an assignment for class. But how would he practice it? For him, as a Christian, the Sabbath was always on Sunday. How would he "keep the Sabbath holy"? He came up with a plan:

> OK, I decided that if I was going to do this right, I would need to change a few things. The first thing I would do would be to finish all of my homework on Friday night. That way I would have nothing to worry about on Sunday, and could just keep my mind focused on God. But this turned out to be easier said than done. On Friday when I tried to get started on my homework, I kept distracting myself, getting up for something to eat, browsing the internet, daydreaming. The book I had to read, or the make-up quiz I had to take, or the course packet I had to review just sat there on the couch while I went off to do something else. It was especially difficult because all my friends were out there in the warm night having fun, and here I was, trapped inside, slaving over papers just so I could "keep the Sabbath holy." Finally, I went outside and jogged around campus to blow off steam.

Even that was not enough for him. He was still anxious, restless, and unable to focus on schoolwork. Feeling defeated, he tried prayer:

> I asked God to help me empty myself of worry and just let things go, to let him take the wheel. I guess he did, because I managed to get a good night's sleep.

> On Saturday I easily caught up on most of my homework. Then came Sunday ...

He found his way to a local church, feeling uneasy, because it had been so long since he had been to church. It turned out to be a peaceful, Sabbath experience:

> The sermon was about being open to God and letting him lead us. As I sat there soaking in everything the minister said through the echoing mic, a sort of peace came over me. It felt right. I was connecting with God again for the first time in years. After the sermon ended, I left the building and noticed just how nice the day was. The sun was warm on my back, birds were locked in harmonious conversation in the trees, and the grass was very green and cushioned my feet as I walked. The world seemed brighter and more cheerful. I felt reawakened. Even though I know that every day can be a Sabbath, I will work to keep this day holy more and more. It has brought me a peace of mind that I have never really felt until now—even if my homework is still unfinished. 99

Another student, who also was dealing with a homework issue, discovered a different way to keep the Sabbath holy. He begins his journal entry with what appears to be a good plan, not only for keeping the Sabbath holy, but also for completing his homework assignments:

> 66 This week I decided that I would literally remember the Sabbath day and not do homework on Sunday. Instead, I would devote my entire Sunday to

worshipping God, reading Bible, and spending time with my friends. I would finish all of my homework on Friday and Saturday in order to enjoy a stress-free Sabbath.

When Sunday came, and he had not managed to finish his homework, he found himself in a dilemma. He wanted to honor his commitment to do no homework on the Sabbath; but he also wanted to complete his homework for Monday's classes. Noticing that he felt anxious, he decided to pray:

> I asked God to give me peace and faith, especially because I still had nagging doubts in the back of my mind about my homework. Even though I was spending my Sunday sitting around in the beautiful weather with my friends, I felt like I could be doing more. Praying was helpful. As the peaceful feelings came, I decided that I would just continue enjoying the day and do homework only if it didn't feel like a burden.

That, however, was not the end. A little later in the day, he received a surprising "answer" to his prayer:

> I don't know how it happened, but all of a sudden, the idea that I could spend some time visiting my grandparents came into my mind. I sensed that, somehow, this was an answer to my prayer. God was giving me an opportunity to reconnect with people I loved, and in so doing, to reconnect with Him.

His grandparents lived nearby. Both had recently been to the hospital—grandma had broken her wrist, and grandpa had developed a serious case of pneumonia. They were home now, and it would be a good time to visit. He went and bought flowers, and, an hour later, he was knocking on their front door:

> When grandpa opened the door, I could tell that he was astounded to see me there with flowers. He invited me in, and I sat down and had a great conversation with him and grandma. When I left, he was almost in tears as he told me what a wonderful grandson I was. Through something as simple as bringing them flowers and visiting for fifteen minutes, I had made them both immensely, amazingly happy.

While driving back to college, he reflected on the miracle of being connected— to God, and to others, simply by remembering to keep the Sabbath:

> As I drove back from my grandparents' house, I felt a wonderful connection to the Lord. I understood that the Lord had used me to brighten up my grandparents' day. He had used me to bring them joy. Just to see the joy that the Lord was able to give them through me was an amazing gift—one that I could never have received if I had spent the day holed up in my room doing homework. 🙾

That evening, in a restful state of mind, he completed all of his homework. But it did not feel like a burden.

81

The Sabbath as a state of mind

While most people think of the Sabbath as a day of the week (Friday, Saturday or Sunday), it is also a state of mind. Keeping the Sabbath "day" holy, then, could mean something as simple as remembering that there is always a state of inner peace—a state of spiritual *rest*, available to us. This is not the same as physical rest, which involves resting the body. The deepest form of Sabbath is a state of *spiritual* rest, or, as Jesus says, "rest for our souls" (Matthew 11:29).

A young woman, who titles her journal entry "A Moment in Green Pastures," talks about her constant state of unrest and her inability to "chill out":

> 66 I am not an easy going, composed person. Rather I am tense and often feel pressed by a sense of urgency. You might say that "urgency" or "intensity" is my false god. This is perhaps because I grew up in an Asian society where life is all about competition and where people often use other people's failures as stepping stones in order to achieve their own goals. I had not noticed this about myself until my American friends told me to "relax and chill out."
>
> In class, when you suggested that we ask a friend about our negative traits, I did that. When I texted my friend, she said, "You never give yourself a break." She is right. I am seized with a "more, better, faster" disease, and I am terrible at taking breaks. So "taking a Sabbath break" and finding peace in the middle of my busy, crazy life seemed like an impossible aim.

Although it seemed like taking a Sabbath break during the day would be an impossible aim, this student had an awakening that changed everything:

> A few days ago, I called my mom and asked her how her relationship with dad was going. She said, "You know your dad. He's always so busy, and he doesn't listen to anyone. I have given up." I understood what mom was saying. It's been over twenty years, and I've never seen my dad put his family first. It's always his work. Everything else comes before family. No matter what we say, he is never willing to listen. My mother's comments reminded me that I've promised myself never to be like my dad. I know how it feels when my dad is so busy that he has no time for me.

After the conversation with her mother, she found herself in an agitated state:

> When I got off the phone, I was shaking uncontrollably from anger toward my dad. Then, the next moment, I realized—as if struck by lightning—that I have been acting the same way that he does. I felt shallow and powerless, never noticing until now the person I have become. In that moment, all I could do was call on the Lord and ask him to take away my feelings of anger and fragility, and to let me be open and accepting of others instead.

Her prayer was answered:

> After my prayer, I could feel the whirling vortex of emotions slowly dying down. At the same time, I felt peace settling into me. I thanked God for

opening my eyes so that I could see my hidden false god. Without God's help, I would have never discovered the false god that had been controlling my feelings and thoughts. I believe that in response to my prayer, God gave me a chance to become a new person. It was a moment "in green pastures." He had "led me beside still waters" and "restored my soul." (Psalm 23:3) 🙶🙶

In Eastern religions, repeating a "mantra," a word or phrase spoken repeatedly, can bring about a sense of inner peace—a Sabbath state.[6] In the following journal entry, a student talks about how she came up with her own mantra, and how it helped her overcome anxiety:

🙶🙶 Last night I was having difficulty falling asleep because of a stressful situation in my life. So I decided to "remember the Sabbath," right there while lying in my bed. I started to pray. I told the Lord why I was feeling so stressed, and how I wanted it fixed. To my surprise, praying about it made me feel even more stressed!

I remembered that one of my professors told us in class that as a child he always ended his prayers saying, "Thank you, thank you, very, very much. Thank you, thank you, very, very much" over and over again as a mantra until he drifted off to sleep. So I adjusted my prayer, and made up a meditation of sorts. I imagined my breath being like waves on a shore, and with each inhale the waves pulled back and I thought, "Thank you," and with every exhale the waves rolled gently up onto the shore and I thought, "Please, Thank you, Please, Thank you, Please."

I realized that this brought me into a Sabbath state, because I wasn't going through the list of what I need and getting all worked up about it. Instead, I was simply acknowledging that I need the Lord's help (Please) and thanking him (Thank you) for all he has given and all he will give me. I used this mantra again today when I was walking back from class and caught myself worrying about the same situation. "Thank you. Please. Thank you. Please." It works!

This student had not only discovered a new way to pray, but also a new way to think about the challenges she faced. Previously, she had believed that worries and anxieties could be relieved by the resolution of problems. Her new realization was that problems could still be there, but she didn't have to be anxious about them. She could still find peace, even in the midst of difficulties. She concludes her journal entry with these words:

This week it really hit home that I need to work on being calm and present in each moment rather than waiting until a perfectly peaceful time when all of

83

6   The Sanskrit word "mantra" is derived from a word which means "thought" or "to think." So, a mantra is a vehicle for thinking, a means of thinking, or "an instrument of thought." Accessed on November 27, 2017 @ www.etymonline.com/word/mantra "Mantra" is the nominative (subject) form, while "mantram" is the accusative (direct object) form. Accessed on November 17, 2017 @ www.jillbormann.com/9.html

my problems are solved. That's because life isn't like that. There are always stresses, and I want to get better at being peaceful and centered in the midst of all the imperfectness. I knew that this problem with worry was going to take a lot of work, and I am proud to have taken one step closer to being a peaceful person. As they say, "True peace is not freedom from the storm; it is peace within the storm." 🙸

Mini-Sabbaths

At the literal level, the Sabbath is a specific day. But at the deeper levels of this commandment, the Sabbath is not a specific day; nor does it require meeting in a specific place. It can occur anytime, anywhere. It only involves resting from worries, concerns, and anxieties long enough to enjoy the present moment—connecting to God, and connecting to others. We call this a "mini-Sabbath." One young lady put it like this:

🙶 The idea of a mini-Sabbath really appeals to me. I don't attend church on Sundays anymore, but I would love to have a Sabbath moment at least once every day. I'm not talking about, "Let's take a moment of silence for ....." Not that kind of a moment. I'm talking about at least once a day, I would love to have a great connection with someone and see that, and realize that, and be aware of what's happening, and thank the Lord for it. That is how I would truly wish to experience the Sabbath. 🙸

Another student, quoting an unknown author, wrote, "Some go to church and think about hunting; others go hunting and think about God." It's true. A mini-Sabbath can take place in unusual locations and at unexpected times. In the following journal entry, a student talks about his experience of a "mini-Sabbath" in the midst of a grueling cross-country race:

🙶 In addition to going to college and working the late shift at a local store, I'm on the cross-country team. This past Saturday, my late shift lasted until 2:00 AM, and I didn't get back to the dorm and into bed until 3:00 AM. Our cross-country meet was the next day, starting at 9:30 AM. Yup, it was on Sunday.

It didn't help that I slept through my alarm and arrived late for the bus. Luckily, I made it just before the bus left for the meet. Once we arrived at the track, another monkey wrench was thrown in. The course we went over on Friday was drastically different from the one we were about to run.

As I was running the course, I started to run out of gas around the fourth mile. I had forgotten to drink water before the race, had no breakfast, and was suffering from a serious lack of sleep. My body was beginning to break down. My mind was screaming, "Stop!" I considered slowing down or even walking. Over and over, my mind screamed "Stop!" Slowly, I reduced my pace. At the same time, I remembered that the Sabbath is about slowing down—not pushing myself so hard. It was like a "mini-Sabbath."

84

The act of deliberately slowing down for a "mini-Sabbath" brought about a small miracle:

> All of a sudden, I felt calm and relaxed. I wasn't thirsty, hungry, or tired. I was just there. I thought about the Sabbath commandment and how God tells us to rest in Him. I asked God to guide my steps. For some strange reason, as I was ascending one of the major hills and saw the downhill, I noticed the sun shining through the canvas of the trees, little light streams hitting the tumbling rocks almost like a guide to my feet. I felt light and focused, sort of like I was being guided around every sharp bend and over the jagged terrain under my feet. An incredible calmness rolled over me and I began to sprint down the hills laughing and smiling with each foot placement. When I realized that I had only a half mile to go, I sprinted harder and didn't stop until I had crossed the finish line.

This student's Sabbath experience continued, even after the meet:

> Afterwards, I looked for a shaded area under a tree and sat down beneath the branches. The coolness wrapped me up, and the breeze swept my hair. In that moment, I realized that no matter what is going on, and no matter how daunting or frustrating the situation might be, I can always have a mini-Sabbath. I can always connect with God—even if it occurs, literally, while I am "on the run." Finding that reconnection with God was like finding an electrical cord that had been disconnected and plugging it back into the Power Source.

He concluded by promising himself that he would always make a place in his life for God:

> I realized that as long as I am connected to God (my Power Source) my mind can be calm and at ease. I will continue to find a place for God in my daily life, even while I'm in the midst of other things. By keeping that connection open, I can reset and re-center myself. I know that this will lead to greater happiness for me and better relationships with others. 🙶🙶

Sacred scripture

Here is something you can try: start your day by writing down some truth from sacred scripture. Just jot it down and carry it with you throughout the day. It could be from the Bible, the Buddha, the *Bhagavad Gita* or the *Qur'an*. Your aim is to notice some circumstance in which you can use this truth to help you. Here is a small sampling of what previous students have experienced:

> 🙶🙶 The quote I chose was, "The Lord is my helper, so I will not fear." Sometimes, for no reason, I become very afraid and feel perplexed. I can't even think what to do and what not to do. But this week, whenever fear came up, I remembered to say to myself, "The Lord is my helper, so I will not fear." Whenever I did this, it made it easier to control myself. I became less fearful. In one situation, when I felt that someone was judging me, I remembered my

85

passage of scripture. It helped. Whether they were judging me or not, I did not care. I said to myself, "If the Lord is my helper, what can anyone do to me? I will not fear." 99

66 This morning I was working out at the fitness center and using many different weights throughout my exercise routine. I know that when I'm done working out, I'm supposed to put all the weights back from where they came from, but I usually don't do it. I'm usually too tired, and a voice inside my heads says, "It's not worth the energy. Someone else is going to do your same workout anyway, so it's best to just leave the weights on the equipment." This is obviously not true, because there are many people who will need more or less weight than me. That's when my passage of scripture came to my rescue: "Do unto others as you would have them do unto you." With this scripture in mind, I put all the weights I used back in their proper places on the rack. Sure, it took a little extra effort to do that, but the extra effort gave me a peaceful feeling. It was what I would have wanted someone else to do for me. 99

66 Here's my quote: "I am with you and will watch over you wherever you go. And I will bring you back to this land. I will not leave you until I have done what I promised you." I chose this quote because every time I read it, it boosts my faith in God. So today, throughout the day, I would read it or think about it whenever I was having a hard moment, or a moment of total exhaustion, and it would allow me to finish the task at hand. For example, it helped me get through a very difficult history class today! This was a great exercise. I plan to carry this quote in my purse always. 99

While most of these examples may come across as "quick fixes," it isn't always that easy. In the following journal entry, a student writes about a failed attempt to use scripture, and what she learned as a result:

66 Since I live at home, my dad drives me to school every morning. Because it's only a five-minute drive to school, if we leave by 9:00 AM, I have enough time to go to the dining hall for a quick breakfast and still make it to my 9:20 class.

Earlier this week, I was all dressed and ready to go at 9:00 AM, but dad wasn't ready. He said that he was "running a little late," and I took this to mean "a few minutes." However, as the minutes slowly, agonizingly, ticked by, I was becoming more and more impatient. First 9:05 passed, then 9:10. At this point I was getting angry. If I had known he was going to take this long, I could have just eaten breakfast at home. Now it was too late to get anything at home, and too late to get dining hall food, and still make it to class on time. It seems like such a little thing, but I hate it when my morning routine is disrupted even a little.

The thought occurred to me that this would be a perfect time for a mini-Sabbath. So I stopped and asked God to give me peace and tranquility, but in the back of my mind I could not stop wishing that my dad would just hurry up already. I tried to honestly clear my mind for several minutes, but I was unsuccessful. On top of being angry because my dad was late, I was also now frustrated that I could not get into a Sabbath mindset.

When my dad finally came down the stairs at 9:15, he asked me if I was ready to go.

"I've been ready for the last 20 minutes!" I replied angrily.

I let my anger get the best of me, and I was instantly disappointed in myself. As we say in class, "I missed the mark." Not only could I not find a Sabbath state within myself, but I was also rude to my dad. In the readings we did for class, people made it sound so easy to find those feelings of peace, but I realized that it's much harder than it might seem—especially when resentment was still controlling me.

She makes a good point. While identifying false gods (first chapter), and accessing the qualities of our Higher Nature (second chapter), may get us back on course, we often need to avail ourselves of even more powerful "weapons" from God's arsenal—in this case the power of sacred scripture. As her journal entry continues, this is exactly what she talks about:

87

Later the next day, I pulled a yellow note card out of my back pack and looked at the sacred scripture quote I had written for the *Rise Above It* class: "He who is without sin among you, let him throw a stone at her first." I thought back to how angry I had been at my dad for being fifteen minutes late. Then I thought about all the times I had been late, and all the people I had inconvenienced, and I realized that if I had remembered this quote in the midst of my anger, it would have helped me to get into the right mindset to accept the feelings of peace and tranquility that I had prayed to receive. I also could have worked it out with my dad in a more peaceful manner. I know that promptness is a virtue, but so is patience. 🥾🥾

This is what it means when spiritual leaders talk about "the power of sacred scripture." The words of scripture can serve as vessels for the inflow of divine qualities, especially the peace and tranquility associated with the Sabbath state. With sacred scripture in her mind, and working in her heart, she could have spoken with her father about her desire to be on time for class. She could even have told him how frustrating it was to wait twenty minutes and miss breakfast. But all of that could have been done kindly and from love—not from resentment and anger. It would have been a "Sabbath" experience.

Remembering your Higher Nature

You might be the kind of student who gets recharged by watching athletic events, jogging around campus, or lifting weights. Or maybe your recharging method is simply to unwind by playing video games, watching Netflix, or surfing the net. Maybe it's hanging out with friends. Or maybe it's just sleeping in after a busy day or a busy week. While these recreational/relaxing activities are important, the focus of this commandment is about *connecting with God*, which can also mean that you are *connecting with your Higher Nature*. You are connecting with who you truly are, at your core. You are connecting with your "Best Self," "Higher Self," "True Self" or "God in you."

In Buddhism this "Higher Nature" is also called our "original nature" or "Buddha-nature." It refers to the essential goodness which permeates the universe and constitutes the core of every sentient being—whether the Buddha or the vilest criminal. As it is written in the Buddhist scriptures, "All beings always have the Buddha-nature" (Maitreya, *Sublime Continuum*, 1:27).

Whenever you realize your "Buddha-nature," "Higher Nature," "Original Nature" or "God-breathed" spiritual nature (Qur'an 15:29), whatever is happening "on the outside" cannot disturb who you are "on the inside." In his journal entry on the Sabbath commandment, one student puts it like this:

> 66 My problems may never go away, or there may always be new ones, but I can learn to see them differently. This can happen if I let go of "my will" and put my trust in "God's will," it may not speed up traffic or make money appear on my dresser (although sometimes I wish it would). But it can create an opportunity for God to flow in with hope and love, despite what is happening at the moment. My peace or Sabbath always comes when I realize that everything is in God's hands, and, no matter how chaotic things are in my outer world, I can remain in a state of inner peace. I think this is what Jesus meant when he said, "Not my will, but thy will be done." 99

According to the Third Noble Truth, as taught by the Buddha, "When the fires of selfishness have been extinguished, when the mind is free of selfish desire, what remains is the state of wakefulness, of peace, of joy, of perfect health, called 'nirvana.'"[7]

To illustrate this concept, we will pass out tea lights for each of you to hold. When the tea lights are lit, we will ask you to imagine that the flame represents the selfish desires of the ego—the lower nature which is so pre-occupied with selfish concerns that it is hardly aware of the needs of others or the existence of God. Next, we will explain that the Sanskrit word *nirvana* means to "blow out" (*vana* = "to blow" and *nir* = "out"). We will then invite you to "blow out" the flame of self-will, imagining that what is left behind is the pure Higher Self—your

---

7   This quotation is taken from the introduction to *The Dhammapada*, introduced and translated by Eknath Easwaran (Petaluma CA: Nilgiri Press, 2007), 44.

"Buddha-nature" or your original "God-breathed" inner spirit—untainted by ego concerns. This is the True Self whose fundamental nature is receptive of what flows in directly from God.[8]

The Sabbath, then, in this highest sense, is an invitation to remember your true nature, to remember that you are born to receive and cultivate your spiritual potential, and that there is a force in the universe—greater than yourself—that will help you do this. When this is understood, the words, "You shall do no work on the Sabbath" can assure you that whenever you clear out whatever may be in the way, the "Force" will not only be *with you*, but will also be *in you*, and *work through you*—to give you rest.

• ● •

The Sabbath is about *unplugging* from that which is temporal and *plugging in* to that which is eternal. It's about taking time to rise above worldly attachments and focus on that which will endure forever; it's about the discovery and development of your spiritual nature, including your God-given desire to serve others without a thought of reward; it's about the peace that is always available to you, and which flows in immediately whenever you allow God to lift you above the promptings of your lower nature. As it is written in the Hebrew scriptures, "If you do not do your own will on My holy day … not doing as you please or following your own desires … then you will find joy in the Lord, and I will cause you to rise above the lofty things of the earth" (Isaiah 58:13-14).

89

---

8 Rick Hanson writes: "It's a remarkable fact that the people who have gone the very deepest into the mind—the sages and saints of every religious tradition—all say essentially the same thing: *your fundamental nature is pure, conscious, peaceful, radiant, loving, and wise*, and it is joined in mysterious ways with the ultimate underpinnings of reality, by whatever name we give That. Although your true nature may be hidden momentarily by stress and worry, anger and unfulfilled longings, it continues to exist. Knowing this can be a great comfort" (emphasis added). In *Buddha's Brain*, op. cit., 15.

The mark to aim at

Remember the Sabbath day, to keep it holy

The focus of this commandment is on *connecting with God*. More specifically, it's about acknowledging God as the "Doer," and seeing yourself as the vehicle through whom the work is done. This is what it means to do "no work" on the Sabbath. The mark to aim at, then, is to *let God do the work through you*. As Jesus says, "I am the vine, you are the branches. If you abide in me, you will bear much fruit" (John 15:5). Similarly, in Hinduism, Lord Krishna says that you must become "an instrument in the hands of the Lord" (Bhagavad Gita 18:50). Therefore, in the context of this commandment your "work" is to put aside worries, fears, and doubts, so that you can align yourself with a power greater than yourself—a power that can work through you. If the idea of "God" is a problem for you, you might prefer to think in terms of a benevolent force in the universe that is seeking to work through you and give you rest. In other words, you are not entirely on your own, and it's not entirely about self-effort. As they say in the movie *Star Wars*, "May the Force be with you!" In your journal, record your experience of practicing this commandment.

Suggestions for further reflection and practice

Remember the Sabbath day, to keep it holy.

The following exercises contain additional information about this commandment. Read through all of them, and then focus on one or two that spark your interest.

1 Activity: attend a religious service

For many people, attending a religious service is the most literal way of keeping this commandment. It serves to deepen their connection with God and with others, and it provides a source of spiritual renewal. If you were forced to attend religious services as a child, you may have developed a dislike for compelled worship. That is understandable. This time, however, no one is compelling you. It's your own free choice. In fact, you may find that the absence of compulsion may help you experience a religious service in a new way. Give it a try. See how it goes.

2 Activity: unplug and enjoy a mini-Sabbath

The introductory story for this chapter described the "Reboot" program—a deliberate effort to go without technology for 24 hours. The idea is to give yourself a chance to unwind from the incessant clamor of the world so that you can focus on what's truly important. Why not give it a try—perhaps for a shorter period of time? 12 hours? 6 hours? 1 hour? Whatever you can manage. During that time, take the opportunity to connect with Someone or Something higher than yourself. Pray, meditate, read and reflect on sacred scripture. Enjoy a mini-Sabbath.

3 Activity: you can take it with you

Toward the end of this chapter we gave some examples of what happened when students carried a passage of scripture with them throughout the day, noticing how it might apply to certain situations. Try it yourself. At the beginning of the day, jot down a passage of sacred scripture that appeals to you; then take it with you as you begin your day. Notice if it comes up for you, reaches out to you, and/or "speaks to you" during the day.

4 Journal reflection: a letter from God

In the commandment on not taking the Lord's name in vain, we suggested that you access God's arsenal of divine qualities by *asking* that these qualities become manifest in you. But communication involves more than just asking. It also involves *listening* for a response. In this commandment, therefore, the emphasis is on listening for a divine response. Write yourself a "letter from God" (or from your Higher Self). In other words, write down what you hear, or (if you don't receive a verbal message) try to put feelings into words. Pay special attention to your opening words and closing words. Keep your mind in an open, receptive state.

5 Activity: practice using a mantra

The repetition of a "mantra" is a time-honored tradition. It can be any scriptural word or phrase that serves to connect you with a Reality that is higher than the fearful, anxious, worried, resentful lower self. In Judaism, the *Shema*, "Hear O Israel, the Lord is One," is a famous mantra. In Christianity, there is the repetition of the name *Jesus*. In Hinduism, there is the repetition of one of the names of God, for example, *Krishna, Krishna*, or *Rama, Rama*, or *Hare, Hare*. In Buddhism, the statement *Om mani padme hum* sums up the entirety of the Buddha's teachings. Select a mantra that works for you and practice repeating it. Memorizing and repeating short passages of sacred scripture (i.e. *The Lord is my shepherd. I shall not want*) can be especially powerful. After you've chosen your mantra or your passage, stick with it, and notice if it brings about a Sabbath state.

6 Activity: stop picking up sticks

In the days of ancient Israel, a man who was caught picking up sticks was condemned for "working" on the Sabbath. On a literal level, his penalty (death by stoning) seems to be unnecessarily severe. When understood more deeply, however, the story symbolizes how each of us can bring spiritual death on ourselves whenever we separate ourselves from the Source of life. When Jesus said, "I am the vine, you are the branches, abide in me and you will bear fruit," he was encouraging us to remember that if a branch is separated from the vine to which it is connected, it withers and dies. It's just a stick. But if it remains connected to the vine, it continues to bear fruit. In other words, the Sabbath commandment is not just about a "day" of rest; it's also about a "state" of inner peace that you can enter whenever you let God work through you. Give it a try and see what happens. Stop "picking up sticks." Let God work through you. Stay connected. Enjoy your "Sabbath rest."

7 Activity: blow out the flame of self-will

The Sanskrit word *Nirvana* means "to blow out." In this chapter, we said that *Nirvana* is not an escape from reality or a state of "nothingness." Rather, it's a deliberate attempt to extinguish self-well, self-absorption, and all things related to your lower nature. When you "blow out" the fires of greed, lust and selfish ambition, you open the way for God's qualities to flow in. Peace, joy, love and the desire to serve with no thought of reward arise—for they were always there, blocked only by self-will. As the flame of self-will is blown out, inner peace arises. It's a Sabbath experience. It's what Jesus meant when he said, "Not my will, but thy will be done" (Luke 22:42).

8 Activity: light the flame of Sabbath peace

In sacred scripture, fire is not only a symbol of greed, lust and selfish ambition ("hellfire," "boiling anger," "burning lust," etc.); it can also be a symbol of God's constant love and wisdom. The gentle, steady flame of a candle can symbolize the presence of a Higher Power who fills us with love (the heat of the candle), wisdom (the light of the candle) and peace (the unwavering candle flame). With this idea in mind, find a quiet place where you can light a candle or tea-light. Set it beside you while you take 15 minutes to read scripture, meditate on a passage of scripture, or simply keep your mind centered on your mantra. In this state, allow your mind to stop jumping restlessly from topic to topic. Instead, let it settle down and enter a state of inner tranquility—a state of Sabbath peace: "As a flame in a windless place flickers not, so is the mind which is under control and united with God" (Bhagavad Gita 6:19).[9]

93

---

9 This translation is based on the commentary of Swami Mukundananda who writes, "The mind is fickle by nature and very difficult to control. But when the mind of a yogi is in enthralled union with God, it becomes sheltered against the winds of desire." Accessed on January 2, 2018 @ www.holy-bhagavad-gita.org/chapter/6/verse/19

"I would just like to apologize to everyone else in the world who does not have my parents, because my parents are literally the best people on this whole planet."

Rise above ingratitude ~ see the best in others.

Honor your father and mother that your days may be long upon the land which the Lord your God is giving you.

Exodus 20:12

A mother's love

Dr. Lonise Bias and her husband James could not have been happier or more proud on June 17, 1986, when they learned that their son, Len, was selected to play professional basketball for the Boston Celtics. During a stellar career at the University of Maryland, he was twice named the Athletic Coast Conference Player of the Year, and in his senior year he was named a first-team All-American. Now he was about to become a professional basketball player. Some sports analysts predicted that he would surpass Michael Jordan and go on to become one of the greatest basketball players of all time. The future looked bright for 22-year-old Len Bias.

Two days later he died of a cocaine overdose.

It's never easy for parents to deal with the death of a child. The family of Len Bias suffered greatly. But that was not the end. Four years later, in the parking lot of a shopping mall in the suburbs of Washington DC, Len's younger brother, Jay, was shot twice in the back. When Lonise found out that her son had been shot, she immediately rushed to the hospital. It was the same hospital where Len had died four years earlier.

In a YouTube interview, Lonise explains what that experience was like:

> *I went to the same waiting room and went to the same door. My daughter opened it.*

"How is Jay doing?" I asked.

She said, "Ma, Jay is gone."

When she said, "Jay is gone," I went completely off. I took my fist and I beat the walls in that waiting room. I beat holes in the wall! I took the lamps and threw them on the floor. I screamed, I hollered. I was so angry with God. I was so mad. It was not fair. ... When I got home I went to my bedroom and shut the door and stayed in there for three days. And every time I thought about what God had allowed to happen to our family again, I would get mad. If someone brought me a cup of water I would take it and throw it up against the wall.

God let me have my temper tantrum for three days. And on the third day I got up and I started to move forward.[1]

Gradually, Lonise, with the full support of her husband and two remaining children, decided that she needed to do something about the drugs and violence that were tearing up families and communities. Believing that God would not let her down, and that there was always hope, she became a motivational speaker, turning her tragedy into a powerful lesson for young people.

Speaking with great conviction, Lonise tells young people that "character is developed precisely at those times when you feel the most pain and disappointment." She tells them that when she lost her two sons she wanted to die. She admits that during that dark time she kept thinking *Why me?* and *Why my family?* Then, moving from the past to the present, she speaks directly to her young audience, saying, "I thought it was all about me and my family. But I came to realize that it's not about me and my family. It's about *you.*"

Well aware of what can happen to young people when they associate with the wrong crowd, she continues: "We need you to be people with backbone and character. We need people who can stand up and make healthy decisions without worrying about what someone else thinks about them."

Lonise knows that making good decisions isn't easy, especially in a world where young people are bombarded with enticing messages about sex, where using drugs is made to seem glamorous, and where gang violence is touted as a solution to relationship problems. She tells them that they are going to have to fight against these temptations. Here's how she puts it:

You are going to have to fight. And you are going to learn that opposition is an opportunity for you to maximize your potential.

---

1 "Dr. Lonise Bias on the Rock Newman Show." See minute marker 36-51. Accessed on November 23, 2017 @ www.youtube.com/watch?v=Xje5arcsDvU

When you are at the gym with the barbell and you pull it up, and you're at the place where you're weak, and you squeeze it, and you keep squeezing it, and squeezing it … you keep working that muscle.

She then compares the development of physical muscle to the development of spiritual character:

You are in the situation you are in to develop muscle, to develop character, to become who you [really] are. If you don't stand for something, you will fall for anything. As Frederick Douglas said, "There is no progress or change without struggle."[2]

Ten years after the deaths of the Bias brothers, Wayne Coffey, a sportswriter for the *New York Daily News*, wrote about the Bias family's campaign to put an end to drugs and violence, the twin demons that had been destroying the lives of young people. The article begins by describing Lonise as "an imposing woman" whose sheer honesty "hits like a freight train." Coffey says that Lonise "not only refuses to succumb to rage and self-pity, but she takes her pain on the road, laying it out for all to see and feel, offering it as a wellspring of hope, and empowerment, a means to spare other families the grief the Biases have known."

During those ten years, Lonise spoke in forty-six states, delivering her powerful message to young people at risk, to school assemblies, at high school and college graduations, and to professional sports teams. Coffey quotes Thomas Sanders, a Hall of Fame basketball player, who remembers the impact she had when she talked to a group of National Basketball Association rookies: "When she was done, the guys leaped up with a standing ovation." Coffey also quotes Kevin Halliman, who, at that time, was the director of player education programs for Major League Baseball: "She is truly gifted. She's speaking as a mother, and it just knocks these guys out. She's like a rifle shot. She comes right down the middle. After she was finished I don't think there was a dry eye in the house."

According to Coffey, this mother's message is not only about drugs and violence. Lonise also encourages young people "to remember their roots, to be accountable for their actions and to remember that every day is a gift." Coffey adds, "Not taking life for granted is at the top of her list."[3]

Len Bias had been a good student in high school, a hard worker who was well-known as a clean-living, religious kid. But things changed when he attended college, especially when he began to associate with students who were "too cool for school." In his senior year, he rarely attended classes, and

---

2   "Dr. Lonise Bias." Accessed on November 23, 2017 @ www.youtube.com/watch?v=MrjMXdLWdJ8&t=328s

3   Wayne Coffey, "Bias Ten Years after His Death: His Mother Delivers a Message," *New York Daily News*, June 17, 1996. Accessed on November 25, 2017 @ www.nydailynews.com/archives/sports/bias-ten-years-len-death-mother-delivers-message-article-1.723715

was flunking most of his courses. Instead of buckling down and studying, he preferred to party with friends. After being drafted by the NBA and securing a potential million-dollar deal to promote Reebok sneakers, he chose to celebrate his success in a dorm room with college buddies who gave him cocaine. It was the last party of his life. The Len Bias story, including his rapid rise to fame and sudden death, became a cautionary tale for young people around the world. The passing of Len Bias was regarded by many as "the most socially influential moment in the history of sports."[4]

• ● •

On June 19, 1986, when Len Bias decided to celebrate with cocaine, he was not honoring his mother and father. His decision to hang out with peers who were "too cool for school" led him away from studies and into pathways that culminated in his destruction. Even so, Len's mother, Lonise, along with his father James (who assisted Lonise behind the scenes), went on to provide words of inspiration for thousands of young people around the world. She taught them that they could bring honor to their families, and to themselves, by living honorable lives.

When asked why she thinks she's so effective with young people, Lonise says, ""Love is my motivation. I truly love them like they're my own sons." [5] "And," she adds, "I believe that Len would be alive today if he had other associations." [6]

4 Michael Weinreb, "The Day Innocence Died." Accessed on November 25, 2017 @ www.espn.com/espn/eticket/story?page=bias

5 Kate Ryan, "Len Bias' mom: 'Love is my motivation.'" Accessed on November 25, 2017 @ www.wtop.com/prince-georges-county/2016/10/len-bias-mom-love-motivation/amp/

6 "Dr. Lonise Bias on the Rock Newman Show." This quote is at minute marker 49:44-50:17. Accessed on November 25, 2017 @ www.youtube.com/watch?v=Xje5arcsDvU

The commandments in world scriptures

Judaism

"Honoring father and mother" is a core value in every religion, and the penalty for its violation can be severe. In the Hebrew scriptures, for example, the punishment for breaking this commandment is death: "If a man has a stubborn and rebellious son who does not obey his father and mother ... all the men of the town shall stone him to death" (Deuteronomy 21:18, 21).

Also, "Whoever curses his father or mother shall be put to death" (Exodus 21:17).

While this punishment seems extreme to most readers, the key takeaway is that this commandment should be regarded with great seriousness because your life depends upon it—perhaps not your physical life, but certainly your spiritual life. For when you mistreat and dishonor your parents, you also destroy something within yourself.

99

It should not be forgotten, however, that the reward for keeping this commandment is the opposite of destruction and death: "Honor your father and mother that *your days may be long* upon the land that the Lord is giving you." In other words, it's a promise of long life.

In Judaism, one should respect parents with a similar respect that one would show to God. In the Talmud, which is considered the authoritative commentary on biblical law, it is written that "the honor you owe your father and mother is comparable to the honor you owe the Almighty" (Talmud Kiddushin 31).

This same section of the Talmud discusses the question of how far one should go in honoring parents. What about a divorced parent who no longer lives at home? To this question, the answer is given that both parents are to be equally honored: "If one's mother is divorced, the same honor is due to both parents and neither takes precedence" (Talmud Kiddushin 31a). Another example of "how far one should go" is given through the following anecdote:

> One day Rabbi Abbahuh said to his son, Avimi, "Give me water to drink." Before Avimi was able to bring him the water, Rabbi Abbahu dozed off. Avimi bent over and stood over him until his father awoke. Because he kept this commandment, God helped Avimi in his studies. (Talmud Kiddushin 31a)

Again, this should not be taken too literally. The point is not about being rewarded in the physical world for good behavior, even though that often is the case. Rather the spiritual rewards for honoring parents—peace, contentment, serenity—all of which are given by God, are beyond number. You open yourself to the inflow of these blessings whenever you are genuinely grateful for everything that is done for you.

Christianity

Like all other religious leaders, Jesus regards the commandment to honor parents as central to one's moral and spiritual development. He also regards the breaking of this commandment as a serious offense. Aware that people were avoiding their responsibility to care for elderly parents, he reminded them about this commandment: "Moses has said," he told them, that 'You are to honor your father and mother,' and, 'Whoever curses father or mother must certainly be put to death'" (Mark 7:10).

The Christian apostle, Paul, also speaks of the central importance of this commandment: "Children, obey your parents," he says, "for this is right. Honor your father and mother—which is the first commandment with a promise—so that it may go well with you and that you may enjoy long life on the earth." Paul adds a warning, not to children, but to parents: "Fathers, do not exasperate your children; instead, bring them up in the training and instruction of the Lord" (Ephesians 6:1-4).

In the Christian tradition, the practice of honoring parents goes beyond parents to all those who have exerted, in some way, a significant spiritual influence upon us. Sometimes referred to as "the communion of saints" or "the community of saints," this concept includes not only Christian saints, but also anyone who has lived according to the will of God. It could be an uncle, a grandmother, a teacher, a close friend, or even an author you've never met but whose words inspired you. This is your community of saints, all those who have had and continue to have an invisible, yet powerful influence on your life—whether they are Christians or not. As Jesus puts it, "Not everyone who says to me, 'Lord, Lord,' shall enter the kingdom of heaven, but he who does the will of my Father in heaven" (Matthew 7:21).

All these people are your "father" and "mother" in so far as they have assisted you in the process of your spiritual rebirth. They are to be honored for the new life you have been given through them. They are the spiritual "father and mother" of your new birth into spiritual life.

Islam

As in Judaism and Christianity, Islam also regards the commandment to honor parents as sacred, although an important distinction is made between worshipping Allah and being kind to parents. As it written through the prophet Muhammad, "Allah has decreed that you worship none but him, and that you be kind to parents .... Say not to them a word of contempt, nor repel them, but address them in terms of honor" (Qur'an 17:23). As is clear throughout the *Qur'an*, divinity can only be attributed to Allah, and Allah alone is to be worshipped.

Nevertheless, while parents should not be worshipped, they are to be respected and honored, especially with shows of gratitude. As it written, "Now [among the best of the deeds which] we have enjoined upon man is goodness towards his parents. In pain did his mother bear him, and in pain did she give him birth; and her bearing him and his utter dependence on her took thirty months" (Qur'an 46:15-16). If one cannot summon up gratitude from one's own resources, one should pray for Allah's help, saying, "O my Sustainer, inspire me so that I may be forever grateful. ... Truly have I turned to you, and truly do I bow to you in full surrender" (Qur'an 46:18-19).

The goods deeds performed by parents should not go without appreciation. Children should in turn do good deeds for their parents: "We have commanded people to be good to their parents" (Qur'an 29:8).

Doing good, not just to parents, but to everyone, is a central tenet of Islam. However, the *Qur'an* gives a definite order for doing good, beginning first and foremost with Allah. Here is the passage: "Worship Allah and none other. Do good to parents, relatives, orphans, those in need, neighbors who are near, neighbors who are far, the person you are with, the traveler you meet, and even captives in war" (Qur'an 4:36).[7]

Clearly, for those who follow the teaching of the *Qur'an*, Allah must be served first; next in line though, are one's parents.

Hinduism

While the Eastern religions also include central teachings about honoring parents, they broaden the idea to encompass not only the honoring of every *person*, but also the honoring of everything in the created universe. This is because, according to Eastern thought, God pervades the entire universe, filling everyone and everything with divinity—each according to the individual capacity to receive. Therefore, to the extent that you honor and respect parents and people—even animals, plants and stones—you also honor and respect God. Because everything originates in God, and is pervaded by God, everything that lives is holy.

The idea that everything originates in God permeates the Hindu scriptures. Krishna (the incarnation of God for Hindus) says, "I am the Father and Mother of the universe, and the Grandfather too" (Bhagavad Gita 9:17). "I am the Creator in all creatures" (Shvetashvatara Upanishad 2:16).

---

7 The translation given here is based on our own reading of over forty generally accepted translations of this verse. For a complete list of the most commonly accepted translations, as well as some of the more controversial ones, see the website "Islam Awakened." Accessed on November 13, 2017 @ www.islamawakened.com/quran/4/36/

Those who attain the highest summit of human consciousness see a manifestation of the divine in all things. Whether it be a clod of dirt, a lump of gold, a tiny child or a magnificent oak, they see in all of creation a reflection of the Creator. Because they keep their focus on what is divine in each person and thing, they remain even-keeled amidst ups and downs, triumphs and setbacks: "They are equally kind to relatives, enemies and friends; to those who support them, to those who are indifferent to them, and even to those who hate them. Through their ability to love and honor the divine in all, they rise to great heights" (Bhagavad Gita 6:8-9).

The Hindu dedication to this ideal—that there is something of the divine in everyone and everything—is at the core of the commandment to honor father and mother. Honoring parents becomes the starting point for honoring everyone and everything as emanations of the divine force that permeates the universe.

According to the Hindu scriptures, however, honoring the universe in a general way first begins at home. One must honor parents. As it is written: "The trouble that a mother and father endure in giving birth to human beings cannot be redeemed even in a hundred years; one should constantly do what pleases the two of them" (Laws of Manu 2:226).

Buddhism

Buddhism, which tends to focus on the here and now, the practical and the non-theoretical, is very explicit when it comes to the necessity of honoring parents. We read, therefore, that "If a person is financially able, but does not support father and mother who are old and past their youth, it will be the cause of that person's downfall" (Sutta-Nipata 1:6). Also, "A wise man should support his mother and father as his duty" (Sutta-Nipata 2:14). In a famous Buddhist saying, it is written, "Of the one hundred wholesome deeds, filial piety is foremost."[8]

In one of Buddha's rare references to heaven, he talks about the importance of honoring parents on earth by taking care of their material needs. As he puts it, "The wise should honor their parents with food, drink, bedding and clothing, anointing them, and bathing them, and washing their feet. In performing these services for their mother and father, the wise receive praise here on earth, and after death they rejoice in heaven" (Itivuttaka 106).

The Buddha, who has little use for religious ritual as a way of honoring God, focuses the attention of his adherents on what it truly means to honor someone, whether it be God, parents, or any person. In a chapter titled "The Thousands," he says, "Better than performing a thousand rituals, month after month, for a hundred years, is a moment spent in honoring

---

8 "Commentary on the Flower Adornment Sutra." Accessed on November 13, 2017 @ www. cttbusa.org/fas40/fas40_9.asp

those whose soul is grounded in true knowledge" (Dhammapada 8:7). As he continues his teaching, the Buddha speaks about the uselessness of making sacrifices to obtain the merit and good favor of the gods. "It is far better," says the Buddha, "to honor those who are righteous" (Dhammapada 8:9). And he concludes the chapter with a specific focus on honoring the elderly: "To one ever eager to honor and serve the elders, these four blessing accrue: long life, beauty, happiness and power" (Dhammapada 8:10).

• ● •

The Buddhist idea that those who honor their parents will have *long life* echoes the promise contained in this commandment: "Honor your father and mother that *your days will be long upon the land that the Lord your God is giving you* (Exodus 20:5). In sacred scripture, the words "*your days will be long*" refer to both physical and spiritual blessings. The physical promise is for a long life in the natural world. In other words, it's about longevity; it's about living to a ripe old age. It's a promise that if you honor your parents you will spend many, long and happy days on earth.

The spiritual promise is even better. When understood spiritually, the term "long days" refers to your increasing reception of greater light (wisdom) and greater heat (love). When you honor and respect your parents, living in gratitude toward them, the periods of time that you remain in sunny states of love and wisdom are steadily lengthened. This results in shorter and shorter periods of time spent in states of coldness (lacking the warmth of love) and darkness (lacking the light of wisdom). It's like moving from the cold, dark days of winter (when there is less warmth and light) to the warmer, brighter days of summer when the sun is shining for longer and longer periods of time.

To sum up: the words "Your days shall be long upon the land that the Lord your God is giving you" are much more than an earthly promise about physical longevity. Seen more deeply, they contain an eternal promise. It's a promise that no matter how long you live *physically*, your states of *spiritual* happiness can continue to increase, depending on your willingness to honor parents, honor others, and honor God. This is the spiritual meaning of what it means to live in "the land which the Lord your God is giving you." This "land"—sometimes called "the Promised Land" (Judaism and Christianity) or "the Pure Land" (Buddhism)—is not a place you can find on a map; rather it's a state of consciousness you enter when you see, honor and love what is good and true in everyone. As Jesus said, "The kingdom of God is within you" (Luke 17:21).

Learning to see the "kingdom of God" or "the presence of the divine" in everyone and everything is a process which begins by honoring your father and mother. As they say in both Hinduism and Buddhism, *Namaste*, which means, "The divine in me bows to the divine in you."

The commandments in the lives of college students

Honor your father and mother that your days may be long upon the land, which the Lord your God is giving you.

I know I should call my parents more often. The unselfish part of me knows this; but I still find it hard to pick up the phone.

Journal excerpt from a college senior

Sometimes it's easy

This might be an easy commandment for you. Maybe it's no problem at all for you to honor your parents. You might be like the following sophomore who describes her parents in terms of their good qualities, and how those qualities have been passed on to her. She writes:

> 66 I would just like to apologize to everyone else in the world who does not have my parents, because my parents are literally the best people on this whole planet. There is not a pair of more loving, caring people in existence. My father is the most supportive man I know. He attended every event I was in growing up, whether it was soccer or softball, singing, or plays. From him I get my intense sense of dedication. I've never missed a practice or a game, because he instilled in me the importance of giving it my all.
>
> My mom has the biggest heart. She would do anything for anyone. She loves everyone unwaveringly, even if those people aren't nice to her (which is probably her biggest asset and flaw at the same time). From her I acquired my big heart. My mom has always advocated resolving disputes and not harboring grudges. It is to her that I owe my willingness to forgive. 99

Another student, with equally admirable parents, talks about what happened when he accidentally dented the family car:

> 66 When I was 18 years old, and living in Germany, I had just gotten my driver's license, but was still learning how to drive a manual transmission. One

night, while trying to parallel park in a tight space, I scratched my father's car on a wall.

The damage was obvious and quite significant. When I came home that night and told my parents about the damage, they were upset. But they also saw that I felt terrible and was very sorry for what happened. After talking for a little bit, my father went into the kitchen and came back with a little bottle of sparkling wine. He opened it, poured it into three glasses and said, "Let's drink to the fact that you've had your first car accident, and there was so little damage."

This is just one of many examples of the kindness, forgiveness, and generosity that my parents have shown me throughout my life. After this event, I decided that the next time I would get upset with my parents for any reason, I would remember this. I would honor them for their kindness to me by being even kinder to them. 🙵🙵

Honoring an absent parent

Then again this might be a challenging commandment for you, especially if you a have difficult relationship with one or both of your parents. In the following journal entry, a student talks about her reluctance to keep this commandment, and how a seemingly harsh law from Leviticus helped her to get motivated:

🙶🙶 I dreaded writing about this commandment. I sat motionless, staring at my blank computer screen. The flashing cursor stared right back at me. I soon noticed that every time I began to type, I would end up pressing endlessly on the backspace key. I finally got around to writing this first paragraph by reminding myself that this commandment is about **honoring** my mother and father. It's not about dishonoring them by expressing negative thoughts about the past.

Unable to think of anything positive to say, she asks God for help:

I needed help from the Lord on this commandment. I needed the strength to find something positive to say about my mother. That's why I chose the quote from Leviticus, "Whoever curses father or mother shall be put to death." I knew I needed something that strong to get me motivated.

She isn't worried about being literally struck dead. She knows that the deeper meaning of this commandment is about what we do to ourselves when we harbor ill-will toward our parents:

Now, I did not take this quote for its literal meaning (that I would be put to death for my feelings toward my mother). I read this quote and looked for a deeper meaning—that I would experience a kind of spiritual death by holding on to these negative views about someone I am supposed to love. I came to the conclusion that harboring negative thoughts can send me into a spiritual nosedive, straight into despair.

> I could write about how much my dad has supported me, loved me, and has given me the world. That would be easy—but this class isn't always about doing what is easy. It's about doing what is right. So I set forth a challenge for myself. The challenge is to rise above the feelings I have toward my mother.

When this student was a little girl, her mother had left the family. Ever since then the student had been struggling with abandonment issues and feelings of resentment. This time, however, it was going to be different:

> I want to honor my mother for the beautiful woman she is. I may never understand the reasons that caused her to leave the family, but I do know that she is a rare gem whose light shines wherever she goes. Her laugh and her smile are contagious. I have never met anyone with such radiance when she walks into a room. She is also honest, and I like to believe that I get my honesty from her. She tells it like it is: "Mom, does this dress look good on me?" "No, this one would look better."

> I often argue with myself, wondering if I am now the one being cruel to my mother—being emotionally distant from her as a punishment for leaving me. Every time I visit, she tries to genuinely connect with me, but there is always something holding me back. I keep thinking, "I can't allow myself to get close to her again. What if she might leave me again?"

The realization that she might be holding herself back to punish her mother was a possible breakthrough for this student. She began to see that the real problem between her and her mother might be within herself:

> It's all going to be different now. It's not her anymore; it's me. It's the old feelings that I have toward my mother. I need to rise above the fear, doubt and hurt that prevent me from connecting with mom. But I especially need to rise above resentment. I must not allow my negative feelings—my "spiritual death"—to take me down. Instead, I want to do my part so that we can rebuild this relationship on a new, spiritual foundation.

Writing this journal entry was a struggle for this student, but when she was finished, her final words described a blessing that poured in through practicing this commandment. She wrote:

> Ahh, that felt nice. :) 🎧

Another student describes a similar situation. This time it's not about being abandoned by a mother. It's about a father who was seldom there for her:

> I come from the inner city, a place where many children do not know their fathers, and most kids are raised by single mothers. Growing up I only saw my father because the judge required him to spend time with me. I can honestly say that I barely know who my father is, and I doubt that he knows much about me. Whenever I'm asked about my father, I just say, "I don't have one." I know he gave me life, but he never raised me. I have always had hostility against my father because once the judge said he wasn't required to come pick me up anymore, I hardly ever saw him.

That's how it had been for twenty-one years. But things changed when she learned about this commandment:

> In the last class, when we were asked to come up with a way to honor either our father or mother, I did what I was required to do. We each had a chance to come up to the front of the room and say something honoring about one of our parents. Our professor said that this was not mandatory, but I decided to walk up there anyway and honor my mother. I had the feeling that I would be standing on "Holy Ground."

> When I walked up to the front of the room I couldn't think about anyone except my father. So I told a story about when I was six years old and my father was teaching me how to ride my dirt bike. I will never forget that day, because it was the first time my dad had ever come to get me and actually spend time with me. Usually, he would just drop me off with my grandmother.

107

> But that day was different. I guess he was tired of my mom complaining to him about how hard it was for her to teach me how to ride the dirt bike. That day my dad taught me how to ride, but now that I'm older, I understand it was much more than that. That day my dad taught me not to ever give up after falling. Every time I fell, I heard my dad saying, "Get up and keep going."

> Even with tears in my eyes I continued to get back on my bike until I was finally riding. It was the greatest feeling in the world! After that day I didn't need my dad to tell me to keep going because I could always hear him in my head. Even now, every time I want to give up on something I believe is too hard, I can hear dad saying, "Get up and keep going."

This was a powerful way to honor a parent who had been absent for most of her life, and the whole class was touched by her story. But the story doesn't end there. The next day she wrote these words in her journal:

> After I left class yesterday, my dad was still on my mind. So I called him. It was the first time I heard his voice since I graduated from high school three years ago. He was so surprised that I called him, and said that he was happy to hear from me. I'm so glad that I did this. I'm going to let the past go and start working on our relationship. I love my father, and with a little prayer and a little bit of patience, I can see our relationship growing stronger over time.

Emotional absence

As we have seen, it can be difficult to honor a parent who has been physically absent. But what about a parent who is physically present, but emotionally absent? In a journal entry titled, "Understanding My Father," a senior describes what it was like to be the son of an emotionally distant father:

> ❝ My father is the most hard-working man I know. He supports my family by working hard every day, and sacrifices his own time to be sure that he can give my mother, my siblings, and myself everything we need. Nevertheless, it is difficult to truly honor my father, because he seems to lack emotion. He says that he loves us, but he has never been one to open up emotionally.

Because of the commandment on honoring parents, this student decided to take this issue deeper. He called his mother and got more background on his father's emotional absence:

> Mom reminded me that when my dad was eleven years old his mother died. I sometimes forget this. But I think it could potentially be a major reason that he has had trouble opening up emotionally to us. I can tell that he loved his mother very much, and all throughout my childhood we grew up calling her "angel grandma." He seems to have had a deep connection with her from the day he was born. It was probably because he was born with a heart problem that is normally fatal. The doctors told my grandmother, "Don't get too attached to him." They thought for sure he would die.

> Every day my grandmother travelled to the hospital to visit him, refusing to heed the doctors' advice, and each day he grew a little stronger. After a long stay in the hospital, he survived, and was athletic throughout his childhood. It is understandable that dad and grandma had a very close bond. It must have been hard to lose her when he was only eleven years old.

> Because of the death of his mother, I suspect that my dad's ability to open up emotionally was difficult for him. Whatever the reason might be for the emotional distance I feel from him, I am truly blessed to have such a hard-working, faithful man as my father, and such a loving, nurturing woman as my mother. They have been incredible role models for their children throughout their 27 years of marriage. I think that this knowledge will help me grow closer to my father, even if he has difficulty growing closer to me. ❞

In the next journal entry, titled "Walls Between Us," a student provides an opposite scenario—a situation in which he chooses to remain emotionally distant from his father. Reflecting on his behavior in the light of this commandment, he writes about the "silent barrier" that he erected between himself and his father:

66 This commandment really hits home for me. I am not always the most loving son. In fact, at the moment there is a wall between me and my parents. We rarely scream or fight, but there is a silent barrier that prevents deep emotional connection from taking place. I can't say when this wall was built, or who laid the first brick, but it's there. I can feel it in the air. I can almost touch it.

I remember a time when my dad and I made an arrangement to give each other a hug every day. We don't do that anymore. I know my parents still love me, and I love them, but over the years a wall has been built up. The fact that we are so busy hasn't helped. In fact, it has kept me from addressing the issues that have come between us. Silent resentments that I did not have time to express have become building blocks as the wall has grown thicker and higher.

After graduating from high school, this student had moved away from home, but a lack of employment opportunities made it necessary to move back in with his parents. As he continues his journal entry, he writes:

I think some of these issues are inevitable when you are twenty-four-years old and still living with your parents. For about a year and a half I lived away from home, and during that time my relationship with my parents was better. Being away from home helped me put things in perspective. I was able to appreciate the love, support, and food that they provided me all my life. But when I moved back in, I admit that I treated them like furniture—especially when I rushed past them on my way to work or class.

He then describes a plan he came up with, not only to practice the commandment about honoring parents, but also to continue practicing the previous week's commandment about honoring the Sabbath:

Last week we talked about remembering the Sabbath, and for me, the Sabbath is all about taking time in nature, appreciating the glorious world God has given us. So this week I came up with a plan to both reconnect with God (Remember the Sabbath) and reconnect with my parents (Honor father and mother).

Here's how it all went down: Since it was Sunday, I decided to not do any work. Instead, I invited my parents, my brother, and my girlfriend to go to a Farmer's Market, and then to a park where we could enjoy the beautiful fall day. While we were at the park we rented rowboats, and had a great time rowing around the lake.

All of this took just a little bit of effort to organize, but it paid off immensely. I didn't have any heart-to-heart conversations with my parents, but I know that in the past it has been these kinds of activities which have opened the door for more relaxed and intimate communication. I now have hope that with regular effort, and with God's help, I can start to chip away at that wall. 99

109

Re-seeing parents

Central to "honoring" your parents is to respect them. The root meaning of the word "respect" is a combination of two Latin words: *re* (meaning "again") and "*spectare*" (meaning "to look"). So, the root meaning of the word "respect" is to "look again" or to "re-see." In other words, you can "re-spect" your parents by learning to "re-see" them in the light of their good qualities and positive attributes.

For example, a parent who was once seen as "too strict" might be re-seen as "principled." A parent who was once seen as a "worry-wort" might be re-seen as "loving and concerned." A parent who was once seen as being "too picky" might be re-seen as a person who is careful, precise, and "pays attention to detail." In the following journal entry, a student describes how his father's behavior used to bother him:

> 66 For a long time, I thought of my dad as silly and over-the-top. He made jokes, he loved explaining things at length, and he had a strong faith in God (he still does). When my friends would come over, he would joke with them and be energetic and positive. Back then, it was embarrassing. I just didn't think of him as being very "cool" at all. He was way too silly. I would just roll my eyes.

As this journal entry continues, dad's embarrassing silliness is re-seen as a positive quality:

> As I reflected on all of this during the week, I realized that I am just like my dad! I love to have fun! Just like him. I love to crack jokes. Just like him! So I have decided to turn it around. Rather than feeling annoyed and embarrassed, I am going to be grateful that dad has passed these qualities on to me, and modeled them so well for me in my childhood. So I have decided to "re-see" my dad as an energetic, positive, fun-loving guy who loves people and loves God.
>
> Looking at him through these new eyes, I can honestly say that he is a spectacular guy. I really look up to him. And I think he deserves to hear that. I don't know if I've ever told my dad just how grateful I am for him, and I think he deserves this praise. I'm going to tell this to him this weekend to his face. 99

Another student, who felt that his parents were "overprotective," attempted to see them in a new way. He writes:

> 66 This commandment has been tough for me, especially this year. Typically, during the school year I live away from home in college housing. This year, however, we were not able to afford the cost of my living on campus, so I've been living at home. In addition, I underwent a complicated shoulder surgery at the start of the term and was under the constant care and surveillance of my parents. It was necessary, and probably a good thing, but it was

also an exhausting experience. I like to be independent and I like getting things done on my own, so I was getting annoyed by my parents' constant overprotectiveness—especially my mom's.

This is where his father stepped in, not so much to protect his son, but to protect his wife.

As the semester continued, and my shoulder began to heal, my mother continued to be overprotective. "Don't do that." "Be careful about this." "Don't lift that box." My relationship with my mother was getting worse and worse. Whenever we talked, it was about something I shouldn't be doing. It was terribly annoying, and I told her in so many words to just "get off my back."

This is when my father pulled me aside and told me that I would not be travelling abroad in the spring, as I had previously hoped to do. This was a massive blow to my ego. He told me that this was a final decision, and one that could only be changed by the restoration of the relationship between my mother and me. He was very clear about the fact that a young man should always treat his mother with respect.

When seen in the light of the commandment to "honor father and mother," his father's firm requirement to treat his mother with respect made a powerful impression:

I have come to the realization that I have been neglecting the commandment that calls me to honor my parents. I have been dishonoring my father, my mother, and God's commandment. While I know that I may not be able to make a sudden change in my relationship with my parents, I have been making a major effort, especially with my mother. This week's focus on this commandment has been a big help. Instead of seeing my mother as controlling and overprotective, I want to start seeing her as loving and caring. I want to treat her with the respect she deserves. 99

111

Everyday saints

You may have experienced times when you were in touch with your own Higher Nature—the place within you where, according to some religions, "God dwells." Whether you call it your "Higher Self," "Source," or "Divine Presence," it is an awareness that there is an Invisible Force that enables you to rise above selfish desire. In religious terms, people who manage to do this are sometimes referred to as "saints."

While you might normally think of "saints" as being people who have been honored for extraordinary religious devotion and humanitarian service (Saint Francis of Assisi, Mother Teresa, Mahatma Gandhi, Saint Joan of Arc, etc.), don't forget the everyday saints in your life—the people who have supported you in your mental, emotional, and spiritual development.

It may have been a beloved grandmother, a first-grade teacher, a neighborhood friend, a coach, or a cousin. It may have been a friendly clerk in a store, or a sibling who helped you through a difficult time. "Saints" and "guardian angels" come in all shapes and sizes, and you never know exactly when one of them might show up in your life. To the extent that they have contributed to your spiritual development, they are your spiritual "fathers and mothers," and they deserve to be honored. These "everyday saints" have been channels of God's love and wisdom in your life.

In the following journal entry, a student includes his older brother as an everyday saint who has looked out for him throughout his life:

> 66 The first person who comes to mind as an "everyday saint" is my older brother. In fact, when you asked us to choose someone to honor, I sent my brother a huge Facebook message thanking him for what he has done for me. In many ways, my brother has been like a second father to me.
>
> So far, my brother has actually saved my life twice. Once, when I was very young and at the beach, I dug a hole in the sand and wanted to see if I could squeeze my head into it. So I slid my head into the hole and got stuck. For some reason I didn't have the strength to pull myself out. When my brother heard my faint cries for help, he ran over and pulled me out.
>
> He also saved my life when I was about to cross a street. There was a truck that I didn't notice was running a red light, and I was just about to cross the street without looking. I would have gotten completely ruined by that truck, but my brother grabbed me just in time, and threw me out of the way. I came about a foot away from being crushed by a speeding 18-wheeler, trailer truck!
>
> Besides actually saving my life these two times, my brother has looked out for me my whole life. Even today, he looks out for me spiritually. We have great conversations about the meaning of life, and I cherish them all. So this week I "honored my father and mother" by letting my brother know how much I appreciated his constant looking out for me, and how much I care about him. 99

Another student describes her spiritual "mother and father" as everyone in her life who has nurtured her on her spiritual journey, but especially four people:

> 66 On the literal level of this commandment, I do not have two parents to honor. I have four! This includes my mom, my step-dad, my dad, and my step-mom. Since my parents got divorced when I was so young, I do not have a memory of them being together. My stepmother came into my life when I was four, and my stepfather when I was twelve. Each one of them has had an impact on me, and I know that some of their good qualities have rubbed off on me. Even though we all have our differences, I respect each of my four parents for who they are, and I love them each dearly. Together they have supported me throughout my life, and still support me.

She then remembers another person who had been a part of her life. She is surprised to realize that she had forgotten about him until she began to think about people who had contributed to her life's journey:

> The biggest shocker for me, when I was reflecting on my past, was the realization that I had left out a very important part of my childhood. From the time I was about five, until I was about nine, my mom was dating and engaged to a man named Ted. He was present during a time in my life when I really needed a father figure. He played games with me and let me help him with projects. Wonderful memories of being with him came flooding back in, and I realized that I had completely blocked him out of my life after he and my mom broke up. I still really look up to him though, and part of me is inspired to seek him out and say, "Hi." Even though he is not in my life right now, he will always be a part of my life. He is one of the "everyday saints" who has supported and nurtured me along the way.

She concludes by dedicating a Bette Midler song to the five people who have been, and continue to be, "the wind beneath her wings":

> Did you ever know that you're my hero,
>
> And everything that I would like to be?
>
> I can fly higher than an eagle,
>
> For you are the wind beneath my wings. 〞

• ● •

Whether it's a friend, uncle, coach, grandmother, or teacher, this commandment calls you to honor all people who have assisted you in your spiritual development. But don't forget to begin by honoring your parents—the ones who gave you life.

The mark to aim at

Honor your father and mother

The first tablet of the Ten Commandments is about *honoring God*, which could also be *honoring those qualities that transcend your lower nature*. As you begin the second tablet of the Ten Commandments, the focus shifts to *honoring others*— everyone and everything through which divinity manifests itself. For this week, the mark to aim at is a simple one: *honor your father and mother*. That's going to be your aim, not just because it's a commandment, but because it will open you to receiving every blessing associated with this spiritual practice. Begin with your parents, striving to see good qualities in them. Then broaden this aim to include everyone who has supported and nurtured you along the way. Practice being grateful for EVERYTHING in your life. Experience the deeper meaning of the words "your days will be long" in the land that God is giving you. In your journal, record your experience of practicing this commandment.

Suggestions for further reflection and practice

Honor your father and mother, that your days may be long upon the land that the Lord your God is giving you.

The following exercises contain additional information about this commandment. Read through all of them, and then focus on one or two that spark your interest.

1 Journal reflection: appreciate your genetic inheritance

Your parents gave you the gift of life. Not just that, but they also passed on to you a specific set of genes which have enabled you to become the person you are today. Whether they supported you along the way, or were not there for you as much as you would have liked, take time to focus on the positive physical attributes, personality characteristics, and spiritual qualities you have inherited from them. Try to give a specific example of a positive physical attribute, a personality characteristic, or a spiritual quality in your father. Do the same for your mother. Then reflect on how these attributes, characteristics, and qualities show up in you. If you don't know much about your biological parents, or find it difficult to deal with this aspect of your upbringing, focus instead on the significant caregivers in your life (step-parents, grandparents, uncles, older siblings, etc.).

2 Activity: re-see your parents

If there are difficult aspects of your relationship with one or both of your parents, you may want to try this activity. First describe what annoys you about one or both of them. Then, make a conscious effort to see the original goodness within that annoying behavior or personality trait. For example, in the case of overprotective parents who may have limited your freedom, try to see the original goodness within their actions—their love and concern for you. Perhaps the indecisiveness of your mom or dad has been especially annoying and irritating. Try to re-see this character trait as an ability to be open-minded, or a willingness to consider all sides of an issue before making a decision. See what impact this practice has on your feelings towards your parents.

3 Activity: re-see your parents (continued)

Continuing from prompt #2, practice re-seeing at a deeper level. What life issues did your parents go through that may have made them especially sensitive to certain situations? For example, if your mother's father died of alcoholism, she might be especially worried when she discovers that you've been drinking every weekend. Maybe you think you can control it, and mom should stop nagging you. However, in the light of this commandment, you may benefit from *re-seeing* your mom, understanding that it is not just about you. It may also be about her past, a fear that the thing that destroyed her father might also destroy you. Instead of reacting with anger, respond with understanding and even respect. Honor her for everything she may have been through and for how much she may really love you.

In fact, as a part of this exercise, you might consider talking with your mom (or dad), and learning from her (or him), what, if anything, lies behind her (or his) excessive worry and concern.

4 Journal reflection: honor the everyday saints in your life

This commandment calls you to honor all those who have supported and nurtured you on your spiritual journey. Select someone from your "community of saints" and describe how or in what way that person has been a positive influence in your life. It could be a school bus driver who greeted you every morning with a warm smile, a friend whose cheerful disposition consistently brightened your day, an elderly relative whose funny jokes never failed to make you laugh, a coach who motivated you to give your all, a teacher who helped you to choose a career path, a writer or musician who inspired you, or a religious leader who helped you on your spiritual journey. Your "saint" could be a living person or someone who has passed on. Honor one of these friends, mentors, guardian angels, inspirational teachers, spiritual leaders and role models. Describe a specific incident that shows the quality (or qualities) you admire in one of these people, and talk about how that person's words or actions has helped to shape your life.

5 Activity: say "thank you"

Following on from prompt #4, think of a way to express sincere appreciation to someone from your "community of saints." What is it about this person that you admire and love? What would you like to tell this person? How will you do it? You could send this person a thank-you card, an email, a text, or a Facebook message. Perhaps you could make a phone call, or arrange a personal visit. If the person you are thinking about has passed away, you could write a thank-you in your journal, imagining that you are speaking "face-to-face" with that person. In some religious traditions, people who are on "the other side" can continue to inspire us as guardian angels. Even if they are not able to read your writing, they might be able to feel your love.

6 Activity: keep a "gratitude journal"

The Roman philosopher Cicero once said, "Gratitude is not only the greatest of virtues, it is the parent of all the others." This week, focus on those things you might normally take for granted. Appreciating your parents, of course, is a first step. But there is much more. For example, if you have a car, someone built it for you. If you're driving on a smooth road, someone paved it for you. If you're listening to music, someone wrote it for you, someone produced it for you, and someone else developed the sound system for you. If you're living in a college dormitory, or eating in a college cafeteria, or sitting in college classes, there's a good chance that someone has paid some of the bill for you. If you're in class, and your professor has taught you well, or a classmate has made an interesting point, be sure to let them know how much you appreciate their contribution to your education. If a teammate or a roommate does something kind or honorable, say "thanks" with sincerity. Be on the lookout for things you can honestly appreciate and people to whom you can express heartfelt gratitude. Keep a list in your journal. You might find that this practice is one of the most important aspects of your spiritual development.

7 Reflection: "too cool for school"

The Len Bias story, which was the introduction to this commandment, is a cautionary tale about what can happen when a good person gets caught up in bad company. As Len's mother puts it, "I believe that Len would be alive today if he had other associations." Peer pressure can be very powerful, and it's possible to get caught up with individuals who can influence you in negative, non-productive—even destructive—ways. As the saying goes, "Show me your friends, and I'll show you your future." Are you easily influenced by people who don't take their studies seriously, who prefer instead to skip classes, sleep in, and slide by? Are you "too cool for school"? In your journal, consider to what extent this kind of behavior might apply to you. And if this does apply, what do you want to do about it? What could you do differently to honor your father and mother?

117

"In examining myself this week, in the light of this commandment, I have come to the realization that I am a spiritual murderer, a back-stabber, a gossip."

Rise above anger ~ be a life-giver.

You shall not murder.

Exodus 20:13

119

The four-minute mile

In 1954, when Roger Bannister said that he was determined to run the mile in under four minutes, there were many naysayers. At the time, no one had ever run a mile in less than four minutes. It had never been done—and many believed that it could *never* be done. Medical professionals and scientific researchers agreed that it was physiologically impossible. A person under that much stress would collapse, even die.[1]

But on May 6, 1954, on a cinder track in Oxford, England, a 25-year-old graduate student proved them wrong. His name is Roger Bannister, and he ran one mile in under four minutes—3:59.4 to be exact. For many, Bannister had achieved the unachievable. The "Dream Mile" was no longer a dream; it had become a reality. [2]

The entire race can be seen on YouTube, including a stride-for-stride commentary written by Bannister himself. In his own words, Bannister describes the important role played by his running mates, and the powerful influence of his coach during the race. The trio of runners, Roger Bannister, Chris Brasher, and Chris Chataway, under the direction of their coach, Franz Stampfl, had spent months training for the race. Here is a portion of

---

1   It was described as "a barrier that defied all attempts to break it, an irksome reminder that man's striving might be in vain." Roger Bannister, *Roger Bannister: Twin Tracks* (London: The Robeson Press, 2014), 102.

2   As an undergraduate at Oxford University, Roger Bannister had been a long-distance runner and a medical student with a keen interest in human physiology. His research focused on oxygen deprivation and how the regulation of breathing could have a direct effect on one's stamina. After graduating from Oxford in 1951, he went on to study at St. Mary's Medical Hospital in London, one of the most prestigious medical schools in Europe. While at St. Mary's, he continued to run competitively under the auspices of the British Amateur Athletic Association.

Bannister's commentary:

> *As the gun fired, Chris Brasher went into the lead and I slipped in effortlessly behind him, feeling tremendously full of running. My legs seemed to meet no resistance at all, as if propelled by some unknown force. … a voice shouting "relax" penetrated to me above the noise of the crowd. I learnt afterwards it was Stampfl's. Unconsciously, I obeyed ….*
>
> *I barely noticed the half-mile, passed in 1 minute 58 seconds. I was relaxing so much that my mind seemed almost detached from my body. It was incredible that we could run at this speed without strain. I was barely aware of the fact that Chris Chataway was now going into the lead.*
>
> *At three-quarters of a mile my effort was still barely perceptible. The time was 3 minutes 0.7 seconds and by now the crowd was roaring. A four-minute mile was possible. Somehow, to do it, I had to run the last lap in 59 seconds.*
>
> *Chataway led round the next bend, and then I pounced past him at the beginning of the back straight, 300 yards from the finish. I had a moment of mixed joy and anguish. Then my mind took over. It raced well ahead of my body and drew me compellingly forward. I felt that the moment of a lifetime had come.*[3]

120

As they say, "the rest is history." The crowd roared as Bannister lunged through the finish line at three minutes, fifty-nine, and four tenths seconds (3:59:4)—a new world record.

• • •

Many years ago, the Rev. George Dole, PhD, was one of Ray's theological school professors. We knew that he was a brilliant scholar, with degrees from Yale, Oxford, and Harvard, but we didn't know that he had been one of the runners in the now historic "four-minute mile." As the race began, Dole had the inside post (lane one), and Bannister was in lane four. Dole got off to a good start. Chris Brasher was in the lead closely followed by Roger Bannister. Right behind Bannister was Dole who was running third in a field of six competitors. Dole finished fifth on that day, but the lessons he learned continue to be significant.

In a recent telephone conversation with Professor Dole, he spoke about

---

3 "Breaking a Belief System … First Four Minute Mile Roger Bannister 1954." Accessed on October 11, 2017 @ www.youtube.com/watch?v=qAXL3waljqo. This is a video of the actual 1954 race, with a commentary written by Roger Bannister. The description of the race, with only a few minor differences, is contained in Bannister's autobiography (cited earlier): *Roger Bannister: Twin Tracks*, 118-119.

those lessons. The first lesson has to do with the importance of a running strategy known as "shadowing." Professor Dole puts it like this:

> Bannister had perfected the art of shadowing. That's when you run as economically as you can. You place yourself just behind the person in front of you, right at his shoulder, and let him set the pace while you follow. First Chris Brasher set the pace, then Chris Chataway, and Bannister shadowed them, letting them pull him along.

Professor Dole is not just a runner; he is also a theologian. Reflecting on the concept of "shadowing" he said, "It's like welcoming those things that flow into your mind from above, and letting them pull you along."

In recalling his experience on that day, Roger Bannister says something similar: "My legs seemed to meet no resistance at all, as if propelled by some unknown force."

Professor Dole also pointed out that individual success depends on the help of others. After a disappointing fourth place finish at the Helsinki Olympics in 1952, Bannister knew that if he were ever going to break the four-minute mile, he would need help. As he puts it in his autobiography, "The Helsinki Olympic games were a turning point in my life. ... I had tried to bear it alone by developing an attitude of isolation. ... A great change came over my running: I no longer trained alone." [4]

It was around this time that Bannister turned to Franz Stampfl, the well-known coach of many Olympic champions. Stampfl, in turn, teamed Bannister up with Olympians Chris Brasher and Chris Chataway—the men who would set the pace for him during the "miracle mile." As Bannister puts it, "The involvement with a group rejuvenated my enthusiasm. The Chrises and Franz made the whole thing much more fun." [5]

Coach Franz Stampfl believed that a coach's main responsibility is to release the latent power in an athlete. [6] Recalling the powerful influence of Stampfl on the trio of runners, Chris Brasher says that their coach "sought to persuade us that we were capable of far more than we thought." [7]

The breaking of the four-minute mile was truly a group effort. It required not only a determined runner named Roger Bannister, but also a field of other competitors, teammates who set the pace, a crowd of roaring spectators, and a coach who believed in him. As Professor Dole puts it, "Coach Stampfl

---

4   *Roger Bannister: Twin Tracks*, ibid., 100, 110.

5   Roger Robinson, "Four Minute Everest: The Story and the Myth," *Runner's World* (May 1, 2004). Accessed on November 6, 2017 @ www.runnersworld.com/running-times-info/four-minute-everest-the-story-and-the-myth?amp

6   *Roger Bannister: Twin Tracks*, ibid., 114.

7   Chris Chataway, "Obituary: Franz Stampfl," *The Independent* (April 5, 1995). Accessed on November 6, 2017 @ www.independent.co.uk/news/people/obituary-franz-stampfl-1614402.htmlhis

played a key role in Bannister's success. He gave him moral support. He believed in him. He convinced him he could do it. Everyone needs that kind of support. Even the biggest, smartest, strongest, and most self-sufficient person needs the understanding, care, and encouragement of others."[8]

• • •

There are many lessons to be learned from the "miracle mile." Perhaps one of the most enduring is that it demonstrates the power of possibility thinking. At a time when the scientific world believed that it was impossible for any human being to run the mile in under four minutes, Roger Bannister did it. In doing so, he demonstrated that both physical and psychological barriers can be broken through.

Six weeks later, John Landy also ran the mile in under four minutes, becoming the second man in history to do so. Within two years, nine people had broken the four-minute barrier. And, today, more than sixty years later, over six thousand people have run the mile in under four minutes—including high school students and people over the age of forty.[9] Because of Bannister's triumph, people around the world gained a new understanding of what can be accomplished when people rise above limiting beliefs. Bannister's accomplishment has been, and continues to be, an inspiration to millions.

In the history of human thought, possibility thinkers have been able to lift our idea of "the possible" beyond what most people imagine is achievable. Galileo revolutionized human thought when he taught that the earth revolves around the sun. The Wright brothers rose above the taunts of their skeptical critics, and successfully flew the first airplane. And sixty years later, astronaut Neil Armstrong became the first man to walk on the moon.

In the realm of spirituality, religious leaders have always encouraged people to elevate their idea about what is possible for the human spirit. The Buddha taught that inner peace is possible for those who rise above covetous desire. Gandhi taught that changing the outer world first begins with striving to change one's inner world. And Jesus taught that instead of hating and murdering, it is possible to forgive and love one's enemy. These spiritual leaders not only taught a higher vision of what is possible—their lives also demonstrated that these spiritual aspirations are indeed achievable.

What Roger Bannister achieved in the realm of athletic endeavor, you can achieve in the realm of the human spirit. "With God all things are possible" (Matthew 19:26).

---

8 Telephone interview with the Rev. George Dole, PhD, October 11, 2017.

9 For a complete list of every person who has broken the four-minute mile since 1954, see "Track and Field All-Time Performances at the "All-time Athletics" website, updated and maintained by Peter Larsson. Last updated on October 25, 2017. Accessed on November 7, 2017 @ www.alltime-athletics.com/m_mileok.htm

The commandments in world scriptures

Judaism

While the exhortation "love your enemy" has been around for a long time, humanity has not always been ready to hear it. That's because there is a long distance between hating and loving. Angry and hateful feelings must first be put away before more loving feelings can flow in. The garden must be weeded before the flowers can be planted.

The commandment, "You shall not murder," speaks to this level of your spiritual development. The first thing to be done, even before you begin to love your enemy, is to put aside anger and stop hating. The Hebrew prophets put it this way: "Cease to do evil; learn to do good" (Isaiah 1:16). Similarly, the Hippocratic oath, sworn to by every doctor who enters the medical profession, reads "First, do no harm."

When it comes to dealing with people who trample upon the freedom of others, especially those who commit murder, the Hebrew scriptures are straightforward: "Anyone who strikes and kills a person shall surely be put to death" (Exodus 21:12). When God delivers Noah from the flood, among his directions for reestablishing order in the earth is the command, "Whoever sheds man's blood, by man his blood shall be shed" (Genesis 9:6). Again, "Whoever kills an animal shall restore it, but whoever kills a person shall surely be put to death" (Leviticus 24:17).

These laws are in a general category called *lex talionis*—the law of retaliation. While that law allows for revenge, it stipulates that the amount of retaliation cannot exceed the original offense: "If there is serious injury, you are to take life for life, eye for eye, tooth for tooth, hand for hand, foot for foot, burn for burn, wound for wound, bruise for bruise" (Exodus 21:23-25). In other words, you are allowed to retaliate, but only in a manner proportional to the offense.

Christianity

Jesus knew the law of retaliation well, but he took a different approach. "You have heard that it was said, 'An eye for eye, and a tooth for tooth.' But I tell you, do not resist an evil person. If someone strikes you on the right cheek, turn to him the other also. And if someone wants to sue you and take your tunic, let him have your cloak as well. If someone forces you to go one mile, go with him two miles. Give to the one who asks you, and do not turn away

123

from the one who wants to borrow from you" (Matthew 5:38-42).

In overturning the law that allowed for a just form of retaliation (an "eye for an eye," but no more than that), Jesus provided a deeper understanding of the commandment about murder: "You have heard that it was said to the people long ago, 'You shall not murder, and anyone who murders will be subject to judgment.' But I tell you that anyone who is angry with his brother will be subject to judgment. Again, anyone who says to his brother, 'Raca,' [you are worthless] is answerable to the Sanhedrin. But anyone who says, 'You fool!' will be in danger of the fire of hell" (Matthew 5:21-22).[10]

In place of revenge, Jesus taught reconciliation: "Therefore, if you are offering your gift at the altar and there remember that your brother has something against you, leave your gift there in front of the altar. First go and be reconciled to your brother; then come and offer your gift" (Matthew 5:23-24). Instead of seeking vengeance, Jesus taught his followers to love those who did them harm: "You have heard that it was said, 'Love your neighbor and hate your enemy.' But I tell you, love your enemies and pray for those who persecute you, that you may be children of your Father in heaven" (Matthew 5:43-45).

Islam

In Islam, to murder even one person is equivalent to murdering all of humanity: "On that account, we ordained for the children of Israel that if any one slew a person—unless it be for murder or for spreading mischief in the land—it would be as if he slew the whole of people" (Qur'an 5:32).

The qualifying phrase, "unless it be for murder or for spreading mischief in the land," is significant. According to the *Qur'an*, this means that it is lawful to execute a murderer. But it is also lawful to execute those who "make mischief," meaning those who mock Allah and his messenger, Muhammad: "The punishment for those who wage war against Allah and his messenger, and strive with might and main for mischief through the land, is execution, or crucifixion, or the cutting off of hands and feet from opposite sides, or exile from the land" (Qur'an 5:33).

The command to "execute," "crucify," "maim" and "exile" can be troubling, especially when interpreted in a literal way. Islamic scholars, however, point out that those who "make mischief against Allah and Muhammad" symbolize states of unfaithfulness within every person—the "infidel within." In this case, all "unbelievers" are called to wage holy war *(jihad)* against states of unfaithfulness and disbelief within themselves.

---

10 In some versions of this passage, it is written, "He who is angry with his brother *without a cause* will be subject to judgment." But the earliest versions of the manuscript do not include the italicized phrase. Jesus said that we should love our enemy and pray for those who persecute us—not be angry at them—even if there is a "reasonable cause."

These unbelieving states must be "executed," "crucified," "cut off," or "exiled from the land." The real war, then, is within you—not outside. When these infidel states are vanquished, you become a life-giver to others: "And if anyone saves a life, it is as if that person has given life to humankind altogether" (Qur'an 5:32).

Hinduism

The idea that inner struggle (*jihad*) is a kind of holy war is not unique to Islam. It is perhaps most clearly illustrated in the Hindu classic, the *Bhagavad Gita*. As Mahatma Gandhi has pointed out, "The *Gita* is not an historical discourse. A physical illustration is sometimes needed to drive home a spiritual truth. It is not the description of war between cousins, but between two natures in us—the Good and the Evil."[11] The *Bhagavad Gita* is primarily a dialogue between Krishna (the incarnation of *Vishnu*, the Supreme God) and Arjuna (who represents each one of us). However, the entire narrative, when seen spiritually, is a description of every person's battle to rise above ignoble impulses in order to live a holy life.[12]

Briefly, the story revolves around Arjuna's unwillingness to fight against people who seem to be his close relatives. In spiritual reality, these "close relatives" are the destructive impulses that have been with him so long that he has grown attached to them. They are his worst enemies, the source of all his misery. If he is to find happiness and peace, he must fight this battle.

The narrator describes Arjuna as one "whose eyes are burning with tears of self-pity and confusion." But Krishna admonishes Arjuna with these words: "It does not become you to yield to this wickedness. Arise with a brave heart, and destroy the enemy" (Bhagavad Gita 2:3).

Krishna's words to Arjuna have echoed through the ages, and have been restated in various ways, perhaps most eloquently by William Butler Yeats who writes, "Why should we honor those who die on the field of battle? A man may show as reckless a courage in entering into the abyss of himself."[13]

125

11 Eknath Easwaran, *The Bhagavad Gita for Daily Living* (Petaluma, California: Nilgiri Press, 1979), Vol. 1, 23.

12 See for example the website www.al-islam.org, especially the article, "The Spiritual Significance of Jihad." An important distinction is made between the *lesser jihad* and the *greater jihad*. The lesser struggle (*jihad*) is about the enemies outside of us; the greater struggle (*jihad*) is about the enemies inside of us. Accessed on October 10, 2017 @ www.al-islam.org/al-serat/vol-9-no-1/spiritual-significance-jihad-seyyed-hossein-nasr/spiritual-significance-jihad.

13 This quotation is from one of Yeats' unpublished manuscripts. It is quoted by Maynard Mack in "The World of Hamlet," *The Yale Review* 41 (1952): 523.

Buddhism

Buddhism regards nonviolence as one of its central tenets. The Sanskrit word for non-violence (*ahimsa*) means, quite literally, "the absence of striking." As the Buddha says, "All tremble at the rod. All fear death. Therefore, one should neither strike nor cause to strike" (Dhammapada 10:5). "Whoever, seeking one's own happiness, harms with the rod other pleasure-loving beings, experiences no happiness in the hereafter" (Dhammapada 10:3).

As the Buddha takes us deeper into his teachings, he speaks about people who have realized that their essential being or "Buddha-nature" is one with Brahman, the Supreme Reality. Therefore, people who put away all craving, all attachment, all self-interest, and are therefore without violence (*ahimsa*) experience the greatest tranquility. The Buddha therefore says, "He who is free from anger ... tolerant amidst the intolerant ... calm amidst the violent ... him I call a Brahman; He who speaks gentle, instructive, and truthful words, whose utterances offend no one ... him I call a Brahman" (Dhammapada 26:18, 24, 26).

In his most famous teaching, the Buddha states that there are Four Noble Truths: (1) there is suffering; (2) suffering is caused by desire; (3) there is a remedy; and (4) the remedy is to follow the *Noble Eightfold Path*. At the center of the eightfold path is this teaching about murder: "Right action is to abstain from taking life."

• ● •

We have come full circle. The Hebrew scriptures begin with the simple, direct command: "You shall not murder." And the Buddha includes, at the heart of the Noble Eightfold Path, the exhortation to "abstain from taking life."

As an alternative to "taking life," you can become a life-giver. You can do everything you can to rise above anger, hatred and any other "murderous" inclination. This could include the malicious desire to destroy someone's reputation, hopes, and dreams, merely because you might gain something from it—the satisfaction of revenge, the delight in another's misery. Instead of being a life-taker, you can become a life-giver; instead of being a spirit-killer, you can become a spirit-lifter; instead of putting people down, you can raise people up. In refusing to murder (or "take life"), you can open the way for the Giver of Life to give life through you.

At the highest level, you can do something equivalent to breaking the four-minute barrier in the mile; you can love your enemy. It can be done. If you do your part, *first* by putting away all anger and hatred, *then* the Giver of Love will flow in enabling you to do the impossible: *you will love your enemy.*

The commandments in the lives of college students

You shall not murder.

The anger I feel when holding grudges against people makes me feel heavy and burdened. I had no idea that while I was holding these grudges, I was spiritually murdering—not just other people, but myself as well.

Journal excerpt from a college junior

The many levels of murder

When this course was taught in maximum security prisons, many of the prisoners were incarcerated for violating this very commandment. As you may know, prisons can be dangerous places. One of the men said that a previous cell-mate had stabbed him in the back.

Many crimes take place behind prison walls, but it was nevertheless shocking to imagine a prisoner stabbing his cell-mate in the back. He explained, however, that it wasn't a *physical* stabbing. As he put it, "He snitched on me." In the prison-setting, "snitching" is one of the worst possible things you can do. It's metaphorical back-stabbing. That's why it is said, "snitches get stitches."

As this story illustrates, "murder" isn't just physical. When murderous words ruin the reputation of others it's called "character assassination." Words can be used to "rip people apart." They can "tear down" a person's good name. They can cut deeper than any knife, and the wounds do not heal easily. Sometimes they can last a lifetime. That's why the word for "murder" in Hebrew is *Ratzach*, which literally means, "to rip apart, dash down, break into pieces." It is deliberate, pre-meditated malice. Whether physical or spiritual, *ratzach* is destructive and deadly.

Sometimes, you may not realize the depth of pain that careless words can inflict. Like a drunken driver who seriously injures a pedestrian, you might say, "I didn't mean it." And yet, whether you meant it or not, the harm inflicted is just the same whether your words were intended "in good fun" or intended to hurt. If you tend to have a sarcastic sense of humor, you may want to carefully consider this aspect of "not murdering." One student, admitting that she likes to make jokes about her friends and family, puts it this way:

> 66 This one was a hard one for me. I'm a college student. Sarcastic. Humorous. Fun. But when do my words become weapons? I find myself making jokes at other people's expense, and then quickly covering myself by saying, "Oh, I didn't really mean that. I was just kidding."
>
> But even if you pull the knife out, the wound is still there.
>
> Yeah, sometimes people can handle it, but I still should be aware of how other people feel. I can tell sometimes, with friends and family, when they are getting fed up with my sarcastic comments. Some people might find my comments funny, and not get hurt, but I am beginning to realize that a little part of me is slowly taking away another person's life. I had never realized that I had been doing this. So when I saw it in the light of the commandment, "You shall not murder," I went into a spiral. I felt awful.

Up until this moment, this student had defined herself as a person who was able to be spontaneous and witty. She had considered herself to be a humorous, fun-loving person. But now she was beginning to see herself differently. She wondered how deep and fundamental a personality change this might require:

> Do I have to change myself completely? My whole humor? Should I apologize? I had so many questions for myself. My life seemed lost. Did I just lose my essence? Could I even change? After doing some deep and honest soul-searching, I realized that I did not have to change who I am, but I did need to change how I said things. I need to learn how to bring people up, not bring them down just for the sake of humor. I need to learn that sometimes my jokes are not that funny, and sometimes they hit too close to home. I need to learn about respecting the border, noticing when a joke becomes more of an insult. There is a line. This is good to know. It's good to know the difference between a harmless joke and spiritual murder.

With her new insight about spiritual murder, she begins to make changes:

> I started to let the people in my life know that I loved them. I wanted to be a life-giver, not a murderer. When uncertain about how people might receive my sarcasm, I refrained from poking fun at them. Even if I did joke with them, I was sure to let them know how much I appreciated them in my life. 99

This tendency to be sarcastic, all in the service of a good joke, is a common form of spiritual murder. In a journal entry titled "Spiritual Assassin," a student writes about his struggle to keep this commandment:

> 66 This week the focus of our class was on "You shall not murder." As a child I had been taught about this commandment and about its deeper meaning. I learned from an early age that, while I was obviously not allowed to kill

anyone, I was also to be mindful of the words coming out of my mouth. My mother used to say all the time that whatever I said needed to be "kind, true, and useful." At my young age, that was practically impossible.

But this week, I heard those words in a new way. This time the words and the teaching really sunk in. I began to realize that although I had heard this commandment many times, I had never really committed to making improvements in that area. I was determined to examine my thoughts before speaking, and if my words were not kind, true and useful—all three—I just would not express them. It would be that simple. **99**

In class, we will ask you to write about and talk about "fresh bread"—a recent incident in your life when you were able to apply a commandment. As this journal entry continues, that is precisely what he does:

66 This weekend I spiritually murdered one of my good friends, and in one of the worst ways possible. I attended my friend's twenty-first birthday party on Saturday night. At the party he opened one of the gifts given to him by his girlfriend. It was a blanket with a picture of him in his hockey uniform, with his name and jersey number. It looked like something that would have been made for a professional player. I was standing near the back of the crowd as he opened his gift and showed it to us. While most people were happy for him, I made a comment about how full of himself he was going to be after receiving that blanket.

Right then and there I had murdered my friend. But I did not realize this until Monday, which was after I had murdered him again. Sunday evening, I got on Facebook and saw on my news feed that he had posted a picture of himself holding the blanket up. Instead of complimenting him, like everyone else was, I decided to write, "Great, one more thing to feed your massive ego."

If what I said before was only a grievous wound, then this comment surely finished him off. I am a spiritual assassin.

Reflecting on what he learned through striving to keep this commandment, he writes:

While we are still good friends, and joke around like that all the time, I still made a terribly mean comment about something he was proud to have, AND I made it on a public forum. It was not kind, not true, and certainly not useful. I still feel bad about it, and plan to make amends with him soon. If I am to be a murderer, which I am actively working to avoid, I hope that I can at least take responsibility for what I have done. **99**

129

Is it kind? It is true? Is it useful?

The student who described himself as a "spiritual assassin" acknowledged that when he insulted his friend on Facebook, his words were "not kind, not true, and certainly not useful." The words "kind, true, and useful" will come up in several of the journal entries you are about to read. That's because one of the main marks to aim for with this commandment is to say nothing critical to or about anybody. Instead, you are encouraged to guard the words that come out of your mouth, making sure that your words pass through three gates: *Is it kind? Is it true? Is it useful?*

This can be a very difficult mark to hit, especially during those times when you are heated up about an issue, and your emotions are beginning to boil over. At such times you can get hotheaded and argumentative, rashly saying things that are unkind, exaggerated, and not useful. In a journal entry titled "Life Drainer," a student resolves to control his out-of-control tongue:

> 66 This commandment has been close to my heart for years. I understand that murder does not only mean physical murder, but it can also come about through the words I say daily to my family and friends. Reading this commandment once again, and taking it to heart, I realize that I often find myself struggling to live up to the high standard it calls for. I continually ask myself, "Why do I allow my tongue to become such a fire?"

> For example, this week my girlfriend and I were arguing about how I prioritize my school work over her. Instead of listening to how hurt she was, and realizing that she was simply wishing that we could be together more, I let my ego heat up and take over. I yelled and screamed about how hard I was working, how little time I had for anything, blah, blah, blah, and then said things that I wish I could take back. I shouted, "You are selfish!"

> I could see that every word I spoke was slowly draining her life, but once I got started it was hard to stop. It was like a fire that had gotten out of control.

Focusing on the commandment, "You shall not murder," helped him to acknowledge how wrong he had been and the damage he had done:

> I'm planning to apologize for my out of control tongue. I want to be a life-giver, not a life-drainer. I think I need to re-read the scripture that says that the tongue is like a small fire that can set a whole forest ablaze. (James 3:5) 99

The reference to his "out of control tongue" is a reminder that although you may think you are free, you might sometimes lose control over what comes out of your mouth. If you get angry enough or upset enough, your high resolve to say nothing critical to or about anyone can disappear and you might find yourself succumbing to the demands of your lower nature.

In moments like this, when you say or do things you afterwards regret, you realize that you are in spiritual bondage, enslaved by the heat of the moment and the relentless desires of the ego. A student, who caught himself "murdering" a classmate, acknowledges that he is a "slave in Egypt," not yet out of the house of bondage:

> 66 Words can be murderous. When I speak biting or cutting words, criticizing another person, those words can do spiritual damage. Even words that are true can be murderous if I speak them harshly or do not deliver them in a spirit of love and helpfulness. I had been taught since a young age that the commandment "You shall not murder" has these deeper implications, and yet before this week I had not been fully aware of all the varied forms that "murder" takes. It has been said that people's words often say more about themselves than about those they are speaking about. I have been skilled at speaking well of others and not engaging in gossip. But spiritual murder is not committed by my words alone. Sometimes it's the attitude within my words.
>
> For example, this week I had opportunities for murdering (or not murdering) other classmates while we were working on a group lab project in my biology class. On Thursday morning, I was tired and not in a smiley mood. While we were working on the project, one of my team members was asking me a lot of questions. Although I didn't lash out at him or call him an idiot, I just answered curtly, "I don't know." That was true—I didn't know. But what I really meant by those three short words was, "Stop bothering me with your foolish questions." While "true," my words were neither kind nor useful. I could hear myself snapping at him impatiently. In my mind I was thinking, "What a stupid question. Why does he think I know the answer to that? He is so frustrating."

This student realized that his words, while true, still had a cutting edge to them. It was uncalled for, especially because his lab partner was not doing anything wrong or mean:

> My lab partner was not trying to frustrate me. He was asking politely. Instead of politely letting him know that I didn't know the answer, I let my mind go on a machete adventure. I gave in to my lower nature, hacking and bashing his intelligence, thinking that he was "stupid" and just too annoying to be around. The truth is, my ego didn't want to be disturbed. It felt superior—like I was a master talking to a slave. In reality, I was the slave—a slave in Egypt, not yet out of the house of bondage. My lower nature was in control, not God. And it was wounding an innocent lab partner with machete-like thoughts and words.

Observing your thoughts, words, and deeds in the light of the commandments is an important step in spiritual development. But there's more. Spiritual development is also about taking responsibility for what you have said or done, and *then doing something about it*. In other words, spiritual development is about choosing to act differently. It's about choosing a new response.

After recognizing how poorly he has been treating his lab partner, he decides

131

that the next time the lab team meets, he will respond in a more life-giving way. He will choose a new response. He puts it like this:

> My lab team met again on Monday night. Once again, I was met with a few questions from the same person. This time, though, I saw the situation differently. He wasn't asking questions because he was stupid. They were good questions, and it showed that he really cared about the project. Also, he was asking because he thought I was smart—and that was flattering! This shift in perspective helped me to think well of him and answer with kindness and patience: "Oh," I said, "I don't actually know the answer to that. It's a good question, though. Let's find that out."
>
> He seemed pleased, and I felt great. By not spiritually murdering him, we were both happier. Instead of taking life from him by thinking ill of him, and acting in a manner consistent with my negative thoughts, I became a life-giver, acting in a manner that is consistent with my Higher Nature. I want to continue examining my thoughts and feelings so that whenever I speak, my words will always be kind, true, and useful. **99**

Murderous gossip

This is not a complicated commandment, and you probably "get it" intuitively. You probably know how destructive words can be—especially if you have ever been "burned" by hurtful words, "cut" by careless criticism, or "wounded" by malicious gossip. In the following journal entry, a student talks about how difficult it has been for her to live in a college setting where her sexual orientation is not accepted. She feels that people are constantly judging her and talking about her behind her back:

> **66** "You shall not murder" is what we are learning. And murder doesn't mean just taking someone's life away. It means to take away their spirit, to attack their character, to destroy their reputation. I know what this means, because I have felt it.
>
> A few of us, including myself, have a different sexual orientation than many other people living on this campus and attending this college. Because a few of us are "different" in this way, we all get lumped into the same category, and no one sees anything else about us. This feels like spiritual murder.
>
> Some people have murdered my reputation so badly that I get to the point where I feel ashamed to be who I am. I want to be viewed as a full person with many different aspects to my life. People who didn't even know my last name were passing judgment on me. One person in particular has made my life so difficult and shameful here that I feel like I have been living in hell. Reading this commandment, and understanding its deeper meaning, I realize that she has been murdering me—my name, my character, my reputation, and my life.

This is a well-written statement of how it feels to be discriminated against, and how it can tear away at a person's self-esteem. But this course is not about recognizing how *other* people break the commandments. It's about recognizing these same tendencies in ourselves, and striving to overcome them. As this student's journal entry continues, she takes a deeper look at herself, learns from her experience, and makes a solemn promise:

> Coming back this year, at the start of a new term, I was hoping that things would be different. But they aren't. People are still the same; the gossip doesn't end; and my spirit is getting wounded all over again. But I have come to a new realization. They may never change; but I can. I can let God's qualities become a part of me. I can even use this experience, including the experience of feeling spiritually murdered by others, to promise myself and God that I will never say anything about others that might hurt their spirit. I will first of all get to know the true nature of a person's character before saying anything about that person. I want to be someone who gives life, not a person who takes it away. I want to stop judging others, even if I feel that they are judging me. And I will ask God to give me the strength to do this.

In this moving journal entry, a young woman has come to the realization that even if other people don't change, she can change. She is not talking about changing her sexual orientation; rather, she's talking about changing her tendency to pass judgment on those whom she believes have been judging her. And she will ask God to give her the strength not only to stop passing judgment on others, but also for the strength to be a life-giver—even toward people who do not accept her.

In the previous journal entry, the thing that hurt the most was the malicious gossip. One of the worst things about malicious gossip is that once it has been spoken, the words cannot be taken back. Even a sincere apology cannot totally repair the damage that has been done. To illustrate, consider the following story:

A man had spread malicious rumors about the local rabbi. Feeling guilty about what he had done, he went to the rabbi and asked what he could do to make amends.

The rabbi said, "Get a feather pillow and take it to the top of the hill overlooking our village. When you get to the top of the hill, cut open the pillow, shake out all the feathers, and let the wind take them in every direction."

The man did just that. He went to the top of the hill overlooking the village. He cut open the pillow, and shook out all the feathers, watching them sail away in every direction.

When he returned to the rabbi, he said, "Is that all?"

"Not quite," said the rabbi. "Now I would like you to go and collect all the feathers."

"But that's impossible," said the man. "The feathers have blown away in every direction."

133

"Indeed, they have," said the rabbi. "And it is the same with the rumors you have spread about me. They cannot be reclaimed, because by now they have sailed away in every direction, and no one knows where they may have landed."

The tale is an instructive one, and may have important implications for your life, especially if you have enjoyed spreading harmful gossip, or just enjoyed hearing about it. In the following journal entry, a student comes to the realization that she has been a gossiper:

> 66 This week we were asked to not murder anyone. At first glance, this seems to be an easy "mark to aim at," considering that murder is usually defined as a malicious act ending another person's life. But the murder we were asked to not commit is that of attacking another person's character. We were to say nothing critical to or about anyone. In other words, don't be a back-stabber.
>
> In examining myself this week, in the light of this commandment, I have come to the realization that I am a spiritual murderer, a back-stabber, a gossip. This comes from a part of me that wants to be connected and to know what is going on in the lives of people around me. There's nothing wrong with that. But I also know that gossip usually turns into something negative and is hurtful to the person being gossiped about.
>
> When I'm with certain friends, I gossip more than when I'm with others. I know that this comes from my need to connect and be accepted, but now I realize that this is more about me than about the person being hurt by my words. And even if I say nothing, it feels like I'm an accomplice.

At this point, after recognizing what she's been doing, she makes a plan to deal with her problem:

> I know this is a problem for me. I want to connect with others, but I don't want to be a gossip. As a solution, I've been trying to find other ways to connect with our friends and see if we can base our friendship on something deeper than a mutual dislike for the same person. Also, before I speak, I have been remembering the story about the feathers. I ask myself, "Do I want to be responsible for the words I am about to say? Would I feel comfortable if the person were standing right here? Would I be able to take my words back once they have been released from the pillow?" This helps me keep my words in check. 99

Another student, also writing about the topic of gossip as a form of spiritual murder, never saw himself as much of a gossip. In fact, he felt pretty good about himself:

> 66 I never thought I had a big problem with murder. I don't spend much time gossiping. I don't like to participate in behind-the-back conversations. I try not to speak harshly to others.

But focusing on this commandment during the week opened his eyes:

134

> Ever since I seriously started to look at ways that I murder others (and myself), the ways seem to multiply exponentially. Just today I was sitting with some people in the cafeteria and they were discussing some rude thing that another college student had done. I won't go into the details, but I could see that there was some justification to what they were saying. But they were still beating on this person, while he couldn't defend himself in any way. I didn't verbally murder him, but I still sat there not saying anything. So, in a way, I was an accessory to the crime. I didn't chime in with something positive, nor did I simply take my leave.

Once his eyes were opened, he noticed multiple ways that he committed spiritual murder. In fact, he titled his journal entry, "I am a Mass Murderer":

> Later in the afternoon, I was driving with my sister. We were just chatting, and a complaint about New Jersey drivers happened to come up. Without even thinking about it, I made a comment about how stupid New Jersey drivers are. As soon as the words were out of my mouth, I realized that I had murdered the whole population of New Jersey drivers. Oops!

> What struck me the most about this experience was how natural it is for me to commit murder. The more I think about it, the more I realize that I've spent my entire life being critical of everyone, all the time, about everything. Up until now I have put on a good front. I even fooled myself! But now I have to start working on the inside. Like Jesus says, it's about cleaning the inside of the cup and dish—not just the outside. So keeping this commandment is going to be "an inside job." **”**

135

Being a life-giver

At first glance the Ten Commandments can appear to be quite negative. Nine of them are stated as "*you shall not.*" The truth is that the Hebrew word translated as "commandment" is "*dabar*," which simply means "to speak" or to "utter words." As such, it can be translated in many ways: as a command, as a message, even as a promise. That's why the ten "commandments" are sometimes translated as "The Ten Words," and are often called the "Decalogue."

With this in mind, it is useful to take another look at the Ten Commandments, or the Ten Words, or the Ten Messages, or the Ten Promises. The usual way, and the way most often associated with the Ten Commandments, is to see them as orders, demands, mandates and decrees. These are things that God says you *must* not do. For example, God says you *must* not murder, you *must* not commit adultery, you *must* not steal, and you *must* not lie.

At the same time, the so-called "commandments" can also be seen as God's promises. These are the things that God will do *through you* if you live according to God's Word. For example, you *will* not murder, you *will* not commit adultery, you *will* not steal, you *will* not lie. This is similar to the many promises given throughout the scriptures: "You shall know the truth" (John 8:32); "You shall receive power from on high" (Luke 29:49); "You will find rest for your souls" (Matthew 11:29). These are not commands; they are promises.[14]

But before you can experience the promises, you need to begin with the commands. Similarly, before you can plant the seeds and enjoy the flowers, you need to weed the garden and prepare the soil. As a human being, then, your first task is to stop doing what is destructive (pull out the weeds), so that God can flow into you with the power to do good (cause the flowers to grow).

To use a different example, if you give up junk food, your appetite for healthy food increases. In spiritual terms, if you refrain from murder in its various forms, your Higher Nature (the place where God "dwells in you" or "operates through you") has an opportunity to receive the inflowing divine life, and manifest it in your outward actions. Instead of being a thoughtless, inconsiderate *life-taker*, you gradually become a kind, considerate *life-giver*.

In the following journal entry, a student writes about his experience of being a life-giver. He is careful to point out, however, that he was only able to be a life-giver after realizing how much of a life-taker he had been:

> 66 For this commandment our challenge was to "say nothing critical to or about anyone for a whole week." To help us get started, we were given a "Star Chart" and a sheet of gummed stars. We were supposed to give ourselves "stars" for each portion of the day (morning, afternoon, evening) we managed to do it. That meant that I could get up to twenty-one stars for the week.
>
> I already knew that this commandment would be a difficult one for me. In fact, while walking back to my room after today's class, I committed murder before I even made it back to the dorm! At that point I knew I was in for a rough week.
>
> I gave myself three stars for the whole week. These are the only times when I felt like I didn't commit any murder. But I did notice something. I discovered that when I didn't commit any murder for a long time (two or three hours), something happened. I started to become a life-giver. I found myself spontaneously saying nice things and doing kind things. Holding doors for people, saying, "Hi," smiling. I remember telling a guest speaker in one of my classes that I really appreciated his presentation and got a lot out of it. This is something that I don't usually do. In my next class I told my professor that I really enjoyed the video he showed us and that it was very instructive. I didn't have any ulterior motive. I wasn't trying to be liked. I just felt like saying these things. And it felt good.

---

14 For an interesting article on this topic, see "10 Commandments or Ten Promises," a paper presented by Mabio Coelho, Department of Theology Centro Universitário Adventista de São Paulo. Accessed on October 11, 2017 @ www.researchgate.net/publication/273130579_10_Commandments_or_10_Promises

In fact, I felt full of life that whole morning. It's interesting to think how goodness can spontaneously arise when I stop being critical of others. Being a life-giver is one of the most amazing things we can do, and it starts with not being a life-taker.

I have learned a lot this week, and I'm not going to let my measly three stars get me down. I'm glad my eyes have been opened toward this evil tendency in my life. It gives me a new mountain to move, and I'm looking forward to the future. 99

In a similar example, a senior writes about what happened when she decided to not let her anger get the best of her. Her story begins with a description of a common problem for college students. It's the notorious "group project"—a good idea when everyone contributes, but also a potential nightmare when "free-riders" avoid doing their fair share. In her journal entry, titled "Group Project Blues," she describes how this commandment helped her deal with a frustrating situation:

66 During this past week I have been with two other students on a group project for our psychology class. We had agreed to do our research separately and then combine them together next time we meet. So I did my part.

But the two other students failed to come through. So she spent the entire night working on the project by herself. When morning came, she was furious:

I was so mad. I had to stay up until 5:00 AM getting the project done. I found myself saying the nastiest things about the two girls who let me down. My roommate, who knew I was taking this course, kept reminding me about my aim ("You shall not murder"). But I was too angry. I couldn't stop myself. It seemed that the evil inside of me was bigger and stronger than anything I could do to stop it from rising up. The more I tried to stop, the angrier I became. And the angrier I became, the more I murdered them. The evil had completely taken over, and it felt like there was nothing I could do to stop it.

Self-effort was not enough. The more she struggled to get rid of her anger, the more she became engulfed in it. Like a person struggling to get out of quicksand, the more she struggled to stop, the deeper she sank into her anger. She eventually fell asleep, but when she awoke nothing had changed:

When I awoke, three hours later, the first thing I thought was, "Those ***********." (You can fill in the blank.) I was late, so I got ready real quick, and when I was going down the stairs, a thought came to me that stopped me in my tracks: "I cannot let myself go outside like this. I need to pray." So I went back to my room and prayed. I prayed for understanding, patience, and strength. I ended up being late to class, but it was worth it.

When I got to school, I saw my project mates. Before I even said, "Hi," they started apologizing. I listened to what they had to say. If my lower nature were still in control, all I would have said was something like, "Whatever"—

and there would have been murderous anger in my tone. Instead, I found myself saying, "Thanks for your apology. I really appreciate it" [kind]. "You should know, though, that I was up all night doing our project" [true]. "Let's see if we can work together next time" [useful].

I was amazed. Those words just came right out of me without any rehearsing. They came out without anger or resentment. It felt so good. It felt like I had been released from an evil state. And it all made me realize that even though it seems hard, even impossible, to rise above murderous anger, I can do it with the help of God. 99

A final example of being a life-giver comes from a student who learned a valuable lesson from her "Star Chart." In her journal entry, she distinguishes between premeditated murder and accidental manslaughter:

66 I never suspected myself to be a murderer. I suppose the small sarcastic comments and offhand critical remarks toward others have seemed harmless enough. At least, no one ever mentioned that my comments hurt them. Up until now, I have hidden it well. Like one of those murderers with a mask, I even managed to hide it from myself. But the truth is, I have come to see this week that I am a very critical person, and my sarcasm can be biting.

All week long I kept my Star Chart and was able to notice all the critical and sarcastic things I say on a regular basis, without even thinking about it. I began to hear it in my tone of voice and in the way I express myself, even in the way I roll my eyes. I am glad that there are "Cities of Refuge"—places of forgiveness where I can go when I realize that so much of the harm that I have done has been unintentional.[15]

Nevertheless, I still need to ask for forgiveness, whether or not the harm I have caused has been intentional (premeditated murder) or unintentional (accidental manslaughter).

While I was reflecting on the pain I must have caused my friends and family with the same comments that were depriving me of stars on my Star Chart, it occurred to me that I should make amends for any outstanding harm I might have caused them in the past. I resolved to clean up any murder scenes I might have created. I also resolved that, going forward, I will stop all forms of murder, even if it means stopping myself mid-sentence when I notice that it is going in a sarcastic or critical direction. At the same time, I will pray for the opposite quality, so that I can reach out to others in love, without criticism and without sarcasm.

15 In the Hebrew Scriptures, there are "Cities of Refuge" where people who have accidentally killed someone can flee for protection from those who seek revenge. See Joshua 20:1-3: "Then the Lord said to Joshua, 'Tell the Israelites to designate the cities of refuge, as I instructed you through Moses, so that anyone who kills a person accidentally and unintentionally may flee there and find protection from the avenger of blood.'"

She comes through with her promise:

> I was gladdened by this idea. The steps seemed so simple. It was like I had just been handed a book with the title, "How to Refrain from Murdering: A Few Easy Steps to Becoming a Life-Giver." I turned to my boyfriend who was sitting next to me and said, "I'm so sorry for any time I might have cut you down and hurt you. (I couldn't think of specific times, but I thought it was worth saying anyway.) And I never want to murder you with my careless comments again." He smiled and said the same to me. I felt like hundreds of stars had just been sprinkled upon us like a blessing, all twinkly and full of hope, no matter what night might surround us. 99

• ● •

The commandment "You shall not murder," then, is a divinely given invitation to become a spiritual life-giver. Through living in accordance with this commandment you can accomplish the spiritual equivalent of breaking the four-minute mile; you can learn to love your enemy. What you once thought was impossible, becomes possible; what you once believed to be beyond your human potential, becomes achievable. As the poet Robert Browning once said, "Ah, but a man's reach should exceed his grasp / Or what's a heaven for?"[16]

---

16 Robert Browning, "Andrea del Sarto," lines 97-98. First published in 1855.

The mark to aim at

You shall not murder: be a life-giver

In this commandment you are called to not murder anyone physically, emotionally, or spiritually. This includes not destroying their reputation, their character, their hopes, their dreams, their confidence, their relationships, their beliefs, and especially their spirit. If you want to say something about someone, and it's not kind, true, or useful, don't say it. This includes destructive gossip, sarcastic put-downs, rude nicknames, even contemptuous eye-rolling. Don't be a killjoy. Be a spirit-lifter, not a spirit-killer. For one week your aim is to *say nothing critical to or about anyone. Instead, let your words be kind, true, and useful.* Encourage. Inspire. Be a life-giver. Give it a try, and see how it goes. In your journal, record your experience of practicing this commandment.

Suggestions for further reflection and practice

You shall not murder.

The following exercises contain additional information about this commandment. Read through all of them, and then focus on one or two that spark your interest.

1 Journal reflection: Ratzach and Nakah

In the original Hebrew version of this commandment, the word for "murder" is *Ratzach*. It means "to maliciously tear apart." When people die in an automobile accident, we do not say that they were "murdered." Rather, we say that they were *killed*. In Hebrew, the word for this kind of accidental death is *Nakah*. As you go through your week, examine yourself in the light of this commandment. Consider to what extent your comments to and about others fall into the category of *Ratzach* (malicious, intentional, pre-meditated, first-degree murder) or *Nakah* (unintentional, accidental, involuntary manslaughter). Keep in mind that whether you murder intentionally or kill unintentionally, the effect on others is similar. The drunk driver who strikes and kills an innocent pedestrian can say, "I didn't mean to do it," but it doesn't make much difference to the person who is permanently disabled or fatally injured. Something similar happens whenever our thoughtless words and careless comments run people over, sometimes doing deadly damage to their character, reputation and spirit.

2 Activity: keep a star chart

In an address given at Hillsdale College, Rabbi Joseph Telushkin asked a group of college students to raise their hands if they thought they could go through twenty-four hours without saying anything critical to or about anyone. Most of the students did not raise their hands. He then told them that if they couldn't go through twenty-four hours without drinking, they were addicted to alcohol. And if they couldn't go through twenty-four hours without smoking, they were addicted to nicotine. He then added, "Similarly, if you can't go for twenty-four hours without saying unkind words to others, then you have lost control over your tongue."[17]

---

17 Rabbi Joseph Telushkin, "Words that Hurt, Words that Heal: How to Choose Words Wisely and Well," from a speech given at the Center for Constructive Alternatives at Hillsdale College, September 1995. Re-printed in *Imprimis* (Hillsdale College, Hillsdale, Michigan) Vol. 24, no. 1 (January 1996): 1.

Try this for yourself. Make a chart for the week, dividing each day into morning, afternoon, and evening. Give yourself a "star" for every period of the day you make it through without saying anything critical to or about anyone. If you need to say something in the spirit of a necessary correction, make sure your words are kind, true, and useful. When you catch yourself being critical, jot down a brief note about what happened. For example, "I got upset with my roommate and called him a 'slob.'" Or, "When we lost the football game, I said, 'That stupid coach should be fired.'"

3 Activity: try a "do-over" (version 2)

This is a different version of the "do-over" activity we suggested for the commandment about taking the Lord's name in vain (see page 68). Therefore, we are calling it "version 2." Here's how it works for this commandment: If you catch yourself speaking critically to or about someone, ask for permission to try it all over again. Just say something like, "I should not be talking this way. I'm sorry. Do you mind if I take that back and start all over again?" *This time make sure your words are kind, true, and useful.*

4 Activity: beware "the temptation to tell the truth"

"Truth alone," when it is neither kind nor useful, can be damaging. If you find yourself in a situation where "telling the truth" about someone might harm them in some way, don't do it. Ask yourself, "What good would saying this do?" "What harm would saying this bring about?" "How useful would it be to share this "truth"?" As Northrop Frye puts it, "A temptation to tell the truth should be just as carefully guarded as a temptation to tell a lie."[18]

5 Activity: switch tracks or stop the train

If you notice that what you're saying is headed in the wrong direction, you can "switch tracks" and then keep going on the new track. There's no need to finish what you were saying, especially if you sense that what you're about to say is not kind, true and useful. Sometimes you can even "stop the train" right in the middle of a sentence. Often, the person you're speaking to may not even notice what is happening! Switch tracks seamlessly or stop the train immediately—before a collision occurs.

---

18 Northrop Frye, *The Educated Imagination* (Bloomington: Indiana University Press, 1964), 136. Frye credits Bernard Shaw as the source for this quotation. See Charlotte F. Shaw, editor, *The Wisdom of Bernard Shaw* (New York: Bretano's, 1913), 245.

6 Activity: avoid being a doormat or a baseball bat

Modern researchers, using sophisticated monitoring devices, have made it clear that holding on to negative emotions can destroy us from the inside. Suppressed emotions can "eat away" at us, leading to a wide variety of physiological problems, including stomach disorders, obesity, arthritis, and cancer. On the other hand, medical researchers have also discovered that venting emotions can be equally destructive. In fact, people who express their anger are three times more likely to have heart attacks.[19] In the light of these findings, it is unwise and unhealthy to be either a doormat (suppressing anger) or a baseball bat (venting anger). Instead, you can "let it go" by calling on a power greater than yourself to help you rise above the negative emotion. From that higher state of consciousness, you can address the situation from a heart of love, using words that are kind, true, and useful. Keep in mind Jesus' words, "Every good tree bears good fruit, but a bad tree bears bad fruit" (Matthew 7:18).

7 Journal reflection: be a life-giver

If you have been diligent in not saying anything critical to or about anyone, you may have found yourself saying and doing kind things spontaneously. This often comes as a pleasant surprise, something that is well worth recording. Write down those moments when you find yourself spontaneously saying things that lift and inspire people. These may be spur-of-the-moment utterances that just seem to come forth on their own from your Higher Nature. In religious terms, these are those moments when "God is working within and through you." In your journal, record one or two of these moments.

143

---

19 Claudia Hammond, "Is it bad to bottle up your anger?" July 30, 2014, bbc.com. Accessed on July 9, 2017 @ www.bbc.com/future/story/20140729-is-it-bad-to-bottle-up-anger?ocid=ww.social.link.email

"I didn't care. I also went to parties where I dressed inappropriately and made out with boys I had no real relationship with. Sometimes I didn't even know their name."

Rise above lust ~ honor marriage.

You shall not commit adultery.

Exodus 20:14

Beyond marshmallows

On May 12, 1987, a young woman stepped up to the podium to deliver a valedictory address on behalf of her college graduating class. It was to be the first valedictory ever given by a woman at Columbia University, ending a tradition that went back to the university's founding in 1754—over 200 years.

It was an exciting and historic day for those who attended. Not only the valedictorian, but also the salutatorian and the class president were all women. In addition, many of the achievement awards on that day went to women. They had broken "the glass ceiling," proving that women can hold their own in academia.

Years later, when this woman was asked to comment on what she remembered most about that day, she spoke about the numerous awards that the female graduates had received. She said that it added to the excitement of graduation day "and to the feeling that women in the class had excelled in uncommon ways. ... Many of the women Columbia attracted in its first coed class were truly intrepid," she said. [1]

The woman's name is Linda Mischel Eisner. During her undergraduate days at Columbia, she majored in computer science, graduated Summa Cum Laude, went on to receive a Juris Doctor degree from Yale University, and eventually became the director of special projects at Columbia University.

Her younger sisters have been similarly successful. Rebecca, who graduated from the University of California, San Francisco, with a Doctor of Medicine degree, specializes in neonatal-perinatal care. Her other sister, Judy, who graduated from the University of Chicago with an MBA, works in the banking industry for JP Morgan Chase & Company.

---

1 "Class of 1987 Heralds New Era at Columbia." Accessed on December 26, 2017 @ www. college.columbia.edu/about/coeducation/classof1987

This is more than a simple success story involving three sisters. In 1968, when Judy was 3, Rebecca was 4, and Linda was 5, they were participants in the now famous "Marshmallow Study." The study, which was conducted at Stanford University and directed by their father Walter Mischel, was designed to study children's ability to delay gratification. In addition to Judy, Rebecca and Linda, 500 other children took part in the study. Each child was led into a room and seated at a table. Then an experimenter would place a marshmallow on the table in front of the child and say,

> Here's a marshmallow. You can either eat it now, or you can wait until I come back. If you wait until I come back, you can have two. OK? So, you can either eat it now, or you can wait until I come back. If you wait, and don't eat this marshmallow, I will give you another one when I come back.

The experiment has been replicated many times and has become a YouTube hit with millions of views. In one case, after the experimenter explains the "eat one now" or "get two later" deal, a young boy says,

> If we wait, you'll give us two?

The experimenter says,

> Yes, you can eat one now, or you can wait. Whichever you want.

The experimenter then leaves the room, and the camera focuses on the child, seated at a table, staring at the lone marshmallow.

Particularly interesting are the various techniques children use to delay gratification. They sit on their hands; they whistle; they roll the marshmallow around; they pick at it; they smell it; they lick it repeatedly. Some, after struggling not to eat it, and struggling to distract themselves in different ways, can no longer resist. They finally succumb and eat the marshmallow. Others do not struggle at all—they eat it right away.[2]

The most interesting aspect of the experiment involves the longitudinal follow-up studies. When those who participated in the study were tracked down in their late teens, again in their twenties, and a final time in their thirties, Dr. Mischel found that those who had been able to delay gratification had significantly better scores on every life satisfaction and achievement test administered. In fact, their scores far exceeded those who were unable to delay gratification. On average, they were more successful at coping with life, and had more stable marriages and families. Among those who had waited for the second marshmallow were Dr. Mischel's daughters, Rebecca and Judy, and their big sister, Linda, the Columbia University valedictorian.

Apparently, "delayed gratification" works.

---

2   See the "Marshmallow Experiment" on YouTube. Accessed on October 13, 2017 @ www.youtube.com/watch?v=Yo4WF3cSd9Q

In a world of quick hook-ups, where all you need to do is "swipe right" on Tinder, it's important to keep the idea of delayed gratification in mind. Relationships that are deep and meaningful are built over time. They're based on two people knowing each other deeply, trusting each other fully, and counting on each other to "be there" in times of need. When knowledge, trust and reliability are the starting point, they become the rich soil in which the seeds of genuine love and intimacy can grow and deepen.

A relationship based on the fleeting desires of the moment can quickly burn out. But a relationship based on a love that is patient can endure forever. That's why the "delay of gratification" is a vital relationship skill, especially in regard to the commandment, "You shall not commit adultery." [3]

Traditionally, when a couple exchange wedding vows, they are making a solemn promise of sexual fidelity. The wedding vow goes something like this:

> *Do you promise to love, honor, and comfort each other, for better or worse, for richer or poorer, in sickness and in health, and forsaking all others, be faithful to each other, for as long as you both shall live?*

It is understood that "forsaking all others" and being "faithful to each other" includes being sexually faithful. Among other things, they are promising to keep their sexual relationship pure, holy, and undefiled. They are promising to never have sex with anyone except their spouse; they are committing to a relationship that will be "unadulterated."

Companies like to advertise their product, whether it be skin cream, maple syrup, or mustard, as "pure" and "unadulterated." This kind of advertising is saying that nothing extraneous has been added to the product; no other ingredients have been mixed in. Similarly, moments of peak experience are sometimes described as "unadulterated." Whether it's walking in the woods on a crisp autumn day, enjoying the quiet beauty of a fresh snowfall, or delighting in the innocence of a child at play, such moments can be experienced as pure and pristine. They are moments of "unadulterated joy" and "unadulterated happiness."

If you look deeply within, you may discover that you possess a God-given desire for what is wholesome, pure, and clean, not only in the products that you buy and the things you experience, but also in your relationships. Because of this, there are teachings in every world religion that protect marriage and caution against the harm that adultery brings—both to society and to the individual. These teachings encourage you to avoid the urge for immediate gratification, to rise above the adulterous promptings of your lower nature, and to wait for the "second marshmallow"—the blessings of a pure and lasting relationship.

---

3   In *How to Avoid Falling in Love with a Jerk* (New York: McGraw Hill, 2007), John Van Epp cites this study. He writes: "Learning about your partner's attention span and impulse control … may be a very strong predictor of what that partner will be like in a long-term relationship with you" (198-199). See also 1 Corinthians 13:4: "Love is patient …"

The commandments in world scriptures

Judaism

In the Mosaic law, the punishment for adultery is severe: "If a man is found lying with a married woman, then both shall die—the man that lay with the woman, and the woman; so you shall put away the evil from Israel" (Deuteronomy 22:22).

Furthermore, even if the individuals are single, sexual relations before marriage are not allowable. Those who engage in pre-marital sex must get married, and they are not permitted to divorce: "If a man finds a young woman who is a virgin, who is not betrothed, and he seizes her and lies with her, and they are found out ... she shall be his wife, and he shall not be permitted to divorce her for the rest of his life" (Deuteronomy 22:29-30).

Sexual attraction is powerful, and at times it takes everything a person has to resist the allurement associated with this commandment. Consider, for example, the story of Joseph who was living as a servant in Pharaoh's house. Joseph's job was to interpret his master's dreams and help him make important decisions about the leadership of his country. Pharaoh's wife, however, found herself attracted to Joseph and attempted to seduce him:

> *Now it came to pass that his master's wife cast longing eyes on Joseph, and said, "Lie with me." But Joseph refused and said ... "You are his wife. How can I do this great wickedness and sin against God?" (Genesis 39:7-9)*

Joseph understood that adultery is not only an offense against the woman's husband; it is also a sin against God.

In another story from the Hebrew scriptures, we read about King David who had it all—wealth, fame, and power. Nevertheless, he allowed himself to be led by the desires of his lower nature. Thinking that it would bring him greater happiness, he longed to possess Bathsheba, a married woman. After arranging to have her husband killed in battle, he took her as his wife, only to realize that he had committed a terrible crime. Acknowledging that he has defiled himself, he turns to the Lord, and asks to be spiritually cleansed: "Have mercy upon me, O God .... Wash me thoroughly from my iniquity, and cleanse me from my sin" (Psalm 51:1, 2).

Christianity

Jesus was well aware of these teachings about adultery. On one occasion, the religious leaders brought to him a woman who was caught having sex with a man who was not her husband: "Teacher, this woman was caught in adultery," they said, "in the very act." They then recited the Mosaic law: "Now, Moses, in the law, commanded us that such should be stoned. But what do you say?" (John 8:4-5). Jesus knew the law, but he also wanted to lift their minds above mere literalism. He wanted them to examine themselves, and to see whether they, who were so adamantly opposed to the impurity of adultery, had any impurities in themselves. So he stooped down, wrote on the ground *with his finger*, and said, "Let him who is without sin among you cast the first stone" (John 8:7; emphasis added).

The image of Jesus writing on the ground "with his finger" is suggestive. It calls to mind the giving of the Ten Commandments, "written with the finger of God." It also suggests that in some way the one who gave these commandments to the Israelites was now in their very midst. He was showing them that although adultery is indeed a sin, it is more important for them to focus on their own sins than to condemn others for their transgressions.

This is the spirit of Christianity; and while it does not abolish the commandments, it demonstrates *how* they can be kept: "Those who heard Jesus, being convicted by their conscience, went out one by one" until Jesus was left alone with the woman. When the accusers had all departed, Jesus said to her, "Neither do I condemn you; go and sin no more" (John 8:9-11).[4]

Although Jesus does not condemn her, he does let her know that her behavior was not in line with the commandments. "Go and sin no more," he says. Adultery is still a sin. She has missed the mark. But, at the same time, everyone who lusts after another person has also missed the mark. As Jesus puts it: "He who looks at a woman and *lusts after her* [cherishes lustful thoughts] has already committed adultery with her in his heart" (Matthew 5:28). Through these timeless words, Jesus invites everyone to "drop the rock" of judgment and examine the hidden lusts that lurk within everyone's heart.

---

4   As we pointed out earlier (p.42), the Greek word translated as "sin" is *hamartia* (ἁμαρτία). This is derived from an archery term which refers to "missing the mark." In the context of this commandment, the "aim" is a wholesome sexual relationship based on genuine love rather than self-gratification. Anything less is "missing the mark."

Islam

For Muslims, both fornication (pre-marital sex) and adultery (extra-marital sex) are forbidden: "The woman and the man guilty of adultery or fornication shall each be lashed with one hundred lashes. Let not compassion move you, for this is a matter prescribed by Allah" (Qur'an 24:2). Adultery, because it undermines and destroys the family, is regarded as a "gateway" evil—a harmful practice that destroys not only the individual but society as well. It should, therefore, be avoided, at all costs: "Do not come near to adultery, for it is shameful, and an evil which opens the way to other evils" (Qur'an 17:32).

It is important to keep in mind that even though adultery is condemned in the *Qur'an*, the death penalty is not mentioned. In Islamic culture, there are many stories about what Muhammad reportedly said and did. The Arabic word for these tales is *Hadith*, and they are given the highest significance, almost equivalent to the authority of the *Qur'an*. According to one of these stories, it is believed that Muhammad included these words in his Farewell Address: "The adulterer must be stoned" (Ibn Ishaq 970). However, because none of these reports appear in the *Qur'an*, it is difficult to determine whether or not they reflect the will of Allah. Whatever one's opinion might be about the punishment for adultery in Islam, both fornication and adultery are against the will of Allah.

Hinduism

In the Hindu scriptures, a wide range of actions are defined as adulterous: "Offering presents to a woman, romping with her, touching her ornaments and dress, sitting with her on a bed, all these are considered adulterous acts" (Laws of Manu 8:357). Even if there is consensual sex, if it is apart from marriage, it is considered adultery: "If one touches a woman in a way she ought not to be touched, or allows oneself to be touched in such a way, all such acts, even if done with mutual consent, are declared to be adulterous" (Laws of Manu 9:358).

While the types of actions defined as adulterous are very clear, the punishment that one receives is less precise. In some scriptures, a preliminary punishment is mentioned, followed by exile: "Men who commit adultery with the wives of others will be punished by the king in a way that is a deterrent to others. Afterwards, these men shall be banished" (Laws of Manu 7:352).

These teachings are quite clear about the physical level of adultery. But Hindu teachings, like Christian teachings, also address the hidden levels of the mind, the abode of our thoughts and feelings: "A man should not *think incontinently [lustfully]* of another man's wife ... for such a man will be reborn in a future life as a creeping insect. Thus, he who commits adultery is punished here and hereafter" (Vishnu Purana 3:11). In this passage, it becomes clear that lustful thoughts are a form of spiritual adultery.

Buddhism

In Buddhism adultery involves the mixing of what is impure with what is pure. In other words, it is possible to "adulterate" something that is pure by mixing in something that is impure or tainted in any way. This becomes a central focus in Buddhism where the emphasis is not just on physical purity, but also on mental and moral purity: "The wise man should remove his moral impurities as a smith blows away the dross from the silver" (Dhammapada 10:5). "Sexual impurity is the blemish of a woman; stinginess is the taint of a benefactor; impurities are indeed evils in this world and the next" (Dhammapada 18:8).

While these teachings primarily focus on impurity in all aspects of the moral life, there is a particular impurity that surpasses all others: "But there is an impurity greater than all impurities—this is ignorance. Rid yourselves of this greatest impurity, O monks, be free from all impurities" (Dhammapada 18:9).

"Why is 'ignorance' the greatest of all impurities?" it might be asked. "What about murder, adultery, stealing and lying?" The Buddha would say that these are all impurities, but the greatest impurity is ignorance because ignorance of truth and the lack of self-awareness leads to selfish desires and materialistic cravings. When one is blindly led by these desires and cravings, it opens the way to all other evils. As Eknath Easwaran puts it in his commentary on the *Dhammapada*, "The worst of all taints is ignorance, because it prevents us from seeing other impurities that consume us from within."[5]

• • •

The commandment against adultery (impurity) calls you to "clean up" those thoughts, attitudes, and intentions that might cause you to stray from the commandments; it calls you to look within and discover the impurities that would gradually destroy you like rust destroys iron; it calls you to pray for a steadfast spirit that will give you the power to resist every sin forbidden by the commandments. That's why David, after asking that God "wash him thoroughly" from the sin of adultery (Psalm 51:2), concludes with this prayer: "Create in me a clean heart, O God, and renew a firm spirit within me" (Psalm 51:10).

The children who were able to resist eating the first marshmallow were on the right track. Self-restraint, impulse control, and the ability to delay gratification are admirable virtues. Ultimately, however, sitting on one's hands, distracting one's self, and other forms of "white-knuckling" are not enough. Like David, you will eventually need to find your strength, not in mere will power, but rather in a Higher Power—one that will give you the strength to resist much more than a marshmallow.

---

5 Easwaran, *The Dhammapada, op. cit.*, 191-192.

The commandments in the lives of college students

You shall not commit adultery.

They say that "times are changing."
But that is not an excuse to throw morals out the window or harden our hearts to being nice, pure, human beings. I think we should stick to basic values, and not give in to the craziness that is our society.

Excerpt from an end-of-course self-assessment

Living in a "hook up" culture

The epigraph for this chapter is taken from an end-of-course self-assessment written by a college sophomore. She begins with a few lines from a familiar Beatles song:

> 66 "HELP! I need somebody. HELP! Not just anybody. HELP! You know I need someone. HELP!" Even though the Beatles wrote this song ages ago, they could not have summed up my generation better. The reason why my generation is so messed up is that everyone is blundering around trying everything and anything to fill the void in their hearts. Some try partying, others copious amounts of sex, and still others try pure selfishness—but all to no avail. What we don't understand is that if we would only take the time to tune into another Beatles song, "All You Need is Love," and realize that we all need God's love to feel complete, we would finally find that piece that is missing inside all of us. God IS the "somebody" we all need in our lives. God will give us the HELP we need, if we ask.

As she continues her self-assessment, she talks about the difficulties she experiences in trying to maintain her own sexual standards in a "hook-up" culture:

> The further and further my generation moves from the Lord's truth, the crazier things get. My generation is in pure chaos right now, and it's all because no one has any morals anymore! According to the most popular opinion, respecting yourself and your body makes you a "rigid, prude

> person"—and there is no worse stigma in society than being labeled a "tease" who doesn't "put out." There are still some good people out there—some that believe the Lord's truth and try to follow his commandments, but those individuals are constantly ridiculed and told that their opinions are old-fashioned and unwanted.

She then gives a specific example of how much times have changed:

> Love, marriage, and family—not promiscuous sex—used to be viewed as the highest goal in society. In the 1950s, if you asked any man or woman on the street what their aspirations in life were, it would be to get married and have children. It is simply not that way anymore. Love and marriage are seen as a damper on one's freedom.
>
> I believe this is why so many marriages from my generation end in divorce. They think that if the going gets rough, they have every right to end the marriage. On top of this, there is social media to exacerbate the problem. As soon as people start to have issues with their partner, they can go on Facebook, Twitter or Ashley Madison and have fifteen possible extra-marital love interests at their disposal. Instead of staying within the marriage and turning to God for help, we are turning to people outside of the marriage to fulfill our needs. ”

Her well-written essay clearly defines the plight of students who feel an increasing pressure to place tolerance—even tolerance for promiscuous behavior—above the sanctity of a truly committed relationship.

The need for connection

On the other hand, it must be acknowledged that sexual desire is real. It is both a God-given instinct, and a heavenly blessing primarily provided for the propagation of the human race. It is as instinctive as the need to eat, drink, and sleep. As a basic biological drive, it's as vital as the impulse for self-preservation, for it involves the preservation of humanity. But like all biological imperatives—especially when driven by your lower nature—it can begin to control you. One student described how he developed a sexual addiction at a young age. In examining himself, he came to the awareness that his pursuit of sex was linked to a misplaced desire for human connection. In his journal entry, he puts it like this:

> “ I was taught by my peers at a young age that the more girls I "got with" the cooler I was. This is how men are supposed to be. So I tried my best, and let my ego run wild, pursuing what I thought was the cool thing to do. I grew to love it. I needed that feeling of connection. I just wanted to be close to someone. Gradually, however, I needed more and more. I was like an addict looking for my fix. Girls made me feel the love and connection I needed. To me, sex meant connection. ”

It is interesting that he is not merely interested in sex for the physical pleasure it affords; on a deeper level, he craves the feeling of connection it gives him, however illusory and fleeting it might be.

Seeking connection through sexuality is a common theme. For example, in the following journal entry, a young woman writes about her need to be comforted after hearing about the death of a friend:

> 66 A friend of mine passed away yesterday. I am still reeling from the pain. I am tired of friends dying. Often, when I am in pain because of death, or loneliness, or self-hate (three of my biggest false gods), I go into comfort-seeking mode. Once I am in this mode, I begin to "act out" in ways that cause negative consequences and pull me away from my relationship with God. Tonight, after hearing the sad news, all I wanted to do was call some boy to come make out with me, and to "make me feel better." 99

Casual sex can provide a fleeting sense of comfort and connection. It offers a momentary feeling of being wanted, valued, even loved. For some it's a remedy for feeling alone and isolated. But it's only a temporary solution—an external remedy for an internal problem.

For example, a student who had never quite gotten over a break-up decided that a "hook-up" might be the answer. In her journal, she puts it like this:

> 66 In my life I have had only one romantic relationship, but I believed it was real, and that we were really in love. We dated for three years. He was my best friend. When we finally broke up, he told me that we couldn't be friends anymore, which hurt almost more than the break-up itself. It's been a year and a half since the break-up and we still don't talk. I tell myself that I'm over it and have moved on, but I still feel lonely and resentful.

> I haven't had a good relationship since the break-up, and I believe that negative emotions connected with that experience have led me down a desperate path. This term I've been going through a phase of feeling extremely lonely and not connected to anyone. It led me into a series of "hook-ups" that I knew would be short-lived and would fail. I didn't care. I also went to parties where I dressed inappropriately and made out with boys I had no real relationship with. Sometimes I didn't even know their name.

She discovers, however, that this lifestyle left her feeling deeply dissatisfied with herself:

> Last week I was at another party. I was in the middle of dancing and suddenly felt gross. I had an overwhelming feeling that I had lost respect for myself. The thought came to me, "I want to go back to a time when my body was respected and the love I gave meant something real."

She concludes by rekindling her hope for marriage:

> In the light of this commandment, I can now see what has been going on. I've been depressed and lonely, which led to the party behavior lifestyle. I thought

it might help, but in reality I was not respecting myself or the boys I was with. Although I'm disappointed by my adulterous behavior, I know that God forgives me, and I have forgiven myself. I am going to fight this urge from now on. I know who I want to become, and the kind of life I want to have. I know that I need to respect myself and respect others because we are all on the path toward a wonderful marriage relationship. Committing adultery, on any level, hurts that journey. **"**

As you can see from these journal entries, what may look like promiscuous behavior from the outside, is, in many cases, a desperate need for closeness and connection. Sometimes it's just about being valued and appreciated.

The problem with "meaningful" sex

While the need for connection, comfort, and attention are powerful forces, it is also possible that the sheer pleasure of sexuality can play a role in the choices you make. In the following journal entry, a student speaks openly about the "great sex" she enjoys with her boyfriend:

> **"** It was a rainy October night, and I was lying in bed all alone thinking about the great sex that my boyfriend and I had enjoyed the night before. I couldn't wait for the next night when we would be getting together again. The way he makes me feel is completely like "heaven on earth."

At the same time, she is aware that her focus on "great sex" (or sex for the sake of sex) may not be appropriate, and that sexuality should, at least, be "meaningful":

> I have been told that this kind of intimacy is a sin. But my father always told me, "As long as it's meaningful, it's OK." He has told me that if I have sex with a guy with whom I share mutual feelings, and if the guy also respects and loves me, the chances of getting hurt are slimmer. That mentality has grown on me, to the point where I don't really care if I have sex outside of marriage. The only thing that is important it that it "means something" to both of us.

As she continues her journal entry, she reflects on her father's advice, and how she has used it to justify her sexual choices:

> To be honest, I sort of know that sex before marriage is wrong, but when my hormones take over, I don't care. I use my father's explanation as an excuse to gratify my needs, and I push biblical teachings into the background.

During the term, however, she comes to a new understanding. In her end-of-course self-assessment, she writes:

> Before taking this course, this was my mentality, and throughout the course I have been struggling to accept the fact that it is **not OK** to have sex outside of marriage. In addition to my father's advice, I had always tried to justify my sexual activity by saying, "People do much worse things," and "It doesn't matter anymore. You have already done it." But no matter what my father

taught me, and no matter how much I have tried to justify it, God has the final say in all things. And he said it in this commandment: "Do not commit adultery." I prefer to live by God's word—not man's, not even my father's. If I can do that, I know I will experience "heaven on earth." 🙶🙶

Struggles with lust

You may have grown up in a family where marriage is considered sacred, and where wedding vows are considered holy—never to be violated. Or perhaps you grew up in a home where your parents did not get along, where wedding vows were ignored, and where physical and emotional abuse led to divorce. Whatever your family situation might have been, or might be, the decisions you make for yourself regarding this commandment are entirely your own.

A student who comes from a family where both partners have loved, honored, and remained faithful to each other, talks about a recent experience of attending a "blessing on a marriage." It occurred during the same weekend that he was working on this commandment. In his church, a "blessing on a marriage" is an opportunity for a married couple to renew their vows and rededicate their lives to one another and to God. He writes:

> 🙶🙶 Just this past weekend I got to witness a husband and wife renewing their wedding vows after twenty-five years of marriage. It was a blessing to see them, to learn about the ups and downs in their relationship, and to hear how they had remained devoted to each other through it all.

He then talks about his own parents, and how much their example of a loving marriage has meant to him:

> I am perhaps most grateful for the example my parents set for me. I have learned so much by watching them work together on their marriage and on their relationship with God. Even when I was a young child and didn't necessarily realize how much effort they were putting forth to love each other, they made an impression on me, even in their smallest actions— offering to do the dishes, giving each other a quick kiss "hello," or saying prayers with me and my sister when they put us to bed at night.

Growing up with such a positive model of marriage, he has decided that he wants the same in his life:

> I want this for my future. I see these great examples of marriage, and it affirms the idea that God created marriage as the greatest of all blessings. When God created the first couple, "God blessed them and said, 'Go forth and multiply.'" This is God's first blessing in the Bible, and Jesus' first miracle is at a wedding. I get the feeling that in God's plan for our happiness, marriage is the way to go. I cannot wait for marriage!

But even with such a positive model, he acknowledges that he struggles with lust:

It is strange to me then, that given this strong desire to have a good marriage, I often entertain lustful thoughts, and sometimes give in to lust. From freely entertaining sexual fantasies to "checking out" a girl when I know I shouldn't, I have fallen prey to this temptation many times. Whenever I entertain these thoughts, and allow them to linger, my mind and body feel physically "impure," and that it is not a great feeling.

Nevertheless, he has not given up hope:

> But I know that the Lord is forgiving, and I know that with God's help I can get through this. I will place my mind on Psalm 51, "Create in me a clean heart, O God, and renew a steadfast spirit within me." 〞

Whether you come from a home that honors marriage or not, struggles with lust may be an issue for you, especially when it comes to pornography. To click or not to click? It is a struggle for many college-age students, especially men. One student describes his addiction to pornography as a "war inside":

> 〝 Pornography is my arch enemy. It has a powerful effect on me because I am a "lusty" person. Because of this, I keep letting myself fall into the pornography trap. Marriage means so much to me, and I want to be a good husband. I want so much—more than anything—for this war inside me to stop.

He knows it's wrong, but he can't seem to stop. He wonders why:

157

> How come I continue to have this problem? I don't know the answer, but I do know that the first step to overcoming it is admitting it to someone else. That's why I am writing this journal entry. I also know that I have been convincing myself that it's not a big deal, and that it isn't a problem. The funny thing is that this is what I tell myself at the exact moment that I feel most vulnerable to this temptation. So instead of resisting the desire to watch pornography, I just let my lower nature have its way, and I give in.

He concludes by reflecting on his inner battle, describing the two opposing camps:

> It is very interesting that the thing I desire most in life—a wonderful, pure, holy, sacred, marriage relationship—is directly opposed to my attraction to pornography. It's like two armies fighting each other. I would think that my strong love for marriage and my desire to protect it would overpower my weakness for pornography, but I continue to fail. I am hoping that this commandment will strengthen me. I need help. 〞

Another student uses the metaphor of "spiritual warfare" to describe a similar addiction to pornography. His journal entry is titled, "This is War":

> 〝 My addiction to pornography started when I was about fourteen. I searched for the most obscene pictures or videos I could find in order to satisfy my curiosity. I felt like I was exploring an exciting, mysterious world, and sneakily masturbated as I did so.

After five years of indulging this habit, I began to develop a religious conscience. At nineteen, I made a determined decision not to indulge myself in watching porn ever again. But it wasn't that easy. In fact, it was a real war. I struggled to restrain myself from watching pornography, but every moment strong impulses attacked me. If I was careless for even a single moment, I would find myself again watching pornography. It was as if some vicious energy was always carefully waiting for any chance, taking advantage of any carelessness, to slip into my mind. Whenever this happened, I couldn't help but give in. It was something I couldn't stop. It was weird. It was like I was hardly conscious of what I was doing, and something else had control of me. It was whispering, even demanding loudly, "This is just curiosity. It's natural. You won't go out and commit sexual acts. You are just watching, and that's all it is."

It has been three years since I first declared war on pornography. Since then my fight has been lonely, persistent, and sometimes dreadful. Sometimes I had desperate feelings that I could never get over it, and that I should just end my life. Millions of times I could not help being defeated in this war. But keeping this commandment, and relying on God to help me win this battle, has been amazing. Even this week the frequency and intensity of the impulses has been less and less.

He concludes by defining the word "adultery" and what it means to him, especially in the context of his "battle":

In class we talked about the basic meaning of adultery. It means "to make impure" or "to pollute" by adding ingredients that contaminate what is supposed to be pure. As I thought about this, I realized that the commandment against adultery is really about keeping my mind clean and pure, and not adulterating it with filthy thoughts.

Jesus said, "Blessed are the pure in heart, for they shall see God." Whenever I am involved with pornography, my mind becomes impure. When this happens, I no longer see people as people but only as physical objects. I do not see God in them because my heart is not pure. For a long time, I thought that just watching did not harm anyone. But now I know how much it harms me, and how much it distorts the way I see the world. I don't want to look at people and only see them as sexual objects. I want to look at people and see God. I am praying that with God's help I can win this battle. 🙶🙶

The battle that this student describes is especially difficult because contemporary culture gives confusing messages about the value of marriage. One student puts it like this in her journal entry:

🙶🙶 It seems that we get conflicting messages all the time. For the most part, there is the extreme of "Sex is bad, don't think or talk about it." Then, at the other extreme, we get the message that "Sex is great. Everything is fine. Chill out. It's all good." In this course we say, "Let's talk about it. Let's share our experiences. Let's talk about where we are confused. What are the standards for good relationships, especially when we are hoping to have great marriages?" 🙸🙸

Forgiving ourselves

As the previous student points out, there is a great deal of confusion around the subject of sexual standards, especially for those who are hoping to have great marriages. Some students seem to feel fine about unrestrained sexual activity, believing that the more sex they have the better. They see no reason to delay sexual gratification. In fact, many seem proud of their "achievements." As far as they are concerned, the idea that "sex is for marriage" may just be a result of social conditioning.

Others, however, sense that sexuality is deeply connected to the idea of love in marriage. They understand that there is something wrong with consenting to a random "hook up," or indulging in sexual fantasies. For them, the idea of sexual restraint is not just a matter of "social conditioning"; rather, it is deeply connected to being human. They know that indiscriminate sexual activity, whether in fantasy or in reality, should be resisted, and that marriage is a sacred covenant that is to be honored.

159

It is perhaps for this reason that many find it hard to forgive themselves for giving in to lust. In the following journal entry, a student writes about a time when he was feeling so guilty that he went to his pastor to confess:

> 🙸🙸 I knew that marriage was going to be the most important thing in my life, but when it came to lust, I felt helpless. Lust was constant, and it was weakening me physically and spiritually. My father had told me that I should stay far away from internet sites that were filled with the lusts and desires of humanity, as any father should. He made the act of watching pornography so bad that whenever I couldn't resist my lusts, I felt like the worst person in the world—headed straight for hell.
>
> When I went to my pastor for the first time, I felt like I was confessing a murder. I broke down in tears, crying and whimpering and said, "I watch porn."

His pastor helped him understand that watching porn was not necessarily a ticket to hell:

> My pastor smiled and let me know that a lot of people my age do this. Throughout our somewhat awkward conversation, he kept reminding me that what I was experiencing was perfectly normal. and it certainly would not condemn me forever. He did, however, let me know that God gives us the power to turn away from this lust. On a piece of paper, he wrote down this

quote from Swedenborg: "The smallest amount of divine power is enough, every time it is called on, to tame instantly the entire devil's crew, even if it consisted of millions."[6]

The meeting with his pastor had good results. It helped him to let go of useless self-condemnation and forgive himself:

> I have learned that lust is dangerous and addictive, but it does not condemn anyone to hell, especially if you acknowledge that it is wrong and try to overcome it. The quote that my pastor gave me has been especially helpful in this struggle. It remains my biggest spiritual tool. 🙶🙶

Self-condemnation comes up often, especially regarding sexual issues. A student who had been raped as a child felt that she would be forever "unworthy":

> 🙶🙶 When I was fifteen years old I was raped, and that has affected my whole life ever since. After people found out about what had happened to me, the person who raped me told me something that has haunted me ever since. He said that I was a "whore" and that I would never live it down.

> He may have been right. After being through that personal tragedy, my false god became lust. I thought that somewhere, deep inside, if people could go through the physical act of having sex with me, maybe they would also love me. Maybe if someone really loved me, I wouldn't feel so dirty and unworthy anymore.

> I am eighteen years old now and have had multiple sex partners. Although I have overcome rape, I have not overcome lust, especially since I have become accustomed to it. I currently have a steady boyfriend here at college and another boyfriend back home. I do realize that what I am doing to both of them is not fair to either, and that this is not the way of the Lord. But lust is the one making the decisions, not me, even when I disagree with those decisions.

> The truth is, I do not think it is right to have sex before marriage. I do not think it is right to have multiple partners. And I do not think it is right to lie to my boyfriend.

It is obvious that beneath a promiscuous lifestyle, she retains a fundamental ethical awareness. It is her lifeline back to decency. In the light of this commandment, she writes:

---

6 Emanuel Swedenborg, *Secrets of Heaven* (New York: Swedenborg Foundation, 1969), paragraph number 8626. Originally published in London in twelve volumes, 1749-1756.

I know that I must identify and get rid of lust as my false god. And I know that I must ask the Lord to help me. Most of all, I must ask for his forgiveness, and I must learn to forgive myself. After reflecting on the readings and listening to the class discussion, I now realize that lust could never fill my need for love. Deep down, I know that God loves me and that if I ask him, he will guide me. I also know that I can't change the past, but I can learn from it. Meanwhile, I will continue to seek the Lord's forgiveness, forgive myself, and pray that my future husband will also forgive me.

With the Lord's help, lust will no longer rule my life, and I will no longer need to feel hopeless that no one will ever love me because of the mistakes I've made. Tonight, for the first time since I was a little girl, I am feeling that I still might have a shot at a marriage that will last forever. 99

This idea, that God is a God of forgiveness, is profoundly important as we consider the feelings of guilt that can arise in connection with this commandment. In a journal entry titled "Neither do I condemn you; go and sin no more," a student reflects on the role of God's forgiveness in his life, especially in relation to lustful thoughts and desires:

66 I'm a 22-year-old college guy. Lust isn't exactly easy to avoid, especially when living far from home, and left to my own rules and regulations. I know I shouldn't be welcoming lust into my life, but I have to be honest: sometimes it gets the best of me.

But there is good news! The good news is that I am not condemned for my lustful thoughts, or even for my lustful actions in the past. I am responsible for right here, right now—this moment. I find extreme comfort in the story about the woman who committed adultery. She destroyed her marriage in a very physical and damaging way, but Jesus did not condemn her. Similarly, even when I have dug myself into the deepest hole I can imagine, God does not condemn me. He merely tells me exactly what I need to hear, not out of anger or hatred, but out of compassion and love: "Go and sin no more." 99

Forgiving others

The word "adultery" is related to the Latin word *adulterare* which means "to make impure what is pure." In religious terms, to commit spiritual adultery is to defile something that is holy. For example, when you harbor grudges and resentments against others, you defile something within yourself that is holy: you adulterate the pure love and compassion that flow in from God. To better understand and overcome this level of adultery, the "Forgiveness Inventory" can be helpful. [7]

Among other things, this inventory offers you an opportunity to think about what you might gain by hanging on to resentments, and what you might gain

161

7 See "Suggestions for further reflection and application" at the end of this chapter for the "Forgiveness Inventory."

by giving them up. After filling out his inventory, one student wrote a journal entry titled "This would be a good class for you, Dad." He begins by discussing the worksheet:

> 66 This is about the "Forgiveness Inventory" you gave us to fill out. I thought of something right away and started writing about it. I don't like to think about this issue because it brings back bad memories, but here goes:
>
> When I was about ten years old, my parents told us they were getting divorced. But it wasn't finalized until much later. So for about a year my dad was not living at home. Since he was just down the street, I would get to see him every once in a while and sometimes sleep over on the weekends. One day, while I was at dad's house, I heard him talking to a lady on the phone, and he got me to talk to her a little bit. Dad asked me if I wanted to make the drive down to Washington to see her and stay the night. I just wanted to be with dad, so whatever he wanted to do, I wanted to do.
>
> We spent the night there and drove back in the morning. I remember this next scene vividly. I was coming home later than I usually would after spending the night at dad's. He dropped me off at home, got out of the car and talked to me in the driveway. He got down on one knee—to my level—and told me that if mom asks me why I'm home a little later than usual to tell her, "We went to McDonald's for breakfast." I asked him why, and he said, "Just do it." I said, "OK," and walked inside.
>
> One of the first things mom asked me was why I was home later than usual. (Dad called it.) I told her we went to McDonald's, and that was the end of that. I didn't feel bad or anything, because I was just doing what dad told me to do.
>
> A few weeks later, mom and I were going to the drugstore. I don't remember how it came up, but I ended up telling her that dad and I went to Washington that one day. She asked me if I spent the night. When I told her, "Yes," she started to cry. At the time, I did not know what was going on.
>
> To this day, I haven't spoken about this with my dad. I love him and everything, and we get along great, but I just can't get myself to forgive him— not yet at least. I don't like thinking or talking about my dad because it brings up too many bad memories (like this one). He completely took advantage of my innocence, and it has changed our relationship greatly. As it stands right now, I don't want to forgive him, because I don't think he deserves it. Maybe my opinion will change. I don't know. Let's give it another ten years and we'll see where we're at. 99

Several years later, while we were working on this chapter, we called the student who had said "Let's give it another ten years and we'll see where we're at." We reminded him about his journal entry, re-read it to him, and said, "If you are willing to talk about it, we would love to know 'where you are at.'" He was willing. So we asked him, "Did you ever speak to your father about this incident?" and, "Did you ever forgive him?"

Here's what he said:

> 66 I think about that memory from time to time. I have spoken to my father about it. I don't know what prompted it, but I'm pretty sure that doing the exercise made me think about it and made me want to have that conversation.
>
> It was so scary to bring up, but so necessary. It was very difficult. We were both emotional about it. I apologized for holding a grudge for so long. Dad apologized too. He said that he remembered that time and said that what he did was wrong. He said he shouldn't have done it.
>
> I'm glad I've forgiven him. I don't like carrying grudges. It doesn't serve anything for me, except helping me stay mad. At the time it actually felt good to be mad at someone who had wronged me, and I wanted to hang on to that anger. But the truth is I don't like being mad at my dad. It doesn't help me grow and change and have good relationships.

We asked if there was anything he wanted to add. "Yes," he said. He wanted to talk about the power of dealing with the past, not just burying it. Here's what he said:

> It felt so good to get all of that out. It has helped me so much. I don't think about it in the same way I used to anymore. It's officially put behind me as something that happened in my life. Before—like when I was in your class—it just brought up sad memories. But now when I talk about it, it actually feels pretty good. 99

We thanked him for the phone conversation and said that this would be a powerful example for future students who take the course. He said, "This has been a powerful phone call for me as well."

163

The mark to aim at

You shall not commit adultery: keep thoughts clean and motives pure

This is a week for honoring marriage. You can do it in the most direct way by not committing adultery, in thought, word, or deed. Your aim is to *keep your thoughts clean, your motives pure, and your actions honorable*. When sexual allurements come up, think in terms of how this might affect your current relationship or potential marriage. On a deeper level, avoid any kind of negative emotion that might pollute and corrupt your heart. This includes any form of bitterness or resentment. Harboring grudges, hanging on to resentment, and persisting in hardness of heart adulterates the pure love that is always available. Forgive yourself, and forgive others, knowing that God is a God of forgiveness— or that forgiveness is your Buddha-nature. In your journal, record your experience of practicing this commandment.

Suggestions for further reflection and practice

You shall not commit adultery.

The following exercises contain additional information about this commandment. Read through all of them, and then focus on one or two that spark your interest.

1 Journal reflection: when desire trumps values

As a human being, it is understandable that you long for love and connection. You have a God-given desire to touch and be touched, to feel significant and be cherished. These are normal, healthy, human desires. Trouble arises, however, when the craving for attention leads to infidelity and betrayal, and when an innocent desire for human connection leads to adulterous "hook-ups." Reflect on those areas in your life where a legitimate need for attention or connection may have led you to the point where you "crossed the line" into adulterous desires, thoughts, and actions.

2 Journal reflection: don't throw stones

In sacred scripture, the word "stones" sometimes symbolizes rock-solid "truth." These "stones" are the universal truths you can use to build the spiritual foundation for your life. You can also use these foundational stones (spiritual truths) to fight against all that is evil and false within you. Sometimes, however, you might make the mistake of using truth to condemn others rather than to identify and rise above your own destructive tendencies. In the biblical account of the woman caught in adultery (John 8:3-11), an angry mob picks up stones to throw at a woman to kill her. In one sense, they are "right" in what they are about to do. The woman has committed adultery, and, according to Mosaic law, she must be killed. But Jesus says, *"He who is without sin among you, let him throw the first stone."*

As you reflect on the meaning of Jesus' words, consider in what ways you may have been using truth ("stones") to justify your condemnation of others. When have you been so focused on being right that you forgot to be compassionate? What resentments might you still be carrying (like heavy stones) that need to be dropped? Is there a relationship where your heart has become hardened (like stone)? Is there a person you need to forgive? (See exercise #6: *The Forgiveness Inventory*.)

3 Activity: forgive yourself

Many people have trouble forgiving themselves for having illicit desires, dwelling on lustful thoughts, or committing adulterous acts. In fact, it is sometimes easier to forgive others than to forgive yourself. But forgiving yourself is essential if you are to start a new life. While it is important to take responsibility for adulterous desires, thoughts, and actions, debilitating guilt is not helpful. Instead, you can learn from the past and move forward into the future with heightened awareness. If this is still difficult for you, pray for the ability to forgive yourself. And if prayer is difficult, think in terms of your Higher Nature and your lower nature, or your Higher Self and your lower self, or your True Self and your illusory self. Know that the "Real You" is not that kind of person. Whatever you may have desired, thought, or done in the past is not part of your Buddha-nature, your Nobler-nature, or the incorruptible *Ātman* within. When you sense that you are succumbing to the allurement of a lustful thought or negative emotion, say to yourself: *This is not me! This is not who I really am.* Or: *I will not do this. I really want to be the person God intends me to be."* (You can, of course, come up with your own version.)

4 Journal reflection: the seduction of negative emotions

Negative emotions and the thoughts they generate may serve an initial use. Like the pain you feel when you place your hand on a hot stove, a negative thought or feeling can alert you to danger. In cases like this, the negative feeling is very effective. It serves a momentary use. But when you allow a thought or feeling to linger too long, when you allow it to embrace you and control you, it is no longer your servant; it has become your master. It has seduced you into slavery. In this regard, notice any negative thoughts and emotions that you may still harbor about a particular incident. Perhaps it was a test that you failed, a friend who hurt your feelings, a parent who disappointed you, or a coach who didn't seem to understand how talented you are. Consider when these thoughts and feelings first arose and why they might have been useful at the time. Then ask yourself why you're still hanging on to them past that point of usefulness. How long do you want to keep your hand on a hot stove? How long do you want to keep committing adultery with negative emotions?

5 Activity: notice mixed motivations

In this chapter we defined "adultery" as mixing what is pure with what is impure. But human motivation is often a "mixed bag" of "pure" and "less pure"—unselfish and selfish. As an example, you may want to get good grades so that you can get a meaningful job, accomplish great things, and help make the world a better place. At the same time, you may also want to get good grades so that you can get rich and be admired by others. In this case, higher motives (wanting to make the world a better place) get "mixed together" with lesser motives (wanting to get rich and be admired). Mixed motives are a regular occurrence—they are present in almost everything that is said or done. This week try to spot some of the mixed motivations that prompt you. Which ones seem to be more noble, genuine, and pure, and which ones seem to be more self-focused and oriented toward "What's in it for me?" See if you can emphasize the nobler motives while holding lightly or even de-emphasizing the less noble ones.

6 Activity: The Forgiveness Inventory

This exercise is designed to help you rise above the negative thoughts and emotions that are no longer serving you; instead, they are now "adulterating" your originally pure spirit. We call it *The Forgiveness Inventory*:

- Describe a situation about which you still harbor negative feelings. These feelings could include disappointment, resentment, anger, hatred, blame, etc. toward a person who offended you or a situation that upset you in some way. What happened? What was said? What was done? Just the facts.

- Describe the thoughts and feelings that arose within you at the time of the incident, as well as any lingering thoughts and feelings that you may still embrace.

- What do you think is the other person's experience of what happened? What do you think the other person may have been thinking and feeling?

- What, if anything, did you do to contribute to the situation? What part did you play? (If you didn't contribute anything at all to the situation, that's OK.)

- What do you gain from holding on to the negative thoughts and feelings? Are they still serving you? If so, how? If not, why not?

- What would you gain from letting go of the negative thoughts and feelings?

- If you are ready to let go of those thoughts and feelings, you may be ready for the following visualization:

    Imagine that the negative thoughts and feelings that you want to get rid of are an "immoveable mountain." Jesus said, "Whoever says to this mountain, 'Be removed and be cast into the sea,' and does not doubt in his heart … will have whatever he says." He then adds, "Therefore, I say to you, whatever things you ask when you pray, believe that you receive them, and you will have them." (Mark 11:24)

    In the light of this teaching, sincerely pray for and envision the removal of the negative thoughts and feelings that are no longer serving you. Visualize them being uprooted like a mountain and cast into the sea. If prayer is difficult for you, this is a chance to practice the "willing suspension of disbelief." Believe that this mountain can be moved. Keep Jesus' promise in mind: "Whatever things you ask when you pray, believe that you receive them, and you will have them."

167

Give this visualization your best effort.

What, if anything, did you experience during the visualization exercise?

- If you experienced a change of heart, however slight, you might now be ready to make amends. One way you can do this is by admitting to yourself, to God, and to the other person that *you are sorry for harboring ill-will*. If doing this will not cause any difficulties for the other person, go ahead and do so. But if making this kind of amends might cause difficulty for the other person, simply release this person from your inner prison of ill-will. While you need not give the other person your trust, you can free him or her from the negativity you've been holding onto. *Blessed are the pure in heart, for they shall see God* (Matthew 5:8).

7 Journal reflection: honoring your partnership with God

Most wedding ceremonies include some form of the promise "to be faithful to one another." In the sacred scriptures of many world religions, there is an indication that a faithful marriage on earth corresponds to a faithful marriage between an individual and God. In the Hebrew scriptures, God says, "Return, faithless people, for I am married to you" (Jeremiah 3:14). In the Arabic scriptures, God says, "I have breathed within you a breath of my own Spirit, that you may be my lover. Why have you forsaken me, and sought a beloved other than me?" (The Hidden Words of Baha'u'llah 1:19). And in the sacred scriptures of India, Krishna says, "Whatever forms are produced in any wombs whatsoever … I am the Father who casts the seed" (Bhagavad Gita 14:4). In the light of these teachings, reflect on your partnership with God, and the promise you have made to live according to your deepest beliefs. Then reflect on these questions, and answer them in your journal:

- How have I remained true to my beliefs, acting from my highest principles, while keeping my motives as pure as I can?

- How have I received "seed" from God—noble thoughts and loving feelings?

- How have I allowed that seed to take root and come forth in a life of love and useful service? Give a recent example.

To the extent that you have done these things, you have been "a faithful partner" in your relationship with God.

"I grew up in the Catholic church, so I always knew that stealing was wrong. Even so, I remember the first time I stole something and how I felt when I did it."

Rise above theft ~ be a credit-giver.

You shall not steal.

Exodus 20:15

The story of a college drop-out

Rodion Raskolnikov, the main character in Fyodor Dostoyevsky's novel *Crime and Punishment*, is described as "remarkably handsome, with beautiful dark eyes ... taller than average, slim and well built."[1] Crushed by poverty, Raskolnikov lives in a tiny, hot, attic room in St. Petersburg, Russia. Behind on rent payments, and dreading a confrontation with his landlady, he must sneak past her every day—something his proud intellect finds humiliating.

A letter to him from his mother begins with the words, "My dear Rodya." She goes on to tell him how much he is loved by his family: "You are everything to us, all our hopes and aspirations rolled into one. How terrible I felt when I learned that a few months ago you dropped out of the university because you couldn't manage to support yourself."[2]

The students at St. Petersburg University had a less sympathetic view of Raskolnikov. Before he dropped out, they saw him as an arrogant, aloof, and unfriendly loner who never took part in their discussions and activities. As Dostoyevsky puts it, the other students "had the impression that he looked down on them all from a certain height ... as though he viewed their convictions and interests as something inferior."[3]

Raskolnikov believes he's an "extraordinary" person whose intellectual superiority gives him an "inner right" to live above the law—even God's law. Convinced that he possesses the truth, he plans to murder an old female

---

1   Fyodor Dostoyevsky, *Crime and Punishment*, trans. by David McDuff (New York: Penguin Books, 1991), 6-7.
2   Ibid., 38.
3   Ibid., 63.

pawnbroker, and then steal her money and possessions. He imagines that he will use the stolen items to do innumerable good deeds for humanity. In his vaunting arrogance he regards the woman's life as having no more value than the life of a cockroach or a louse.

One day, while sitting in a cheap restaurant, Raskolnikov overhears another student talking about the old pawnbroker: "A hundred, a thousand good deeds could be arranged and expedited with that old woman's money, which is doomed to go to a monastery," says the student. "If one were to kill her and take her money, in order with it to devote oneself to the service of mankind ... wouldn't one petty little crime like that be atoned for by all those thousands of good deeds?"[4]

Raskolnikov is shocked. These are "precisely his own thoughts." He interprets this coincidence as a sign that he needs to take action: "It was as though some form of predestination, of augury, had been at work."[5]

The next day, under the cover of darkness, and with an ax concealed within his heavy coat, Raskolnikov makes his way to the pawnbroker's house. Thinking he has come to redeem or pawn something, the old lady lets him in. Raskolnikov has brought a silver cigarette case tightly wrapped in a cloth. He offers it to the woman, pretending that he wants to pawn it. But it's merely a decoy. As soon as the pawnbroker turns away to unwrap it, he strikes her with the ax, killing her instantly. Then he takes a ring of keys from her jacket pocket and goes into the bedroom to steal the treasures that she has locked away.

Meanwhile, the pawnbroker's half-sister, Lizaveta, comes home and discovers her sister's body in the living room, lying in a pool of blood. Raskolnikov is frightened and confused. Believing that he has no choice but to murder Lizaveta, he rushes into the living room, and with one blow of the ax sends her crashing to the floor.

Raskolnikov escapes with the stolen goods, but leaves behind him two dead people. He had convinced himself that he had the right to do so, because he had come to the intellectual conclusion that the money could be used "in the service of mankind."[6]

For the next 300 pages, Raskolnikov wanders the streets of St. Petersburg,

---

4 Ibid., 80.

5 Ibid., 81.

6 Ibid., 495-496. This is known as the "Extraordinary Man Theory." Basically, it is the belief that an extraordinary person can determine whether or not the end justifies the means. For example, Raskolnikov could use the stolen money to complete his education at St. Petersburg University, and then dedicate his life to helping others. The end (completing his education and getting a useful job) would justify the means (murdering an old woman and stealing her money). As an "extraordinary man," Raskolnikov had the "right" to do this.

tormented by his crime, constantly afraid of being discovered. Along the way he meets Sonya, a beautiful young woman with an unshakeable belief in God. Unfortunately, she has been forced into prostitution to support her destitute parents and siblings. Beyond the taint of her lifestyle, Raskolnikov senses something deeper. Dostoyevsky writes, "And yet not one drop of lust had penetrated her heart; he could see this; she stood before him exposed in her reality."[7]

On one occasion, after dark, Raskolnikov decides to visit Sonya in her apartment. They have a long discussion about the existence of God, with Sonya affirming God's existence, and Raskolnikov trying to reason her out of it. After many unsuccessful attempts at challenging her faith, Raskolnikov finds himself both moved and confused by Sonya's inner strength and purity of spirit. He doesn't understand how she can believe in God, especially in the face of all her troubles. *Why doesn't she just end it all and throw herself in the canal?* he wonders. *She's a fool! A holy fool!*[8]

Just then, Raskolnikov notices a book lying on a dresser-top in Sonya's apartment. It's a copy of the Bible, given to Sonya by a woman named Lizaveta: "Someone murdered her with an ax," says Sonya. "She was a righteous woman. ... She and I used to read and talk. She will see God."[9]

Hiding his surprise at this mysterious coincidence, Raskolnikov shrugs it off, saying to himself, *Holy fools, the two of them. I'll be turning into a holy fool myself, soon. It's catching.*[10] He then abruptly turns to Sonya and says, "Go on, read it!" He wants her to read the part about the raising of Lazarus. "What do you want me to read it for?" asks Sonya. "I mean. You don't believe in God, do you?" Raskolnikov avoids her question, repeating his demand: "Read it! I really want you to! You read it for Lizaveta, after all."[11]

Sonya hesitates, then starts to read aloud. Her words are filled with meaning. The more she reads, the more excited she becomes, until she reaches the final lines:

> *And when Jesus had thus spoken, he cried with a loud voice,*
> *"Lazarus come forth." And he that was dead came forth.*

After the reading, there is a long, silent pause. Raskolnikov has been moved, but he's far from convinced. Sonya might just be a "holy fool," he thinks. Nevertheless, he says to Sonya, "If I come back tomorrow, I will tell you who murdered Lizaveta. ... You I'll tell, and you alone."[12]

173

---

7   Ibid., 384.
8   Ibid., 386.
9   Ibid., 387.
10 Ibid., 387.
11 Ibid., 388.
12 Ibid., 393.

Raskolnikov does come back the following evening and confesses to both murders. Shocked at first, Sonya begs and pleads with Raskolnikov, urging him to confess not only to her, but also to the authorities. "Go, immediately, at this moment," she says. "Stand at the crossroads ... and tell everyone, out loud, 'I have killed.' Then God will send you life again."[13]

Reluctantly, Raskolnikov agrees. He confesses to the authorities and is sentenced to eight years of hard labor in Siberia. But the confession does not lead to genuine remorse. Still believing that his "extraordinary person" theory has validity, he regrets that he turned himself in. Instead, he should have had "the courage of his convictions."[14]

Then, one night, during his first year in prison, Raskolnikov has a dream:

> He dreamt that the entire world had fallen victim to some strange, unheard of and unprecedented plague that was spreading from the depths of Asia to Europe. Everyone was to perish, apart from a chosen few, a very few. Some kind of trichinae had appeared, microscopic creatures that lodged themselves in people's bodies. But these creatures were spirits, gifted with will and intelligence. People who absorbed them into their systems instantly became rabid and insane. But never, never had people considered themselves so intelligent and in unswerving possession of the truth as did those who became infected. ... Each person thought that he alone possessed the truth.[15]

The dream has a profound effect on Raskolnikov. He realizes that the dream is about him. He had been one of those who thought that "he alone possessed the truth." He believed that his philosophical reasoning was higher than God's law. Dostoyevsky writes:

> In place of dialectics, life had arrived, and in his consciousness something wholly different must now work towards fruition. Under his pillow there was a copy of the New Testament ... the same one from which she [Sonya] had read to him the raising of Lazarus .... Until now, he had never opened it.[16]

"Life had arrived," says Dostoyevsky, a new life based on something higher than mere intellect. Like Lazarus, who had been resurrected from death, love had raised Raskolnikov into a new, resurrected life. God had come to him through the purity of Sonya's love, raising him above the arrogance that had nearly destroyed him. And now, because of his faithful love for Sonya,

---

13 Ib id., 501.
14 Ibid., 649.
15 Ibid., 652.
16 Ibid., 656. The word "dialectics" in this passage refers to philosophical reasoning that leaves out any consideration of God, higher influences, or spirituality. It is based on intellect alone without reliance on faith or revelation.

and Sonya's faithful love for him, Raskolnikov would serve the remaining seven years of imprisonment "as if they had been seven days."[17]

• ● •

Rodion Raskolnikov is one of the towering figures in literary history. Within the first few chapters of the novel, he has not only stolen the money and possessions that rightfully belonged to an old pawnbroker, he has also stolen her life and the life of her sister. On a deeper level, as an impressionable young man, he allowed spiritual thieves and robbers to creep into his mind, and take away his faith in God, and in God's law—replacing it with faith in his own intellect.

In his book, *Losing Moses on the Freeway*, Pulitzer Prize winner Chris Hedges writes, "It is the tragedy of secular belief, indeed the tragedy of all man-made attempts at utopia, to place unbridled and total faith in the intellect." Hedges goes on to describe faith in one's intellect—rather than in God—as "the worst form of self-devouring idolatry." He concludes with these words: "Raskolnikov, like many of us, believed that intellect was enough to order his life. He substituted intellect for faith. He made a god of his intellect and served this god. Like all false gods, his intellect betrayed him." [18]

As Hedges points out so skillfully, Raskolnikov is a universal symbol for the various kinds of stealing. On the most literal level, he has not only stolen from others; he has also stolen from God, claiming the gift of intellect as his own, and using it to reject God's law. This kind of intellectual arrogance is one of the surest paths to self-destruction. As it is written in the sacred writings (*Hadith*) of Islam, "Those with even a seed's weight of arrogance will not enter heaven.... Arrogance means rejecting the truth and looking down on people" (Sāhih Muslim 91).

175

17 Ibid., 656. Dostoyevsky is using language with religious overtones as the novel comes to its conclusion. The reference to "seven years as seven days" is suggestive of the love between Jacob and Rachel in the Hebrew Bible: "So Jacob served seven years to get Rachel, but they seemed like only a few days to him because of his love for her" (Genesis 29:20).

18 Chris Hedges, *Losing Moses on the Freeway: The 10 Commandments in America* (New York: Free Press, 2005), 165.

The commandments in world scriptures

Judaism

The first theft recorded in the Bible takes place in the Garden of Eden. Adam and Eve have been told, in no uncertain terms, that they may eat of any tree in the garden, "but of the tree of the knowledge of good and evil you shall not eat, for in the day that you eat of it, you shall surely die" (Genesis 2:17). As the story goes, Eve listened to the voice of the serpent who said, "You will not surely die. For God knows that in the day you eat of it, your eyes will be opened, and you will be like God, knowing good and evil" (Genesis 3:5). Convinced by the serpent's clever reasoning, Eve ate the forbidden fruit and persuaded her husband, Adam, to do the same.

This story has long been regarded as "the fall of man," and has been interpreted in various ways. At the most literal level, it's simply about obeying God. If God says, "Don't do it," it means "Don't do it." If God says, "You shall not steal" or "Do not take what is not your own," it means just that.

At a deeper level, the story speaks about your tendency to disregard the teachings of scripture and the moral order of the universe, believing (like Raskolnikov) that you know better than others and better than God. This is what it means to believe the voice of the serpent that whispers, "You will be like God knowing good and evil," or, in other words, "You are self-sufficient, independent, and capable of using your own intellect to determine what is right and what is wrong." As you begin to serve the false god of intellect "eating from the tree of the knowledge of good and evil" you succumb to the illusion that you do not need the teachings of scripture—or even a human teacher for that matter. In this condition you believe yourself to be totally independent, not needing God or any person to help you determine what is good and what is evil. Your own intellect is enough.

As the illusion deepens, you begin to believe that life is your own (not a gift from God) and that the benevolent emotions and true thoughts that flow in are your own (not a gift from God). In brief, you "take the credit" or "steal the credit" that rightfully belongs to God.

This idea—that your noblest thoughts and most benevolent emotions flow in from God—can be found in a deeper understanding of scripture. This is the reason why there are severe penalties for theft in the Hebrew scriptures, especially when it involves the things that belong to God. Consider, for example, the biblical story of Achan, who had just returned from battle. It was customary in those days to dedicate the pillaged objects, won in battle, to God. As it is written, "All the silver, and gold, and vessels of brass and iron, are consecrated unto the Lord: they shall come into the treasury of the Lord" (Joshua 6:19).

Achan, however, did not do this. Instead, he kept some, gold, silver, and a beautiful garment for himself, even though they "belonged to God." When Achan's theft was discovered, he was stoned to death together with "his sons and daughters, oxen, donkeys, sheep, tent and all that he had ... and they burned them with fire after they had stoned them with stones. Then they raised over him a great heap of stones that is still there till this day" (Joshua 7:24-26).

At first glimpse, Achan's penalty may seem barbaric. But when understood more deeply, this biblical story contains essential messages about your spiritual development. The physical punishments described on the *literal* level correspond to punishments you inflict on yourself at a *spiritual* level. What may strike you as harsh and overly punitive is not intended as a *prescription* for a twenty-first century legal code, but rather as a *description* of what the violation of a commandment does to your spirit.

When read in this way, the death of Achan symbolizes the importance of removing every desire to steal—that is, *to claim as your own*—those spiritual things (loving feelings and true thoughts) that belong to God. In sacred scripture, the people of God are called to destroy this kind of theft by burning it with "fire" (a symbol of God's love) and burying it under a mound of "stones" (a symbol of God's many truths). In this way, the desire to claim as your own what belongs to God will not return. You will no longer be in danger of committing spiritual theft. The part of you that desires to take what is not your own will be, metaphorically speaking, "dead and buried."

Christianity

In Christianity, Jesus speaks about spiritual thieves and robbers who make a mockery of spirituality and try to lead people away from the truth: "All who came before me," he says, "are thieves and robbers. The thief does not come except to steal, and to kill and destroy. I have come that they might have life, and have it more abundantly" (John 8; 10). It is well-known that thieves and robbers prefer to operate under the cover of darkness. Therefore, Jesus says, "The light has come into the world, but men loved the darkness rather than the light ... for everyone practicing evil hates the light and does not come to the light, lest his evils be exposed" (John 3:19-20).

In some traditions, these inner thieves and robbers are considered "infernal

177

spirits," "evil spirits" or demons. In other traditions, they are considered personifications of your lower nature—your tendencies to be ruled by egotism, envy, greed, fear, lust, etc. And sometimes they are simply called, "the enemy." The Christian apostle Paul writes, "Our struggle is not against flesh and blood, but against principalities and powers, against the rulers of darkness, against spiritual wickedness in high places" (Ephesians 6:12). These are just some of the many ways to describe the destructive thoughts and feelings that sneak into your mind—like robbers—convincing you that there is no power greater than yourself, and that the benevolent affections and noble thoughts that flow into your mind are all self-generated.

When Jesus chased the deceitful moneychangers out of the temple, he said, "You have turned a house of prayer into a den of thieves" (Matthew 21:13). A "house of prayer" is a symbol of the human mind when focused on higher things, along with an acknowledgment of their source. It should not be turned into a darkened abode filled with self-serving schemes for material advancement—a "den of thieves." Nor should it shut out one of the deepest truths to be learned along the spiritual path: without God (or a Higher Power), we can do nothing.

Jesus puts it this way: "I am the vine, you are the branches. Abide in me and you shall bear fruit, for without me you can do nothing" (John 15:5). The idea is that all life flows in from God, or from a Higher Source, including every loving emotion you feel, and every true thought you think. To claim that these loving affections and true thoughts are self-generated is to commit spiritual theft. They belong to God, not to you.

The other way to say this is, "With God all things are possible" (Matthew 19:26). In the context in which this teaching is given, Jesus is talking about casting out demons (evil desires, negative thoughts, etc.). "With men," he says, "this is impossible." But "with God all [*spiritual*] things are possible."

In other words, God has the power to remove *all* bad feelings and *all* negative thoughts, replacing them with good feelings and positive thoughts. This is what is meant by "all things" are possible. This is not necessarily about obtaining a new car, or winning an Olympic medal, or obtaining a 4.0 grade point average. It's about identifying and casting out demons so that you can love enemies, serve unselfishly, and find peace even in the midst of emotional storms. These are the things—*the spiritual things*—that are, indeed, possible with God.

Islam

In Islam, the commandment against stealing is straightforward: "As to the thief, male or female, cut off his or her hands" (Qur'an 5:38). Islamic scholars disagree about how to interpret the Arabic word *eqta'u*. While most translate it as "cut off"—meaning, quite literally, "to amputate"—some scholars assert that it simply means "to cut" which has the meaning of leaving a mark or a scar. According to this minority view, the punishment for theft would entail having a distinctive mark put on the hands of the thief as a deterrent and warning for others.

Whichever view one holds, it's clear that the *Qur'an* regards stealing as a serious trespass—especially when it involves devious behavior.

In this regard, it must be proven that the thief acted in a manner that was sneaky, secretive, or cunning. In the *Qur'an*, the word "stealth" is used specifically to describe the way "obstinate, rebellious, evil spirits" strive to insinuate themselves into people's minds. These infernal spirits deny truth, make a mockery of spirituality and insist that there is no life after death (see Qur'an 37:6-16). In doing so, they secretly endeavor to lead you away from right living and into spiritual death. The *Qur'an* declares, however, that these spirits cannot harm those who follow Allah: "Those who seek to snatch away something by stealth are pursued by a flaming fire of piercing brightness" (Qur'an 37:10).

The bright light of truth drives evil spirits away.

Islamic scholars have different theories about what this might mean. Some conjecture that it is a meteorite, or a shooting star. However, it could also refer to the idea that the piercing brightness of sheer truth is overwhelming to evil spirits. When someone has been in darkness and a bright light is turned on, the "piercing brightness" can be intolerable. If this is multiplied a thousand or a million-fold, imagine the unendurable pain it might cause. Evil hates the light, much preferring to dwell in the darkness where its crimes cannot be seen.

In this way, it can operate by stealth.[19]

---

19 The word "stealth" describes the way stealing takes place. It is sly, secretive, and silent. A thief who operates by stealth is like a fox that quietly creeps up upon its victim, ready to devour its prey. Today, "stealth bombers" are designed so that they cannot be easily detected by radar. Similarly, we need "spiritual radar"—the teachings of sacred scripture—to detect the approach of spiritual thieves and robbers that quietly seek to invade our minds.

Hinduism

Turning to the Eastern religions, we see similar teachings about the human tendency to take what is not one's own. In Hinduism, "taking what has not been given," along with murder and adultery, are listed as "the three kinds of wicked bodily action" (Laws of Manu 12:7). In a list of famous aphorisms, the practice of "not stealing" is considered one of the five basic virtues (Yoga Sūtras of Patanjali 2:30).

An important distinction is made between two kinds of thieves. "Open thieves" are those who use the marketplace to cheat people out of their possessions: "These open deceivers live by various sorts of shady trading" (Laws of Manu 9:257). These "open thieves" might be compared to "white-collar" crimes such as tax fraud, embezzlement, money-laundering, and illegal insider trading. The other kind of thieves are called "concealed deceivers." These are the robbers who, under the cloak of night, break into homes and businesses in clandestine ways. They are called "evil-minded thieves, who secretly prowl over the earth" (Laws of Manu 9:263).

The idea of a sneaky, deceitful, evil-minded prowler calls to mind similar warnings in both Christianity and Islam. These are the warnings about the deceptive thieves and robbers that can enter people's minds by "stealth," attempting to rob them of their faith in a Power greater than themselves. These spiritual thieves and robbers can silently slip into human minds with the suggestion that human beings are sufficient unto themselves, that success on the horizontal plane of material existence is all that matters, and that there is no need of a Higher Power. In doing so, they are seeking to steal from you the belief that there is something beyond yourself. These "concealed deceivers" are also stealing from God that which belongs to God—you!

The delusion that you can be completely self-sufficient, and therefore have no need of God, is directly addressed in the Hindu scriptures: "He who knows me as his own Divine Self, as the Operator within him, breaks through the belief that he is the body" (Bhagavad Gita 4:9). Simultaneously aware of your unity with God and acknowledging your dependence on God, you can say, "I am always the instrument" (Bhagavad Gita 5:8).

When you are grounded in scriptures like these, and in a life according to them, it is more difficult for the "thieves and robbers" of egotism or arrogance to lead you astray. You know that you "do nothing" from yourself, and that everything you do is done in you and through you by a Force greater than yourself. As Swami Mukundananda puts it in his commentary on the *Bhagavad Gita*, "Whatever I have achieved and whatever I wish to achieve, I am not the doer of these."[20]

---

20 Accessed on November 26, 2017 @ www.holy-bhagavad-gita.org/chapter/2/verse/47

Buddhism

In Buddhism, the fourth precept on the *Noble Eightfold Path* speaks directly about theft: "Right acts are to abstain from taking life, *from stealing*, and from lechery" (Pali Canon).

Going deeper, the Buddha gives the remedy for the evil of theft. The goal is to get beyond all worldly attachments, especially attachment to the idea that you are your body, or even that you are your thoughts: "Let a man put away anger. Let him renounce pride. Let him get beyond all worldly attachments. No sufferings will befall him if he is not attached to mind and body, who calls nothing his own" (Dhammapada 17:1).

In Buddhism, the golden key to freeing yourself from every attachment is *awareness*. The relationship between awareness and theft is illustrated in a short Buddhist tale called "The Thief":

> One day a thief approached a great Buddhist master, looking for spiritual guidance. Although the thief wanted to grow spiritually, he had one condition: "I will do whatsoever you say," he told the master, "but I can never stop being a thief. I have accepted my destiny. So don't talk about it. From the very beginning let it be clear."

> The master agreed, but he too had one condition: "Now you can go and do whatever you like," he said to the thief. "But I only ask one thing: Be aware! Go, break into houses, enter, take things, steal; do whatsoever you like, that is of no concern to me—but do it with full awareness."

> The thief agreed.

> After three weeks he came back and said, "I cannot steal. I have tasted awareness, and it is so beautiful. Just the other night, while prowling through a rich man's home, I found a box of precious diamonds. I could have become one of the richest men in the world—but when I became aware, those diamonds looked like stones—just ordinary stones. I could not even touch them because the whole thing looked foolish, stupid. Master, thank you. I have lost the desire to steal. I will stay here and do whatever you say. I will be your disciple.[21]

As the thief became aware of his Higher Nature, the urgency of satisfying his lower nature subsided. As he reached full awareness, he lost all desire to steal. He had touched his True Nature—his Buddha-nature; he was no longer a thief.

• ● •

---

21 This adaptation is based on a short story by Shree Rajneesh (Osho), a modern teacher of Indian spirituality. Accessed on July 5, 2017 @ www.spiritual-short-stories.com/spiritual-short-story-77-the-thief/

This brief survey of the commandment "You shall not steal" in world religions has taken us beyond the literal level of stealing into deeper and deeper spiritual levels. We have seen that all evil desires are like thieves and robbers who sneakily creep into your mind to steal your happiness, take away your joy, and rob you of contentment. These "spiritual pickpockets" must be identified and removed. At the deepest level, the focus of this commandment is upon those thieves and robbers *in you,* who would delude you into claiming as your own what rightfully belongs to God.

These concepts rise above mere literalism. The harsh punishments for thieves and robbers described in the literal texts serve as wonderful symbols of deeper truth. We begin to see that these scriptures are not about eradicating people and animals, or amputating hands and feet; rather, they are about the eradication of evil in ourselves. In the words of the Buddha, "A tree that has been cut down will grow again, unless its taproot is destroyed. In the same way, if evil desire is not destroyed, it will return to us again and again" (Dhammapada 24:5).

The commandments in the lives of college students

You shall not steal.

During sixth grade, my friends and I started stealing. We became so good at it that it was almost second nature.

Journal excerpt from a college sophomore

Have you ever stolen anything?

The epigraph to this chapter contains an excerpt from a journal entry about stealing. The student says that at a certain point stealing became "second nature." He was responding to the question we often ask when our students begin to study this commandment: "Have you ever stolen anything?"

In the past, after giving students a few minutes to think about it, we ask for a show of hands, saying, "Please raise your hand if you have ever taken anything that didn't belong to you." Hands go up all around the classroom. Almost everyone has stolen something, and their stories are fascinating. Here are a few examples:

> ❝ While growing up, Pokémon was the thing that all the kids were playing. We were a poor family, just trying to get by, so I didn't have any cards. But my friend had almost all of them. So one day, while I was at his house, and he wasn't looking, I took them. When he noticed that he was missing his cards, I didn't say anything, but I felt terrible. My stomach felt like someone was punching it, and my body felt hot. When I got up to leave, the cards fell out of my pocket. The moment we made eye contact I ran as fast as I could out of his house. I realized that I didn't only steal his cards, but I also lost his trust. ❞

Another student recalls an early experience of stealing candy cigarettes:

> ❝ I grew up in the Catholic church, so I always knew that stealing was wrong. Even so, I remember the first time I stole something and how I felt when I did it. At the time I was in second grade, but I was hanging out with the fourth graders in my school who would go to the corner store and steal stuff. At the time, I thought it was cool that they could steal stuff and not get into trouble, so I wanted to try it myself.

I walked into the store, looked around, and noticed that no one was watching me. At the time, "smoking" candy cigarettes with those little red tips was the coolest thing in the world. When I saw my chance, I grabbed a pack and ran out of the store. As I ran out of the store, I was excited because I knew that my fourth-grade friends would really be impressed. My house was very close to the store, and during that short run I felt like the coolest person alive. It felt great to do something like this and get away with it. 🙶

It's interesting that there is a certain feeling of pleasure, satisfaction, or delight that sometimes accompanies the breaking of a commandment, but it is a feeling that does not last long. Consider, for example, the story of a student who describes his early experiences of stealing as "exhilarating":

🙶 When I was fifteen years old, my friend and I began to steal CDs from Best Buy. I don't remember how we learned to do it in a store loaded with security cameras, but we became very good at it—improving our loot from the initial one or two CDs to three, four, or even five CDs each for a total of ten!

Not only was this extremely exhilarating, fully knowing how careful we must be with cameras watching us, but it was exciting to see just how much we could steal and get away with. Even getting caught, which eventually happened, was also exciting. I remember feeling very egotistical and powerful as the store security interviewed me. I figured they would just take the CDs away and let us go.

But when the police came and put them in the back of squad cars, his feelings changed:

I will never forget the humiliation of all those people watching me with strong eyes of judgment, as if I was a pathetic and unworthy human. But that wasn't even the worst part. Even now, I get tense with shame when I think about it. After waiting in a holding cell for what seemed like half a day, my mother came to pick me up. There are no words to express the embarrassment I felt when my mother, a deeply good person, saw that her son was a person without integrity. There is no pain like hurting someone you love. 🙶

Thieveries like these, when committed in childhood, are forgivable because they take place before a person becomes a fully rational adult. Researchers inform us that the rational mind is developing all through adolescence, and even into the college years. In some cases, the rational mind is not fully developed until the age of 25.[22] It is understandable, then, that some college students find ways of committing petty larceny. It could be as trivial as stealing food from a community refrigerator:

22 "Is 25 the New Cut-off Point for Adulthood" (BBC News Magazine, September 23, 2013). Accessed on October 15, 2017 @ www.bbc.com/news/magazine-24173194

66 I am a dorm student, and one of the most annoying things that happens is that people take your food out of the refrigerator and eat it without asking. Well, last Thursday, just before the *Rise Above It* class, I was looking for something to eat, and there was nothing in the refrigerator except one "Hot Pocket." I was hungry, and there was no time to go to the dining hall, so I ate it.

I didn't really think of it as a theft, and I didn't feel the need to tell the person who put it there, because right after class I went to Food Giant and bought a replacement. "She will probably never realize it," I told myself.

But she did.

What happened was that I bought the wrong kind. Another friend told me that the girl I had taken the Hot Pocket from was really mad. She couldn't believe that someone had secretly replaced her food with another item. I felt bad. Even though I had no intention to steal, I did. I eventually bought her the right one, but I know that replacing the item does not replace the fact that I stole it. 99

This act of "petty larceny" might be classified in the same category as using detergent that is left in the laundry room, shampoo that is left in the shower, or "borrowing" things without remembering to return them. The tendency to forget to return items is sometimes known, not as theft, but more euphemistically as "permanently borrowing." One student, who becomes aware of this tendency in himself, puts it like this:

185

66 I'm forgetful. I borrow things from people a lot. The problem is I hold on to whatever it is for days, weeks, months, years—until I conveniently "forget" who I borrowed it from in the first place. I'll justify it any way I can, saying things like, "I've had it for so long, they probably have forgotten about it by now," and "They would've asked me if they wanted it back." I tell myself, "It would be weird to give it back now, since they expected it to be returned two months ago." I come up with every excuse in the world to justify why it's more practical for me to just keep the item, whether it's an item of clothing, a movie, or a book. I can see that my habit of "permanently borrowing" is a form of theft. 99

Another student talks about his tendency to steal from a fast-food restaurant:

66 One of my favorite fast food restaurants is Chipotle. The prices are reasonable, but when you add a soft drink to your purchase, the bill adds up. So when the person at the counter asks me if I would like anything to drink, I just say, "A cup of water is just fine." I do this because an empty water cup is free. But when I get my water cup and go over to the drink station, I fill it with soda!

According to this commandment, that is stealing. And it feels like it too. It's not a major crime, but as I stand there filling my cup, I feel self-conscious and worry that someone might be looking at me. Deep down I know that what I am doing is wrong. Next time I go to Chipotle, I will fill my cup with water. I need to rise above these petty actions. If I want the soda that much, I should pay for it. 🙶

Academic theft

The basic definition of stealing—"to take something that is not your own"—can have various levels of meaning. At the most basic level, it refers to the theft of a physical object: a book, an article of clothing, a computer. Sometimes, however, the stolen item is not a physical possession. For example, students break this commandment when they take grades they do not deserve:

> 🙶 My brain works better in the arts and humanities, and not so well in math and science. Numbers just don't make sense to me unless it is something as basic as two plus two. Math is the biggest hurdle for me, and since it is required I worry that it will bring my GPA down. That's why I have started to get other people to do my homework for me.
>
> I started making friends with the good math students, and some were willing to help me out. Since my professor grades our homework, my math grade began to increase dramatically. I hate to admit it, but in the light of this commandment, I have been stealing—I have been taking something that does not belong to me: high grades on my math homework. Because of this I am promising to stop stealing and work harder at understanding math. 🙶

When students get someone else to do their work, and then take credit for what that person has done, they are stealing. They are taking a grade that is not their own. In the following journal entry, a student describes her side of the story— the perspective of the good student who does homework for others:

> 🙶 Some of the girls in the dorm who are not academically minded asked me if I could help them with their homework. At first it was just normal helping, giving them guidance on how to do it. But then it led to me giving them the answers, and eventually just doing the homework for them.
>
> Was I breaking the commandment that forbids stealing?
>
> Yes! I was stealing their chance to actually learn the material. Even though they were the ones getting the answers from me—thus stealing credit and grades that did not belong to them—I was equally in the wrong. When it came time for them to take the test, they did not know how to do it, because they had relied on me for their homework. I felt bad, not just because they had failed the test, but because I had been their "accomplice." 🙶

While there are many forms of academic cheating, one of the most notorious is plagiarism:

186

❝ In our *Rise Above It* class, we learned that plagiarism is derived from the Greek word, "plagios," meaning "treacherous." That's a strong word. It means "deceitful," "unfaithful," "two-faced." I don't want to be that kind of a person.

Last week I started a research paper. During my research, I was looking for good quotes to back up my thoughts and ideas. As I found ones I liked, I wrote them down and would decide later which ones would really help benefit my paper. Then I came across a quote that was perfect. It not only said what I was trying to convey, but as a bonus it had elements of writing that my English teacher said to be aware of in our own writing.

The thought came to me that I could pretend this was my quote. I spent a good deal of time trying to figure out how I could work this quote into my paper while making it seem like I wrote it. But this commandment has heightened my awareness. I knew that this would not only be plagiarism, but it would also be breaking one of God's commandments—taking someone else's hard work and pretending that it is mine. That is stealing. ❞

These journal entries on academic cheating point to a problem that you or your friends might be confronting, perhaps more intensely than any other generation before you. Overwhelmed by crowded work schedules, inundated with emails and text messages, swamped with friend requests and status updates, pressured to maintain good grades or lose your scholarship, enticed by addictive video games, worried about the need to keep up your Facebook and Snapchat reputation, anxious about getting into grad school, fearful about getting a job in an increasingly competitive job market, and concerned that you may never get out from under a growing mountain of college debt, you might be tempted to revert to a survival skill of your lower nature: it's called "cheating."

Research studies indicate that cheating habits can begin as early as elementary school and intensify in high school, where 95% of students admit to cheating in some form. By the time they get to college, cheating behavior has become so habitual that they no longer see it as wrong or immoral. Rather, it is regarded as an essential survival skill. For some, coming up with creative and ingenious ways to cheat is considered a badge of honor, and sharing answers to a test is seen as "collaboration." It is not surprising, then, that two out of every three college students admit to cheating on a test or written assignment.[23]

Nevertheless, many students refuse to cheat. While they may not receive academic rewards or cheat their way to the head of the class, the rewards they receive are much deeper. A college senior reflects on her persistent resistance to plagiarism:

---

23 In an extensive research study involving 71,300 students from four-year colleges, 68% admitted to cheating on a test or written assignment. In a similar survey of 70,000 high school students, 95% admitted that they had cheated at some time. They had either plagiarized, copied someone else's homework, or cheated on a test. Accessed on July 7, 2017 @ www.academicintegrity.org/icai/integrity-3.php

66 I've done my share of stealing in my life, but one thing I have never stolen is someone else's work. I have never plagiarized. Of course, there have been times when I was under a lot of pressure, and didn't have time to finish a paper, or I didn't have enough words to make the required word count. At those times it would have been easy to cut and paste an extra paragraph into my paper and change up the words so that it looked like my work, but I didn't do it. So I can say that I am proud that I have gotten through this much school and can still say that's true for me. Many people cannot say the same.

She then talks about how she can continue to be a person of integrity for the rest of her life:

I have decided to make it a goal of mine not just to get all the way through college, but to get all the way through life, without stealing in any form. With my strength from God, I know I can accomplish this. 99

Work ethic

Many people are quickly dissatisfied if they do not perceive their job as "meaningful." The reality, however, is that the most meaningful jobs still require a considerable amount of what old-timers call "grunt work."

This is especially the case with a great deal of "student work," which often includes less than glamorous jobs like washing dishes, emptying waste baskets, and cleaning bathrooms. Every now and then a student might land a paid internship, but the greater part of student work is basic, unskilled labor. For example, consider this journal excerpt from a student whose assignment was to do vacuum cleaning in a college art museum:

66 I didn't think this week's commandment, "You shall not steal," would be too hard for me. In fact, I thought it would be pretty easy. I have never had a problem with stealing. Then I saw the section in today's readings for class that said, basically, "If you are slacking off at work, you are taking money that does not belong to you." This really struck me. So I have to admit it: I have a problem with stealing. Every time I go to work, I am stealing money from my employers.

My student work job is at the Art Museum. I dread going to work, and I put it off as long as I can, so I am usually at least fifteen minutes late. Since there is no supervisor on duty, no one notices anyway. My main job is to carry around a heavy, clunky vacuum cleaner and make sure the carpets are done well. There is usually a list of other things to do as well, and (when I can get away with it) I just do some of the things on the list and vacuum as quickly as possible—sometimes missing whole areas. And I spend a lot of time texting friends.

This week, after I realized that I was stealing from my employer, I made a serious effort to change. I earnestly worked as hard as I could, and guess what? It felt pretty good. The time went by quickly and I didn't even mind vacuuming that much. 99

In keeping the commandment "You shall not steal," this student experienced an attitudinal shift—a shift that brought about a wonderful result. When she changed her focus from cutting corners on the job to doing the job well, a job that she had previously perceived as boring drudge work became something quite different. As she puts it, "I earnestly worked as hard as I could." And she adds, "It actually felt pretty good."

In a similar journal entry, a student whose work assignment was cleaning a college dormitory talks about how much he disliked his job, and how he also found ways to cut corners:

> ❝ I clean Miles Hall for student work. At the beginning of the year I was very religious when cleaning, and I did it very well. But now, whenever I go to my job, I can't wait to get out, so I do half-hearted work. I guess I would have kept doing it well, but every time I went back to work, the stuff I had cleaned the previous day was dirty again. My supervisor, of course, never knew the difference, since dormitories get dirty every day.

Thinking about the commandment on stealing, however, helped him see things differently.

> I had been telling myself, "It doesn't matter whether I clean or not, because they are just going to mess it up anyway." But I know this is the wrong attitude. I need to realize that I am lucky to have a job where there is always something to clean, so the opportunity to earn money never stops. No matter how much I clean, the next day it all comes back, which means more money in the pocket for little old me.

> More importantly, though, I hadn't even realized that this was a problem, or that I was stealing from my employer. I need to start looking at things in the light of the commandments, and if I am breaking them, I need to stop.

With his new insight about not stealing from his employer, he resolves to not only do his job well, but to take his work to a new level:

> I'm ready for a whole new approach. I'm planning to clean Miles Hall so well, they won't want to make it dirty—or else they'll be answering to me! ❞

Rev. Martin Luther King, Jr. said something similar:

> *If a man is called to be a street sweeper, he should sweep streets even as Michelangelo painted, or Beethoven composed music, or Shakespeare wrote poetry. He should sweep streets so well that all the hosts of heaven and earth will pause to say, here lived a great street sweeper who did his job well.*[24]

There is joy in doing one's job well; there is joy in living an honest, sincere

---

24 There are several versions of this quotation. This one was accessed on July 9, 2017 @ www.quotationspage.com/quote/31363.html One of the earliest versions can be found at www.old.seattletimes.com/special/mlk/king/words/blueprint.html

life. Those who cut corners, by cheating at school or at work, find that life is a constant effort to find "the easy way out"—an effort that can become tiring. But those who put in the work, and do the best job they can, come to realize that this commandment is given so that they may enjoy their lives, whatever work they may be doing.

Becoming the Buddha

Once you get beyond the more obvious aspects of this commandment, you might be surprised to discover the subtler ways that stealing shows up in your life. It may come as a realization, an awakening, or even a sudden shock. In this section and in the sections that follow, you will read about several "awakenings" and "realizations." Perhaps they will prompt awakenings in you.

In the following journal entry, for example, a student realizes that he has spent the last thirteen years "robbing" his father:

> 66 My parents divorced when I was six. Throughout that time, I huddled up and hid myself from the rest of the family. I was so scared of everything, having my family ripped away from me. I felt as though my family had been stolen from me.
>
> But what I haven't realized until now is that I have also been stealing from my family—especially my father. I have been depriving him of my love. I show him little or no emotion. In fact, my father has not seen me smile in thirteen years, and it's because of the day I watched my mom drive down the driveway and out of my life.
>
> My dad stayed behind to raise me, but I was not a son to him. I have stolen that from him. It sounds a little far-fetched, but I never gave him a chance. And the saddest part is, he has given me every opportunity to succeed in this world and has supported me unconditionally ever since I was born.
>
> Scripture says, "Anyone who has been a thief, let him steal no longer" (Ephesians 4:28). It's time for me to stop stealing. It's time to let my father in. 99

Another student talks about her growing self-awareness, especially in an area which she describes as "one-upping":

> 66 Often, when hearing others talk about their successes and new possessions, it's hard not to try to "one-up" them, steal the conversation, and tell them about my successes and my new possessions. This week I worked on listening to people, letting them have a full opportunity to talk about what is making them happy—without adding my two cents, and without stealing their happiness from them.

She speaks about self-awareness as the key to her spiritual practice:

> What I've gotten out of each of these commandments is the ability to be aware

of myself. Being aware of how I'm communicating is such a key part of the Ten Commandments. Stealing energy or stomping on someone else's joy can happen without people even noticing. That's why awareness is so important.

She then gives an example of how she practiced awareness in the light of this commandment:

Recently I was in a conversation with a friend who was working through a lot of insecurities. My other friends get frustrated with her because they say she is always talking about herself, and whatever you say, she will "one-up" you. In the conversation she was talking about the new college she is attending and how glad she was to be able to transfer from here. Her words made it sound like those of us who did not transfer were just missing out on all the great fun she was having. I was aware that my ego was feeling put down as she went on "one-upping" me and my college.

Because of this commandment, however, I decided not to steal her joy. Instead, I decided to be supportive of her and tell her how great that decision must be for her, and how happy I am for her. I was sincere, and it felt so good. It came to me that she was not trying to attack me or put me down. Rather, she was just searching for acceptance. I treated her the way I would want to be treated if I were expressing excitement.

As she continues her journal entry, she admits that she was not immune to the desire to steal her friend's joy. But her determination to keep this commandment gave her the strength to resist:

I was amazed that I was able to rise above my urge to steal her energy and bring her down to my level. Instead, by keeping this commandment, I was able to support her by honestly feeling her joy. After that conversation, I was so glad that I did not let my ego control me or create a barrier between us. It has taken me many years to get to this point, and I plan to use this practice in all of my other relationships. 🙻

As already mentioned, we begin this commandment by asking students to raise their hands if they have ever stolen anything. Almost everyone raises a hand. After that, we brainstorm the various ways people steal from one another, and make a list on the whiteboard. In his journal entry, a student writes about why he didn't raise his hand, and what happened when we did the brainstorming exercise:

66 Growing up in a Hispanic household, the most degrading and disrespectful thing is to steal. So, when we were asked to raise our hand if we had ever stolen anything, I kept my hand down. But afterwards, when we had jotted a trillion things on the whiteboard about various ways we could steal, two words stood out to me. I mean they really stood out to me, as though they were in 72-point font. These words were "CONVERSATION" and "OPPORTUNITY."

191

> I just kept looking at those two words and thinking of situations where I had stolen the conversation by not giving the other person an opportunity to speak. I am the type of person who thinks he knows what is best for everyone, so I tend to cut people off during conversations. This happens a lot when I have something important to say and want to say it before I forget it. I know this isn't right. I should be listening to what other people have to say rather than thinking about what I want to say. I do not listen to understand. I listen to respond. I have to stop stealing the conversation. 🙶

Another student, noticing the same tendency to "steal the conversation," writes about how she used this new awareness in conversations with her family and with a close friend:

> 🙶 I had an opportunity to catch up with a lot of people on the phone today. First, I called my mom to ask about a recipe and to find out how her day was going. Then I called my dad to ask him to help me with travel plans. After that I called my sister and we talked about the plans we are making to celebrate mom and dad's anniversary. Everything was going great and I was practicing my new skill of "not stealing the pauses." The scripture, "Let every person be swift to hear, and slow to speak" (James 1:19) was in my mind.
>
> Then I called my best friend, Julie. Julie and I have been great friends ever since she moved from Canada to Ohio and started going to the middle school I was attending. All through high school we were very close, and we've remained close ever since, even though we are attending different colleges.
>
> It had been a long time since we last spoke, so we had a lot of catching up to do. At one point, I found myself rambling on and on about something I was so excited about. While I am sure that she wanted to hear about it as much as I wanted to hear about how she was doing, I suddenly became aware that I had been stealing the "microphone" and not giving her a chance to speak. Honestly, I hadn't even thought about it. I was being quick to speak and slow to listen!
>
> I realized that I needed to not let my excitement about all the things I had to tell her take the spotlight, because I really was very excited to hear how she was doing as well. So I finished my thought and followed it right up with a question for her. I learned a lot about what she has been up to. In the past, we have been so excited that we have run over each other, and that has been OK. But taking time to listen and give her my full attention was so much better. I feel like today I became not just a better listener, but, more importantly, a better friend. 🙶

These journal entries are peppered with statements like, "I realized,""It dawned on me," and "I suddenly became aware." It's a good reminder that in keeping these commandments you may experience real, "Buddha-like" moments—sudden flashes of self-awareness. The more "Buddha-like" moments you experience, the more you are *becoming the Buddha.*

Stealing from oneself

As you become aware of the many ways you can steal from others, you may also realize that you might be stealing from yourself. In the following journal entry, a student focuses on how she tends to rob herself of a good education:

> 66 Most parents tell their children that stealing from others is wrong. But what about stealing from one's self? I have heard people say that they wish they had done more when they were younger, and that they had robbed themselves of certain experiences, but I wasn't sure how this applied to me—until yesterday, when I caught myself in the act.
>
> Here's what happened: I was doing my homework for Education class, which consisted in a lot of reading. I was thinking that maybe I would just skim the chapter to get the main points, since there wasn't going to be a test. This was when I caught myself red-handed. There is a reason why I am in college. I am attending college and taking classes because I want to be a teacher. I want to work with kids and do a great job. But first I need to learn. I chose all of my classes for a reason, and I chose the degree I want to pursue. But if I don't study, I am stealing from myself the very education I seek.
>
> So I decided to read more thoroughly, and I am very glad I did. Once I got into the reading, it was very interesting. It was all about the topic of teaching children to read—one of the most important things I will be doing. If I hadn't decided to do this reading, I would have been robbing not only myself, but also the children that I someday hope to teach. 99

Writing in a similar vein, another student describes her tendency to sleep in and skip class. She begins by describing the battle to get up for an early morning class:

> 66 As my alarm cut into the pleasant waves of sleep, my first awareness was an overpowering feeling of resistance. When I finally struggled up into some semblance of consciousness, getting out of bed seemed even less appealing than usual.
>
> "I went to bed late last night," I told myself. "I'm ahead of what we are doing in class, and lectures aren't even required. I really need the sleep. Skipping this one class won't be a big deal."
>
> Already I was drifting backwards. The agony of awakening was swiftly being replaced with the warm blankness of much-needed sleep. My thoughts grew indistinct ....

Suddenly, she remembers the commandment for the week:

> "You shall not steal." All of a sudden, I remembered that we had talked about stealing from tuition-paying parents. "But I am paying most of my tuition," I told myself. "My parents wouldn't care. They hate getting up early too. This won't affect my grade, so it doesn't matter."

193

The commandment, however, would not leave her alone. She could not get back to sleep:

> It was no use. I dragged myself out of bed and set a world record for shower speed. I made it to chemistry and dropped into my seat, wondering why I had chosen to wake up. "I could be asleep right now," I told myself.

But, to her surprise, keeping the commandment paid off:

> It was the best chemistry class all year. It was fascinating. I usually like chemistry, but this class was amazing. I even forgot to be tired. If not for the commandment, I would have missed it. I would have stolen from myself a great learning experience. This has been a real "awakening"—in more ways than one. 99

Acknowledging the Source

As you explore the deeper levels of this commandment, you may discover that "taking what is not your own" has broader and profounder implications. For example, you may begin to realize that taking too much pride in your abilities is a form of spiritual theft. One student puts it like this in her journal:

> 66 I have always believed that nothing can be done without my effort, and therefore, I usually don't give credit to God for what I have achieved. Moreover, when my friends credited God for their accomplishments, I derided them in my thoughts. I thought, "They are too weak because they need to rely on God."
>
> A few days ago, one of the dorm girls asked me if I could help her with her math homework. At first, I was glad that she was comfortable enough with me to ask for help. But as I was helping her, I began to get frustrated. She couldn't understand the basic concept of math, even though I explained it to her repeatedly. Since math comes to me naturally, I couldn't understand why she struggled with a simple math concept. I was thinking, "Wow, she is so dumb!"

Suddenly, she has an important realization:

> As soon as this degrading thought came into my mind, Jesus' words came back to me: "Without me you can do nothing" (John 15:5). I realized that I was committing the crime of spiritual theft. I understood that although I may be better at something than others, this is a gift from God. Claiming it as my own is theft, and using it to condemn others is a crime. 99

Do you see what she means? Do you see the link between excessive pride and spiritual theft? Perhaps another illustration will help. This one comes from a sophomore who is shocked when she realizes how she has been breaking this commandment:

66 This past Tuesday night, I was putting off doing my homework and was sitting in the dining room while my mom was proofreading my sister's history essay on the desktop computer. I enjoy proofreading essays and learning about history, so I started reading it with my mom and giving her some comments to write down. When I came across an unclear sentence, I thought, "Man, she can't write. If I had written this, I would have done much better."

Suddenly, she notices that her attitude of superiority is a form of spiritual theft. As she continues her journal entry, she writes:

The thought that I was better than my sister immediately brought to mind our class discussion on healthy pride and genuine humility. We spoke about the problems that can arise when we think "I know better than others." In the light of that discussion, I suddenly saw what I had been doing to my sister. I was surprised and appalled that the thought of my superiority over my sister even came into my head. I don't know if it had appeared before in similar circumstances, and I hadn't noticed it, or whether this was the first time it had ever appeared, but it was a shock. My sister is actually an excellent writer. I was nit-picking to show how smart I am. Not only was I discrediting her, and her ability to write, but I was taking credit for a gift that the Lord has generously given me. I had forgotten that "I do nothing at all" (Bhagavad Gita 5:8). 99

"Acknowledging the source" can be confusing, especially if you believe (as it appears) that YOU are the source. In other words, you might find yourself asking, "Why should I be giving God credit when it feels like me?" Or, "How am I supposed to know if God is doing it through me, or if I am doing it myself?" In the following journal excerpt, a student describes the process he went through to answer these questions for himself:

66 I consider myself an obsessive-creative type. When I get in the creative zone, it feels like the story is spilling straight from my heart through my fingers and onto the page. Hours will pass by like seconds, and I'll forget to eat. When I've learned a piano piece to the point where I can just feel it without thinking about it, I lose myself in emotion. Just typing this out right now, I've noticed something about the language I've used. I *lose* my *self*. It's as if I'm channeling or tapping into something deeper or higher than myself. And *wow*! Does it make me feel alive! I feel high—not the destructive high of cocaine, but a spiritual high of connecting with something larger than myself.

I once emailed a famous author asking for career guidance, and he gave me advice which, at the time, was disappointing. He said, "Ignore money and success, and realize that your work is not your own but a manifestation of something deeper and bigger." When I reflect on his advice today, especially in the light of this commandment, I understand that I'm just a channel for some bigger force. My aim, then, is to hone my skills so that I can be the clearest channel possible.

In the end, though, my creative accomplishments are not my own any more than the life force which propels my limbs is my own. And then, if I've produced anything of value, the glory belongs to someone, or something greater than myself. Maybe I should just say, "The glory goes to God." 🙶

Accepting praise

Here comes the next question: if all the credit goes to God, how do you accept praise? Shouldn't people just be praising God rather than complimenting you? It's another good question. A student who had a part-time job teaching Hip-Hop to elementary school students describes how awkward he felt when some of his students praised him:

🙶 I've been teaching Hip-Hop dance to sixth and seventh graders at a nearby elementary school. It's not easy teaching a whole gym of raucous kids who all want to do different things. Well, on Thursday morning I had just finished teaching my first class which started at 8:30 AM. After the session, a group of girls from the class all came up to me, thanked me, and let me know how much they appreciated my taking time off from college studies to teach them. They also said that I was a very good dancer.

I've always been bad at taking compliments. I always find a way to dispute what people are trying to tell me, and I never accept that they might be telling me the truth. I realize that putting myself down is a bad habit, and that habits are hard to break. But after thinking about this incident I've come to a realization: I am bad at accepting compliments because I forget that the talents I have come from God. If I were more aware of that, and really believed it, taking compliments would be much easier. I would not think it's about me. I would think, "They are appreciating a talent that God has given me."

As he concludes his journal entry, he describes a new attitude that he will adopt toward his dancing:

It's funny how happy I've been to use all the gifts God has given me, but not as quick to give him thanks for those gifts. Now that I'm more aware that my dancing ability is a gift from God, I will work even harder at improving myself. It will be a way of saying, "Thank you, God, for giving me this gift." And when people tell me I'm a good dancer, I will simply say, "Thank you," and remember that "In Him we live and move and have our being." (Acts 17:28) 🙶

In the *Rise Above It* class you will have plenty of opportunities to practice the gracious art of saying, "Thanks." This may become important to you when you receive awards and honors, or are otherwise recognized for your achievements. In the following journal entry, a gifted student athlete explains what it was like to win an athletic award, and how she handled the compliments that followed:

🙶 I recently won "Athlete of the Year." I kept thinking, "How can this be? I'm only a sophomore. Why would they pick me over all those juniors and

196

seniors?" These were the thoughts that streamed through my mind that day, as I was surrounded by family, friends, coaches, and teammates.

As it began to sink in that they really did pick me, I kept thinking about all I had achieved during the past year in three sports, and how hard I had worked. I thought it was all about me and my wondrous talent. The more I thought this way, the more full of myself I became. As people kept congratulating me, my pride kept rising. It was all about myself.

In *Rise Above It* class we've been learning that we have no power from ourselves, even if it doesn't look that way. In other words, I cannot achieve anything without God. So I need to become a credit-giver, even though (up until now) I have always been a credit-taker. On that day, I was acting as if all the talent I had was from my own doing, and that all the good fortune I had was from within myself. But after studying the deeper meaning of this commandment, I now realize that although my name is on the stat sheets, God has given me everything—including the ability to play sports.

In the Bhagavad Gita it says, "I am always the instrument." I like that statement. It brings up numerous thoughts and revelations for me. It helps me realize that I just might be God's instrument, whether on or off the playing field. The next time people say, "Good game!" I'll just smile and say, "Thanks!" But that thanks will also be a thanks to God. 99

197

On another occasion, several students from the *Rise Above It* class were on a ski trip together. They were joking about our discussion of how important it is to be a credit-giver (offer compliments sincerely) and to be a gracious credit-taker (receive compliments graciously). One of the young men on the ski trip describes what happened:

66 This was a good weekend to practice this commandment, especially since several other members of the class were on the college ski trip. Whenever we complimented each other on a good turn or a nice jump, we would smile, say "Thanks," and point upwards. We had a good laugh about that. Even though we were joking, it still served as a reminder that we owe everything to God. 99

It wasn't me

As we close this chapter, we invite you to read a particularly moving journal entry from a young woman who describes herself as a person who "grew up in a religious family, and always attended church." She was quite familiar with the teaching that we should always praise God, because without him we can do nothing. She was taught, from a young age, that "it is good to be humble." And she knew, intellectually, that taking credit for the good things she did was "stealing" God's credit.

Nevertheless, there were times when she *wanted* to take credit for things, and sometimes she felt like she *should* be getting the credit she deserved. One day, however, she had an experience that helped her understand the deeper significance of this commandment. Her story begins with a friend who asked her if she was free to talk. In her journal, she says, "I knew something was up, so I invited him to come to my dorm room." She continues:

> 66 When he got there, I could sense that he felt afraid. He shut the door and told me, "You can't freak out." I was calm and tried to reassure him. It took him a few tries, but eventually he pulled up his shirt sleeve and showed me several razor cuts on his arm. "I did this," he said.
>
> I was by his side in a second and suddenly something felt right. Somehow, this was the right place for him to be, and somehow, I found the right things to say. Or did I? No, it wasn't me.

She titled this journal entry, "It Wasn't Me." What she meant was that God had somehow used her as an instrument of his love, and whatever words came out felt like they were the right words. Nevertheless, a few months later, things got worse. There was more cutting; more desperation:

> It got to the point where I knew that it was time to tell someone. I remember feeling that he might see this as betraying him. He had told me that I was the only friend he felt comfortable talking to about it. That made it harder. But I knew that in the bigger picture, the right thing to do was to tell someone, even to get help from a qualified professional, even though in the smaller picture it might look like betrayal.

She spoke to the Dean of Students who took note of the problem and gave her some pointers. The dean told her to say things like, "You are too important," and "You are worth more than this." After the meeting with the dean, she sent her troubled friend a text message saying, "Can you hang out? Can we talk?" He agreed.

> I was shaking the whole time I waited for him to show up. I was so scared and nervous. He had walked away from and hated other people for trying to do interventions. He had heard it all; he perceived his friends as being attacking and confrontational. They said things like, "You are making everyone so worried." "How can you do this to your mom?" "This is so stressful to your friends."
>
> So when I said, "We need to have a conversation. We need to talk," he said, "Oh, no. Are you serious? You too?"
>
> I said, "It's fine."
>
> He sat down. He agreed to talk. I don't know what happened next. I don't even remember exactly what was said. I do remember using the pointer from the dean, telling him, "You are important. You are worth more than this." I also remember asking him to talk to his mom and to get help. But everything

else came from a Source beyond myself. As the words came out of my heart and mouth, he listened, and in the end, he agreed that it was time to get help. It was a miracle, and, I swear, none of it was from me.

In reflecting on this experience, she describes what it was like to be an instrument of the Lord's love and wisdom, and how it compares to taking credit for the good that she is able to do:

In that moment I could see and feel what it means to be "an instrument for the Lord." I've learned that, yes, sometimes it feels nice to attribute good things to myself. But this is not real happiness. That experience was one of the scariest times of my life, but it was also the most humbling. I <u>know</u>, with all of my being, that the things that helped my friend were not from me. I'd had the privilege of letting God work through me.

I discovered that there is a happiness available to me that I can't quite imagine in my day-to-day life. Even a glimpse of it is amazing. Who knew that "it wasn't me" could be so inspiring? 🙶🙶

Four years later, while preparing this book, we called this student to get more details, and to find out how her friend did. "Did he get help?" we asked. "Yes," she said, "and he is much happier now." She then shared the rest of the story:

🙶🙶 A few weeks after that meeting with him, I was in an Abnormal Psychology class. The subject for that week was "Mental Health Disorders," and the topic for that day was "Suicide." I was almost crying. At the end of class I tried to get out as quickly as possible because I was so emotional. He had been sitting next to me in class and I knew it must have been hard for him too. As I headed out the door and into the hallway, I felt a tap on my shoulder. It was him. He said, "Thank you for giving me back my life."

I sort of smiled and nodded. Then we walked off in separate ways to our next classes. It felt good to know that I had saved someone's life. But it felt even better to know it wasn't me. 🙶🙶

The mark to aim at

You shall not steal: be a credit-giver

The literal level of this commandment is straightforward: Do not steal. Do not take what is not your own. Do not take things that belong to others, whether objects, or ideas, or anything else. This includes not cheating in school (taking grades you don't deserve) or at work (taking payment for a shoddy job, spending time texting rather than working, putting extra time on your time-sheet, etc.). On a deeper level, this commandment invites you to practice humility, acknowledging that every ability you have comes from a higher source. So your aim for this week is to *be a credit-giver—not a credit-taker.* Give credit to God for the loving emotions you feel, the noble thoughts you think, and the useful deeds you do. If the idea of God is uncomfortable for you, just remind yourself that there is a power in the universe, as pervasive as the heat and light of the sun, filling you and everyone with the warmth of *love*, the light of *wisdom*, and the *power* to serve—as much as you are willing to receive. Give credit where credit is due. In your journal, record your experience of practicing this commandment.

Suggestions for further reflection and practice

You shall not steal.

The following exercises contain additional information about this commandment. Read through all of them, and then focus on one or two that spark your interest.

1 Journal reflection: a time when I stole something

Describe a time when you stole something. What were your thoughts and feelings before, during and after the incident? What did you learn? How do you feel about that incident today? How does your current level of awareness regarding stealing compare with your level of awareness when you stole that thing?

2 Journal reflection: stealing on campus

Notice the various ways you're tempted to steal during the week. This could involve borrowing a video or a book without returning it, sneaking a free meal at the dining hall, using shampoo that was mistakenly left in the shower stall, doing a half-hearted job at work, or cheating on a test or written assignment (stealing a grade that does not belong to you). Expand this list to discover other ways that you are tempted to steal. You might even catch yourself red-handed—with your hand in the cookie jar (or in your roommate's refrigerator)!

3 Activity: identify the inner "know-it-all"

"Taking what is not our own" has a long history. It goes all the way back to the biblical story about the Garden of Eden. According to the story, Adam and Eve took what was not their own—the forbidden fruit. God had told Adam and Eve not to eat from the tree of the knowledge of good and evil; but the serpent had a different suggestion. He said, "In the day that you eat of it, your eyes will be opened, and you will be like God, *knowing* good and evil" (Genesis 3:5; emphasis added). This is a divine warning, cautioning us to avoid being a "know-it-all." Whenever we fail to heed the warning, contempt arises, along with arrogance and disrespect for others. We believe that we are always right ("knowing good and evil") and we may have a hard time admitting that we could be wrong. As one student put it: "When I admit that I'm wrong, it's a slap in the face to the false god of needing to be right." This week, be aware of the "inner know-it-all" (a.k.a. "the false god of needing to be right"). Before offering your opinion in any setting, add phrases like, "I might be wrong about this," or, "This is just the way I see it," or, "I still have a long way to go before I fully understand this," etc. The abbreviation IMHO (in my humble opinion) might be especially useful!

4 Activity: "That's interesting. Tell me more."

Give the gift of total attention. This is especially powerful in a classroom setting where the best discussions can take place when you're deeply listening to others around you. This means rising above the temptation to rehearse what you want to say, or text a friend, or surf the web while pretending to be paying attention. Giving the gift of full attention can also go a long way toward improving friendships and making new ones. Practice listening deeply and without interrupting. Leave a pause of a few seconds after people finish speaking so that you can allow what they've said to sink in. Rather than responding immediately with your own views, or "one-upping" them, you can say, "That's interesting, tell me more." Don't steal the conversation.

5 Activity: give credit to others

At the deeper levels of this commandment, stealing is *to take credit for things that do not belong to you*. Plagiarism is good example. When you plagiarize, copy someone's homework, glance at someone else's work during a test, or buy a pre-written essay online, you are taking the credit that belongs to someone else. Instead of being a credit-taker, be a credit-giver. Look for things that you honestly admire in others. When you notice people doing kind, gracious, and charitable deeds, praise them for what they've done. Appreciate what other students achieve, whether it be in campus leadership, community service, academics, art, athletics, or anything else. Give credit where credit is due.

6 Activity: develop self-awareness

The Buddha taught that the key to inner peace is to practice self-awareness, especially an awareness of how thoughts and feelings arise and perish—how they come and go, how they arrive and depart. In the context of this commandment, notice those moments when a desire to take credit for what you do or think arises within you, and you forget to give credit to God or a higher source. This kind of self-awareness will help you avoid "stealing from God." It will help you avoid attributing goodness or wisdom to yourself. While it is fine to enjoy and even revel in your accomplishments, watch out for things like excessive pride, arrogance, and superiority. Be aware of these things as they arise within you, and let them depart without getting attached to them.

7 **Activity:** acknowledge the Source

When we believe the illusion that goodness is from ourselves, and not from God or a Higher Power, it's like believing that the electric outlet in the dorm room is the source of electricity. We tend to forget that electricity is generated in a power plant. Jesus was saying something similar when he told his disciples, "The words I speak are not my own, but my Father who lives in me does his work through me" (John 14:10). In this activity, you have a chance to acknowledge the source of all the noble thoughts that arise in you, all the loving feelings that flow in to you, and all the honorable things that you say and do. If someone compliments you, say a simple "Thank you" while inwardly acknowledging the Source. Depending on your religious tradition or affiliation (or even if you don't have one), you can develop a habit of saying to yourself, "Praise the Lord," "Allah Akbar (God is Great)," "Thank you, Jesus," "Hare Krishna," or simply, "It wasn't me." This is the essence of humility.

"My aim this week was to (1) not be lazy and (2) exercise every day. Trying to "hit the mark" really made me notice some of the lies I tell myself."

Rise above lying ~ tell the truth.

You shall not bear false witness against your neighbor.

Exodus 20:16

The case of Steve Titus

On October 12, 1980, a 17-year-old girl was hitchhiking on Pacific Highway South, near Seattle, Washington. Around 6:45 PM she was picked up, taken to a secluded location, and raped. According to the police report, the rapist was a bearded white male, 25-30 years old, with shoulder-length brown hair, driving a blue car. After the rapist abandoned her, she found her way to a nearby home where she called the police to report the assault.

The Seattle police began a hunt for the rapist.

Six hours later, at 1:20 AM, the police spotted a blue car parked outside the Raintree Restaurant and Lounge on Pacific Highway South. They waited to see who would come out of the restaurant and get into the car. Eventually, a bearded white male and a young woman left the restaurant, got into the blue car, and headed in a southbound direction.

After allowing the couple to drive a short distance, the two police officers turned on their flashing lights and made them pull over to the side of the road. The police officers searched the car, questioned the couple, and took individual photographs of the man and the woman—front and profile "mug shots."

That night a team of detectives assembled a photographic "line-up" of six bearded men, including the mug shots of the man in the blue car. The next day they showed the six photographs to the victim and asked her to point to the picture of the man who looked like the man who raped her.

"That one's the closest," she said.

She had pointed to the same person the police officers had stopped the night before—the man in the blue car. At the time, the man was 31 years old and employed as the district manager for a seafood corporation. He had worked there for five years and had 100 employees under his supervision. On the night that he was pulled over, questioned, and photographed by the police, he and his fiancé were heading home after an evening date. They were planning a June wedding.

Five months later, in a Seattle courtroom, the prosecutor called the rape victim to the stand, and once again showed her the line-up of mug shots.

"Do you recognize these pictures?" the prosecutor asked.
"Yes," she said.
"And do you recognize the person who raped you on October 12?"
"Yes," she replied.

The prosecutor then asked her if the person who raped her was in the courtroom.

"Yes," she said, and she pointed at Steve Titus.

The prosecutor then asked her to walk toward the man she believed had raped her, and get as close to him as she was on the night she was raped. The defense protested, but their objection was overruled. The victim started walking in the direction of Steve Titus, who was sitting at the defense table. But before she was able to get near him, she burst into tears.

The jury, after hearing the evidence produced by the prosecution, and witnessing the emotions that were generated in the courtroom, were understandably moved. Based on the evidence they had heard, the display of emotions they had witnessed, and twelve hours of deliberation, on March 4, 1981 the jury reached their verdict: Steve Titus was found guilty of first-degree rape, a crime that could send him to prison for the rest of his life.

Steve Titus could hardly believe what had just happened. He had been convicted of rape in the first degree. His parents were shocked; they screamed at the jury. Steve's fiancé sobbed uncontrollably. They all believed that Steve was innocent.

Steve vowed that he would not rest until he was cleared of the false charges and his name was vindicated. As an initial step, he contacted Paul Henderson, a reporter for the *Seattle Times,* and asked for his help. Henderson, who was moved by Steve's sincerity, began an intensive investigation that quickly led to the capture and confession of the actual rapist—a man who was implicated in the rape of over 50 other women in the Seattle area.

The evidence proved conclusively that Steve Titus was an innocent man. On June 8, 1981, just four months after he had been falsely accused, the case against Steve Titus was overturned. Steve was set free, and Paul Henderson won the Pulitzer Prize for Investigative Reporting.

It would be a good story if it ended there. But it doesn't.

Tormented by the thought that he had been falsely accused, and obsessed with the desire to have this wrong righted, Steve Titus launched a lawsuit against the police, the legal system, and everyone else who he believed had caused him so much pain and suffering. He spent every waking moment thinking about his vindication, mulling over the evidence, and figuring out what he would say when he had his "day in court." In the process he lost his job (because he could no longer focus on his work), and his fiancé (because she could no longer endure his incessant complaining).

From that point on, Steve Titus devoted his entire life to righting the wrong that had been done to him. Working with his lawyer, Paul Hansen, they put together a 20-million-dollar lawsuit against the Port of Seattle. When asked what it was like to work with Steve on the case, Hansen said:

> *Time, it is clear, does not heal all wounds, at least not Steve Titus's. He spends every waking moment and every sleeping moment consumed by this case. It rips him apart, still, that nobody apologized to him. ... They ruined his life, and they won't even say, "I'm sorry."*

Hansen was then asked, "Will he ever be able to put it all behind him?" Hansen replied:

> *That's the question the rest of us are asking. We watch this man's ceaseless struggle and we ask, "Why can't he get on with his life?"*[1]

Steve Titus believed that those who had given false witness at his trial had shattered his life into a million tiny pieces that could never be put back together again. Those who knew him well during that time said that he wasn't able to sleep or eat. To all outward appearance his life was in ruins. Perhaps, when he had his day in court and was fully vindicated, it would all be different.

The court date was set for February 19, 1985. All in all, Titus and his attorney would be presenting the results of nearly four years of gathering evidence and preparing their case for trial. Steve Titus would finally be able to turn the tables: he would accuse those who had falsely accused him. But, for Steve Titus, that day never came. On February 8, 1985, just eleven days before his "day in court," Steve Titus died of a stress-related heart attack. He was 35 years old.

As we will see in this chapter, false witnesses are of two kinds. In the case of Steve Titus, *external* false witnesses (the victim's testimony, the police report, etc.) may have led the court to a false conviction; but *internal* false witnesses (the belief that his entire life had been ruined by this event) may have led Steve Titus to his death.

---

1   Elizabeth Loftus, *Witness for the Defense: The Accused, the Eyewitness, and the Expert Who Puts Memory on Trial* (New York: St. Martin's Press, 1991), 58. See also the TED talk by Elizabeth Loftus, "How reliable is your memory?" Accessed on October 22, 2017 @ www. youtube.com/watch?v=PB2Oegl6wvI&t=223s

The commandments in world scriptures

Judaism

In the literal sense, the commandment "You shall not bear false witness against your neighbor" refers to saying things that are untrue about someone in a legal setting. In the Hebrew scriptures the punishment for making a false accusation can be severe: "If the witness proves to be a liar, giving false testimony, he must be punished in the same way the other person would have been punished" (Deuteronomy 19:18-19). In other words, if the false witness had falsely accused someone of murder, and the accused person was found innocent, the false witness would suffer the death penalty: "Show no pity: life for life, eye for eye, tooth for tooth, hand for hand, foot for foot" (Deuteronomy 19:21).

The Hebrew scriptures, however, are not merely about legal matters. Reading a little deeper, it becomes clear that false witnesses can refer to "inner accusers," the lies that arise in our minds, the messages of discouragement that, if believed, lead to feelings of worthlessness, hopelessness, and despair. In the *Book of Psalms*, David experiences a moment of helplessness: "Lord how they have increased who trouble me! Many are those who rise up against me. Many are they who say, 'There is no help for him in God'" (Psalm 3:1-2).

David, however, refuses to succumb to those who bear false witness against him. Whether the false witnesses are external (people who accuse him) or internal (false messages that enter his mind), he rises above it. In the next verse, he writes, "But, You, O Lord, are a shield for me, my glory and the One who lifts up my head" (Psalm 3:3). Rather than believe the accusations of others, or the false messages that arise in his mind, David trusts in God: "False witnesses have risen against me, and they breathe out violence. I would have lost heart, unless I had believed that I would see the goodness of the Lord in the land of the living" (Psalm 27:12-13).

Christianity

The commandment "You shall not bear false against your neighbor" was one of Jesus' central teachings. When the rich young ruler approached Jesus, and asked what good thing he should do in order to have eternal life, Jesus took him back to the commandments: "You shall not murder," "You shall not commit adultery," "You shall not steal," "*You shall not bear false witness*," "Honor your father and mother," and, "You shall love your neighbor as yourself" (Matthew 19:18-19; emphasis added).

When the religious leaders complained that Jesus' disciples did not wash their hands before eating food, Jesus was clear that what goes into the mouth does not defile a person, but rather what comes out of the heart: "For out of the heart proceed evil thoughts, murders, adulteries, fornications, thefts, *false witness,* and blasphemies" (Matthew 15:19; emphasis added).

When Jesus speaks about what comes "out of the heart" in regard to false witness, he is speaking about a desire to judge people before knowing the whole truth about them. In a teaching that reflects the legal aspect of this commandment, he says: "Judge not, that you be not judged, for with what judgment you judge, you will be judged; and with the measure you use, it will be measured back to you" (Matthew 7:1-2).

At first glance this might seem to be an echo of the Hebrew law of retaliation regarding false witness ("an eye for an eye"). But Jesus explains it in a whole new way: "And why do you look at the speck in your brother's eye, but do not consider the plank in your own eye? Or how can you say to your brother, 'Let me remove the speck from your eye'; and look, a log is in your own eye? Hypocrite! First remove the log from your own eye, and then you will see clearly to remove the speck from your brother's eye" (Matthew 7:3-5).

209

Because you seldom see the whole picture, your judgments of others will often be slanted, partial, and incomplete. Even worse, your judgments can be biased by prejudice, partiality, or personal interest. In such cases you may inadvertently or deliberately bear false witness against your neighbor. This is why it is so important to "take the log out of your own eye." Only then will your judgments be coming from love rather than contempt, spoken from wisdom rather than ignorance, and offered in the spirit of helpfulness rather than harmfulness. This is what Jesus means when he says, "Do not judge according to the appearance, but judge with *righteous* judgment" (Matthew 7:24; emphasis added). Only then will you be bearing "true witness."

Islam

According to the *Hadith*, Muhammad said, "Do not testify until you are as certain as you are about the palm of your hand." When someone asked Muhammad, "What qualifies a person to be a witness?" Muhammad answered, "Can you see the sun?" When the person answered, "Yes," Muhammad said, "Testify like it or do not."[2] In other words, if you are to bear witness for or against anyone, you should only do so if you can see the truth as clearly as you can see the palm of your hand, or the sun in the sky. Otherwise you should not testify at all.

While the *Hadith* strongly influences Islamic thought, the *Qur'an* is the final authority in all matters. There it is written that every lie and every falsehood is designed to undermine the pure truth of Allah's teaching. The language is strong: "We hurl the Truth against falsehood, and it knocks out its brain, and behold, falsehood doth perish!" (Qur'an 21:18). Moreover, the *Qur'an* makes it clear that the origin of every lie and every falsehood is from a diabolical source. The only escape is to take refuge in Allah: "If a suggestion from Satan assail your mind, seek refuge in Allah, for he hears and knows all things." This is done by bringing Allah to remembrance: "When a thought of evil from Satan assaults them, they bring Allah to remembrance, and lo! they see aright!" (Qur'an 7:200-201).

According to the *Qur'an*, the term "Satan" (also known as *Iblīs*) refers to the leader of the "evil ones"—those who persistently conspire to drag believers into deeper and deeper falsity: "The evil ones plunge them deeper into error, and never relax their efforts" (Qur'an 7:22). At the same time, there is always hope; there is always refuge from "the evil of the slinking whisperer, who whispers evil into the hearts of mankind" (Qur'an 114:4-5). That refuge is found in Allah: "I seek refuge with Allah, the sustainer of all people, the ruler of all people, the God of all people" (Qur'an 114:1-3).

Hinduism

In Hinduism, the evils of bearing false witness are directly addressed. As it is written, "Abusing others, *speaking untruth*, detracting from the merits of all men, and talking idly shall be the four kinds of evil verbal action" (Laws of Manu 1:7). "All things are determined by speech; speech is their root, and from speech they proceed. Therefore, he who is dishonest with respect to speech is dishonest in everything" (Laws of Manu 4:256). On the other hand, truth-telling is held in the highest regard: "To tell the truth is consistent with righteousness. There is nothing higher than the truth" (Santiparva 109:4).

---

2   While not included in the *Qur'an*, the *Hadith* (reports of what Muhammad said and did) have great influence on Islamic thought. This information was accessed on July 11, 2017 @ www.al-islam.org/greater-sins-volume-2-ayatullah-sayyid-abdul-husayn-dastghaib-shirazi/nineteenth-greater-sin-false

Truth, and its role in protecting you from delusion, becomes a major theme in the *Bhagavad Gita*, a Hindu classic which is often regarded as the epitome of Hindu thought. In this work it is taught that nothing can disturb the person whose mind is established in the truth: "They are not elated by good fortune or depressed by bad. With mind established in Ultimate Truth, they are free from delusion" (Bhagavad Gita 5:20).[3]

As the *Bhagavad Gita* comes to an end, Krishna asks Arjuna, "Have you fully understood my message? Are you free from your doubts and delusions?" (Bhagavad Gita 18:72). In his response to Krishna's question, Arjuna speaks about the blessed state he now experiences—a state that is available to everyone who is no longer blinded by the delusions of the ego, but rather is ready to fight against them: "You have dispelled my doubts and delusions," says Arjuna to Krishna. "You have made me ready to fight this battle." Because he knows the truth, Arjuna is no longer susceptible to delusion: "My faith is firm now," says Arjuna, "and I will do your will." (Bhagavad Gita 18: 72-73.)

Buddhism

Ordinarily, the Buddha avoids terms like heaven and hell because his theology is grounded in the here and now. But there are times when he uses these terms in the most direct way, especially when speaking about false witness. According to the Buddha, "He who speaks what is not true goes to hell. ... He also goes to hell who having done a thing says, 'I did not do it'" (Dhammapada 22:1). People who accuse others falsely, or find fault when there is no fault, also go to a terrible place after death: "Beings who imagine faults in the faultless and perceive no wrong in what is wrong, embrace false views and go to a woeful state" (Dhammapada 22:13). [4] But those who speak the truth are regarded as a "Brahman"—a holy person, a cosmic soul: "Him I call indeed a Brahman who *utters true speech*, instructive and free from harshness, so that he offends no one" (Dhammapada 26:26; emphasis added).

In addition to the lies you tell others, the Buddha also speaks about the lies you tell yourself: "A liar lies to himself as well as to the gods. *Lying is the origin of all evils*; it leads to rebirth in the miserable planes of existence, to a breach of the pure precepts, and to the corruption of the body" (Maharatnakuta Sutra

---

3   The Sanskrit phrase that is translated "Ultimate Truth" is *brahmani-sthitah*. This passage is also translated "With mind fully situated in Ultimate Truth, poised in spiritual intelligence, devoid of delusion." See "Jnana Yoga: Knowledge of the Ultimate Truth". Accessed on October 22, 2017 @ www.dubjockey.co.uk/bag2.html

4   The Sanskrit word translated as "hell" is *Naraka*. It is also translated as "the downward course" and "the place of darkness." In some ways it is similar to Jewish, Christian and Muslim concepts of hell, except that it is not eternal. Although it is a place of suffering, it is also a place of learning. And when enough lessons have been learned, the individual returns to earth for another incarnation.

27: *Bodhisattva Surata's Discourse*; emphasis added). The *Noble Eightfold Path*, the core of Buddhism, addresses lying directly in the teaching that is referred to as "Right Speech": "Abstain from false speech; do not tell lies or deceive" (Pali Canon). False speech, according to the Buddha, is so sinister that it can lead to all other evils: "He who speaks falsely, or scoffs at the life to come, is capable of any evil" (Dhammapada 13:10).

• ● •

The commandment against false witness deals with many levels of the human mind. On a literal level you are called to be honest in all your dealings, never bearing false witness in a courtroom, never falsely accusing anyone, and never telling a lie. More deeply, every judgment you make about others, if not grounded in a clear and full understanding of another's situation, is a lie. And, on the deepest level, you lie to yourself every time you allow the "slinking whisperers" referred to in Islam, or the "false prophets" referred to in Christianity, or the "delusions of the ego" referred to in Hinduism and Buddhism, to insinuate lies about who you are, and who you may become.

In Islam, the emphasis on not being led astray by "the slinking whisperer" calls to mind the words of Jesus: "Beware of false prophets, which come to you in sheep's clothing, but inwardly they are ravening wolves" (Matthew 7:15). These "false prophets" and "ravening wolves" are not merely *people* who give false information about the scriptures and the circumstances you find yourself in; they are also the *inner accusers* and *slinking whisperers* who try to convince you that life is purposeless, that you are hopeless, and that there is no help for you in God.

The truth is just the opposite. Help is *always* available; there is *always* hope; and your life *always* has meaning and purpose. After all, you are made "in the image and likeness of God" (Judaism), "the kingdom of God is within you" (Christianity), and you are filled with "the breath of God" (Islam). As your consciousness expands, you come to realize the incorruptible *Ātman* within (Hinduism), as well as your Nobler-nature (Buddhism).

As you continue to dwell in the truth, you realize that in every situation you always have a choice. You can listen to the false witnesses who want to destroy you, or you can listen to the true witnesses—the perennial wisdom that is always available and is especially contained within the sacred scriptures of all religious traditions. To everyone who lives according to the words of these "true witnesses," the message is clear: false witnesses may attempt to enslave you with lies about yourself, about others, and about a Power greater than yourself, but *"the truth shall set you free"* (John 8:32).

The commandments in the lives of college students

You shall not bear false witness against your neighbor.

I need to practice achieving self-knowledge. I would like to not be so attached to every thought that arises.

Journal excerpt from a college senior

Lies you tell to others

When we discussed procrastination as a false god, we quoted the Buddha who said, "In giving up a lesser happiness, the wise person beholds a greater one. Therefore, let the wise person give up the lesser happiness, so that the greater happiness might be attained" (Dhammapada 21:1). In the following journal entry, a student talks about the "greater happiness" he experienced when he decided to rise above dishonesty and tell the truth:

> 66 Yesterday, in one of my classes, we had a quick multiple-choice quiz. The quizzes were graded immediately and then handed back to us, so we could go over them. When I got my quiz back, I noticed that one of my answers was wrong, but there was no "X" next to it. So instead of getting a "10" on the quiz, I should have gotten an "8."

In the context of this commandment, he believes that saying nothing about the unearned quiz grade would be dishonest:

> For a moment I thought it would be best to say nothing, since it wasn't my fault. But this commandment is about bearing true witness. So I said to myself, "I need to be honest about this." When I told my professor that I should have gotten a lower grade, she was so happy with me for being honest that she gave me credit for the question! When I think about it now, I would have been happy even if my grade had been reduced. It just feels good to be honest. It may seem like a small thing, but it gave me a great sense of relief and inner peace. Like the Buddha says, in giving up a lesser happiness, I experienced a greater one. It will be a good memory. 99

In this case, telling the truth helped a student through a morally challenging moment and brought a sense of inner peace. Sometimes, however, the stakes are a little higher than two points on a quiz grade. In the following example, a student was asked to come to the dean's office to discuss whether or not he had been drinking on campus. Writing in his journal, he talks about his experience:

> 66 When I went into the dean's office this morning, he told me that he had reason to believe that I had been drinking alcohol on campus. I suppose he was giving me a chance to confess. But I said, "No, I hadn't been drinking." He just said, "OK," and let me leave. When I left his office, I didn't feel good about what happened, especially because I had gotten away with a lie. In fact, I felt sick about it.
>
> All morning long my conscience was still nagging me, and I knew that it would continue to nag at me for a long time. I knew that it was unlikely that the dean had any evidence to prove that I was drinking, but that didn't matter. Whether he could prove it or not, I knew the truth about what I had done. And I knew that I had lied about it. So I decided to go up to his office and admit it.
>
> I knocked on his door and waited. When he said, "Come in," I entered his office and sat down. I could tell that he was glad to see me again. Without hesitating, I told him that I had lied to him in the morning. "The truth is," I said, "that I had indeed been drinking and that when I was confronted about it, I didn't know what to do, so I lied." I also said, "I realize that instead of hiding it, I should just 'be a man about it,' tell the truth, and deal with the consequences."
>
> He was very appreciative that I had voluntarily come out with the truth. He smiled and said, "I already knew that you had been drinking, but I wanted to give you a chance to admit it on your own."
>
> The punishment was not that bad. I got written up and given a warning, but that's not the part that matters. I felt good. I was happy I had gone in. I didn't know what the consequences would be, but I knew that whatever they were, I wouldn't mind dealing with them. It actually felt good to sit there in the dean's office and admit that I had screwed up, and that I was willing to make it right again. Honesty is still the best policy. 99

Writing in a similar vein, another student describes what it felt like to be honest with his parents. His journal entry is titled "Truth Therapy":

> 66 I was texting with my mom this week, and she was asking me the usual questions: "How are you?" "How is school?"—questions to which I usually reply with a simple, "Good," or "Can't complain." But realizing that this week is about honesty, I thought that I would be honest with her, even if it wasn't exactly what she wanted to hear. I told her that I've been in a rut lately, and that I'm not too happy with life. I even told her that the expectations I've placed on myself—getting all B's this term so I can be eligible for sports this

winter, and not wanting to let my parents down, or the people who gave me a second chance—are all weighing heavy on me. On top of that, I said that I'm having a serious problem with sleep. I admitted that I didn't know whether it's because of this rut that I'm in or vice versa, but it has caused me to miss too many classes.

She listened. And she was glad that I had shared all of this with her. We felt closer to each other. As we talked, I experienced a new wave of more positive thoughts coming over me. All the stress of the day seemed to melt away, and the worries that had so weighed me down seemed to disappear. I didn't know telling the truth could be so relaxing! 99

Lies you tell about others

Have you ever blamed others (falsely accused them) for your own irresponsible behavior? This form of false witness goes all the way back to the Garden of Eden when Adam blamed both God and Eve: "The woman you put here with me—she gave me some fruit from the tree, and I ate." And Eve, in turn, blamed the serpent: "The serpent deceived me, and I ate" (Genesis 3:12-13). Rather than take responsibility for what he had done, Adam placed the blame on others; similarly, Eve placed the blame on the serpent. In other words, they both placed the blame on someone or something outside of themselves.

215

In the following journal entry, a student notices her tendency to blame people and circumstances for her inability to get to class on time, rather than take responsibility:

66 I'm really good at being late for things, and I always make excuses. They aren't straight-up lies—they are just little twists on the truth. For example, just today, when I was late for my sociology class. I put the blame on the other girls in my apartment: I said, "I was waiting for my turn to use the sink." I also blamed the traffic: I said, "I got stuck behind a trash truck, and then had to go through a school zone."

Even though these things really happened, they are not THE REAL REASON why I was late. The real reason is that I just don't pay attention to the clock, I don't plan ahead, and I don't leave enough time for things. That's the real reason why I'm usually late. I have to start being more accountable for my actions, and I have to stop making up lies to defend my irresponsibility. 99

Perhaps you, too, tend to falsely accuse others, holding them responsible for your own irresponsible *behaviors*. It's very common, especially when others seem to be interfering with your schedule or interrupting your plans. It's even worse, however, when these interferences and interruptions open the way for negative *thoughts* and *feelings* about others. In the following journal entry, a student identifies as "false witnesses" the condemning thoughts and feelings that flow into his mind:

66 I work in the College Gardens. On workdays, I normally go to breakfast at 7:30 AM (right when the cafeteria opens). This usually gives me enough time to eat and then make it to work on time. On Monday, when I showed up at 7:30 AM, the gate wasn't opened yet. I decided that they were just running a little late and would open it soon. A few more minutes went by and I started thinking, "Maybe they are down a person, and they are struggling to get everything set up." Then people around me started complaining and saying things like, "We pay for this food," and "It's unprofessional for them to be opening the gate this late."

These comments must have had a negative effect on me, because I found myself thinking things like, "These workers are incredibly rude," "They are just taking their sweet time in there." "They don't care about any of us," and "They are so lazy." The condemning thoughts kept coming: "They have no regard for people like me who have so little time to eat and then get to work." The madder I got, the more the accusing thoughts flowed in.

Finally, at 7:50 AM—twenty minutes late—they opened the gate. By now I was really mad. I couldn't believe how rude they were being. And to make matters worse, when we walked in we could see that there was no hot food. We were all furious. I didn't even look at the workers when I passed them, just to show them how angry I was. I wolfed down some cold cereal and raced off to work.

216

Later that day, I came back for lunch and was talking to Debbie, one of the managers. She was very apologetic and told me that the night before, a pipe had burst, making it impossible for them to cook or wash dishes. On top of that, they had been scrambling around since early in the morning trying to get the kitchen mopped up and set up for service. When I heard that, I realized how foolish I had been. I felt like such an idiot for getting so worked up over not getting a hot breakfast and for assuming the worst of the workers. This was a clear-cut case of bearing false witness against my neighbor. I was thinking, falsely, that they were lazy. In truth, they were probably more stressed out than I was. 99

The human mind, like nature, abhors a vacuum. In the absence of truth, it fabricates stories and makes assumptions to fill the void. For the most part, these assumptions are false, or at best, only partially true. In the following journal entry, a student examines her tendency to make assumptions about people, judging them before knowing them:

66 Last night I was out with some of my friends at a restaurant. In walks this guy that I like and am planning to get to know better. But he wasn't alone. He walked in with this girl who used to have blonde hair, but has now dyed it red. She was wearing provocative clothing. The thought immediately popped into my head, "She's skanky." From there, all sorts of random thoughts raced through my mind about her slutty personality and her sleazy lifestyle. The funny thing is, I don't even know her name!

Recognizing that she was "bearing false witness" against this young woman, she decided to do something about it:

> I immediately recognized that the false god of jealousy was driving all of this, but just naming it was not enough. I also had to see that I was making all sorts of excuses for why I had a right to be jealous and negative. I know that I will probably see both of them around campus, and when I do, I will introduce myself to her and get to know her, so that I don't have to go around with a negative—and probably false—image of her in my head. 🙶🙶

Although you may intuitively understand that false witness is a violation of ethical law, you may find that the testimony of other students will help you see the subtler ways that this commandment might apply to your life. In the following journal entry, a female athlete has a sudden realization as she listens to another student talk about how he applied this commandment to his own life:

> 🙶🙶 I was sitting in my *Rise Above It* class listening to all the stories about how people had tried to keep this commandment during the week. To be honest, I didn't see how this commandment applied to me. I try to live my life as honestly as I can; I don't lie to other people; and I try my hardest not to lie to myself by making up rationalizations to justify my behavior.
>
> But when I heard the story my classmate shared, I immediately knew the way in which I was breaking this commandment. He told the class about how during his hockey years growing up, he had a rival on another team. It was someone he hated so much, when, in fact, they had never even had a conversation with each other. Later in his career he was on the same team with this player, and they became close friends!
>
> Suddenly it all became clear to me: I understood that making a judgment about another person before I really know that person is a form of false witness.

These Buddha-like moments of spiritual awakening are most valuable—especially when followed by an application to one's own life. As this student continues her journal entry, she talks about a time when she faced a similar situation:

> I have done the same thing in my life. When I played travel volleyball, there was a certain girl that I played against all the time. She was the setter for my club's biggest rival, and the leader of her team. I hated that club with all my heart, and always looked for chances to put their players down, especially their team leader. I hated how loud she was, and I always took her cheering for her own team as being derogatory toward my team.
>
> As we grew older, we ended up coaching for rival volleyball programs, and now we both play volleyball for different colleges that also happen to be rivals. In brief, I grew up hating this girl; I have continued to hate her my whole life; and I continue to hate her now as a rival at another college.

217

> But here's the crazy part: I don't even know this girl. I have never had a single conversation with her! After hearing my classmate's story, I suddenly realized that my rival could be a great person. Sadly, I never bothered to find out, because I was too busy bearing false witness against her. 99

These students learned valuable lessons. Whether it involved condemning food service workers, or judging someone as "skanky," or hating a rival, they learned that the stories they fabricated about others—especially about people they hardly knew—opened the way for a flood of negative feelings and thoughts to flow in. They also learned that putting the best interpretation on the actions of others is not just a way of "being nice"; it's also a protection against the barrage of false witness that can arise the moment there's an opening.

Lies you tell yourself

As you go deeper into this commandment, you may discover subtler forms of false witness—especially the rationalizations and justifications you use to defend your lower nature. Here are some examples: "I've worked really hard, so I deserve to zone out playing mindless video games." "There's no use going to practice today. The coach will never put me in anyway." "Why am I trying so hard? Nobody really cares." And so it goes.

To help you address this aspect of the commandment, we will ask you to give yourself a specific aim for the week. For example, "This week I *will not* (eat sugar, skip class, text during class, sleep late, gossip, take short-cuts at work, etc.)." We will also ask you to phrase it the other way around: "This week *I will* (eat healthy, go to every class, get up early, speak positively about others, do a thorough job at work, etc.)." Once you have determined your aim, notice the stream of justifications and rationalizations that prevent you from achieving your goals. Here is an example of what previous students have said:

> 66 My aim this week was to (1) not be lazy and (2) exercise every day. Trying to "hit the mark" really made me notice some of the lies I tell myself: "I'm too tired." "It's too cold outside." "There isn't enough time." But the most subtle and persuasive lies were those that twisted the truth: False witnesses somehow know how to take something that is true, (I need to focus on school), and use it against me to justify not exercising (therefore you don't need to exercise). I have to realize that a lot of truth-twisting like this goes on in my head. 99

The aims that students choose for themselves are broad and varied. One of the most common aims is to avoid procrastination and get assignments done on time. In her journal entry, titled "Where Did the Time Go?" a sophomore writes:

> 66 I lie to myself all the time. Every day I tell myself that I will do homework, and yet every day I do everything possible to avoid doing it. One of my biggest avoidance techniques is to turn on the TV. Whenever I do this, I lie to myself

> with rationalizations and justifications like, "Watching a little TV will help me relax." And then, after I've watched for a while and another show is coming on, I say to myself, "Oh, another hour can't hurt," and "I've got plenty of time later." However, there are only so many times that I can use that excuse. Eventually, there is no more time left, and my homework is still not done.

Recognizing that she has been justifying her procrastination with lies, she gives herself a specific mark to aim at:

> I decided that my aim for this week would be a positive one. I would not give up television completely, but I would make it a reward for completing my homework.

The practice of giving oneself a specific mark to aim at—in this case watching TV as a reward for completing homework—can be very powerful. As she continues her journal entry, she reflects on how her ingrained TV habit rises up to sabotage her plan:

> Today when I got home from school, I automatically made a snack and went straight to the television. When I caught myself in this old pattern, my first reaction was to justify it: "Maybe I can study for my history exam and watch my show at the same time," I told myself. "That's better than not studying at all."

> I tried. I even muted the commercials and tried to squeeze in a few paragraphs during the commercial breaks, but it was impossible.

Remembering the mark she is aiming at, and determined to not give in to false witness, she manages to follow through on her commitment:

> So I turned off the television and focused on completing the study guide. I was really focused, and I absorbed a lot of material. Then, when I was completely finished with the study guide, and felt ready for the upcoming exam, I gave myself a nice reward: I watched one episode of my favorite series. It was a good feeling. Remembering this commandment and my commitment helped me push through. 🙶

Because your aim will be self-chosen, you will need to *compel yourself* to do what you know is best for you. While it may seem paradoxical, this kind of self-compulsion leads to the highest form of personal freedom. At first, this may be difficult. Long-term, deeply engrained habits do not disappear overnight. That's OK. We all start like that. However, as your consciousness begins to expand, and you start to notice that you have been controlled by the unconscious reactions of your lower nature, you may feel a desire to change things. In other words, you may decide that you no longer want to be ruled by merely selfish impulses, but rather by something higher. While your behavior may not change, *at least you notice* how you have been behaving, and you have a genuine desire to change.

This is a crucial step in your spiritual development.

219

Gradually, as you use higher truth to rise above the promptings of your lower nature, you begin to think and act in new ways. As you continue to do this, *thinking* in accordance with higher truth, and *acting* in accordance with higher truth, a miracle takes place: you begin to *feel* differently. Unpleasant circumstances no longer trigger ego-based reactions in the way they used to. Instead, as the deeper truths of sacred scripture become a part of your very being through habitual practice, you *enjoy* responding in loving ways. At this point, it no longer feels like self-compulsion. Rather, it feels like "second nature." As it is written in the Hebrew scriptures, "I will put my law in their minds and write it on their hearts" (Jeremiah 31:33). In Christianity, this is called being "born again."

But this takes a while. We begin, as always, by noticing the various manifestations of our lower nature. One of those manifestations is a tendency to be apathetic about life. Students who are apathetic are inclined to believe a lie that sounds something like this: "Nothing matters, so why try?" The more you tell yourself this lie, the more it becomes an excuse to do nothing except eat, sleep, and perhaps play some video games. In a journal entry titled "The Root of Apathy," a student talks about what came up for him when he wrote down a specific aim that might help him counter this lie:

> 66 I don't know how it happened—I was always a pretty religious kid—but at some point, I let myself become obsessed by the notion that life is empty and meaningless. This became a point of pride for me, and I had contempt for people who let their religious faith completely consume them. I wondered, "How could they be so stupid and naïve? How could they be so ignorant?" I was slipping into a nihilistic world view where nothing mattered. I felt proud of myself and superior to others.

> That all changed after our last class. We did this simple little exercise, where we wrote down something we wanted to accomplish (our "aim" for the week), as well as the false ideas associated with it that would prevent us from achieving our goal. Then we wrote down, beside each false idea, a "truth" that would support us in reaching our goal. Although incredibly simple, and beneath my superior position as a nihilist (or so I thought), the exercise was a real eye-opener for me.

> Here's what happened: My aim was "Be more active." To be honest, I was growing tired of the "life is meaningless" routine. So I decided that, at least for one week, I would try to actively engage with life, and even enjoy it. The other way of wording this was, "Be less apathetic." I then wrote down the false ideas that support my apathy. "Nothing has meaning," "Apathy is not addictive," and "You can always start caring tomorrow." On the other side, next to each false idea, I wrote down what I KNOW to be true—not just believe. I wrote, "EVERYTHING has meaning," "Apathy IS a vicious cycle," and "You are most effective if you START NOW."

> As simple as this exercise was, it was a wake-up call. I realized that I had,

220

indeed, been lying to myself, using the philosophy of nihilism to justify my laziness, my fear of failing, and my feelings of superiority. The false ideas infused by my "demons" had been keeping me in an apathetic stupor where I was of no use to anyone, and on a slow path to self-destruction.

As the week progressed, and as I kept my aim in mind, it came to me that I had fallen into the trap of spiritual apathy because I had falsely believed that all religious people were hypocrites living in a "fake reality." But I suddenly realized that I was the one who was ignorant. I was the one who had been living in a fake reality. I was the one who had been the hypocrite, condemning others with a broad brush, while thinking that I was superior to them. I was the one who needed to wake up and stop ignoring the parts of life that are positive. For me, God was dead because I had killed him. But the truth is that God is very much alive. 🙶🙶

Feeling stupid, worthless and inadequate (at times)

According to a study conducted by the American College Health Association, 32% of college students admit that there are times during their college experience when they feel so depressed that "it is difficult to function"[5] There are times when even the brightest, happiest students feel stupid, worthless and inadequate. It could be in a classroom situation when you are unprepared for a test; it could be at a social gathering where you find it uncomfortable to make small talk; or it could be on the athletic field where you made a mistake that hurt your team. These are all opportunities for "false witnesses" to fill you with depressing messages about your value as a human being.

Let's focus for a moment on the idea of "socializing." This can range from feeling slightly awkward at a party to being petrified if called on to speak in class. In the following journal entry, a student talks about his struggle to engage in a simple conversation:

> 🙶🙶 I have social anxiety that cripples my ability to communicate with others. Most days I would prefer to be alone and speak to no one. It is excruciatingly painful for me to talk to other people. I have all these voices ringing in my head. They tell me that I'm stupid and inadequate. They tell me that other people hate me and feel that I'm annoying them when I try to initiate a conversation. They make me afraid. They make me want to avoid people. When all I want to do is say, "Hello," they tell me not to. As a result, I'm scared to death of speaking to people.

This student talks about "voices ringing in my head." In some religious systems these "voices" are called "the enemy," "satanic influences," "evil spirits," or

221

---

5   Lindsay Goobersoly, "The Top 50 Colleges with Stressed Out Student Bodies" (May 9, 2016). Accessed on October 22, 2017 @ www.universityprimetime.com/top-50-colleges-with-the-most-stressed-out-student-bodies/

"whisperings of the devil." As he continues his journal entry, he quotes from the *Qur'an*:

> In the readings for this week, there was a powerful teaching from the Qur'an. It said, "If a suggestion from Satan assail thy mind, seek refuge with God." The passage goes on to say that when this happens, we should "bring God to remembrance, and then we will see aright" (Qur'an 7:200-201). I like that phrase—"a suggestion from Satan"—because that it is exactly how it feels when these lies are ringing in my head. Sometimes it's pure torture to be in a classroom, dreading that I might be called on. Sometimes it takes everything I have in me to just remain seated in my chair and not bolt out the door!

As we mentioned in the previous section, we will set aside class time for you to write down "the mark" or the target you are aiming at—in other words, the goal you have in mind. In the case of the student who said he struggles with social anxiety, his aim was "to have a meaningful conversation with someone this week." In addition, he identified the false witnesses (negative, disempowering statements) that might deter him from "hitting the mark." Here is his list: "I am stupid," "People don't like me," and "People think I'm annoying." He then refuted each false witness with a true witness—a positive statement or empowering scriptural message that would support him in hitting the mark he was aiming at. Here's how he used this exercise:

222

> The truth is, I love other people and want to overcome these things that prevent me from relating to them. So today I sought refuge in a Higher Power. I did this by thinking of three positive things about myself that I believe to be true—three things that would help me refute the false witnesses that assail my mind. Here they are: I am creative. People like me. People would like to have a conversation with me.

These "true witnesses" can take a variety of forms. You could also make use of a scriptural passage such as "God is my strength," "I am with you always" or "Peace comes from within." You can also choose a positive statement that has truth within it: "I am loveable," "I can choose wisely," "God knows my heart," "I can be a good friend," etc. The possibilities are unlimited, and the choice of passage often depends on what you need to hear in the moment. The main point is that truth, wherever it may be found, has the power to overcome falsity.

Even so, truth has no power until it becomes a "living truth"—that is, until it is put into your life. Returning to the student's story about overcoming social anxiety, he writes about what happened when he decided to make use of those three positive statements about himself:

> I took a deep breath. Then, on four separate occasions, I approached four different people that I wanted to talk to. My goal was to come out of each conversation having learned at least one new, meaningful thing about that person. This would be a simple task for most, but for me it would be a major accomplishment. Remembering my list of "true witness" statements from class helped.

I'm happy to report that it went very well, and I learned a lot from this exercise. I would be lying if I said that I did not feel frightened during these conversations, but in my heart, beneath this feeling, learning something new about someone was quite thrilling. It made me happy. It helped me feel that I was expressing and showing love. Instead of making up a story in my mind that they did not love me, I turned it around. I learned something that is true about others. Instead of getting caught up in the lies Satan was telling me about myself, I focused on learning the truth about others. 99

Another student, also dealing with a tendency to isolate himself, titles his journal entry "Live Your Life, Man, You Can Do It":

66 The in-class "mark to aim at" was to pick something that we want to work on in our life. One side lists the reasons we think are stopping us or make us believe we can't do it. These are the "false witnesses." The other side lists counter-arguments for why we can accomplish what we want. These are the "true witnesses."

I want to work on enjoying life to the fullest. I've had a really hard time with this because of my depression. I'm on meds and everything, but sometimes I'm just in a bad state, and it's hard to get out. One of the things I wrote down on the "I can't do it" side is "I have a fear of opening up to people and letting them in." Also, I said that when I'm in a bad state, these are the thoughts that come to me: "I will never get out of this," "I'm useless," "I'm worthless," and "Nobody actually likes me." Whether those thoughts make me depressed, or my depression brings on those thoughts, I don't know. But it can be depressing to say the least!

On the bright side, however, I listed some good counter-arguments. I said, "Hey, I've been happy before, and I can be happy again." Just writing that down helped me to remember last spring when there was a jump in my step and I loved the weather every day. My goal for this week was to get back to that state and start enjoying life again. I also knew what I had to do. I would need to talk with the Lord every day, first and foremost, but I would also need to talk to my friends. My counter-arguments helped with this. I wrote: "I have friends!" "I'm close to my family!" "There are people out there who love me!"

I almost gave a chapel talk last year about how "Help is All Around You–You Just Have to Open Your Eyes." It was too late in the year (the spring), so I didn't get a chance. Maybe once I feel good again, I'll have that opportunity. Wait a minute! I feel good right now. Oh wow! I am enjoying life! 99

In the next journal entry, a student talks about how a low grade in a political science class plunged her into the depths of despair:

66 I'm taking a lot of credits this term, so I've been working very hard, and, up until recently, maintaining an A average in all my classes. But last week we had midterms. Because I'm taking an overload, I had four midterms within

the same week and not enough time to study for them all. I stressed myself to the utmost trying to cram in just a few more facts for each class.

On Friday morning, during my first class, we got back our political science midterms. I got a B. I was so upset that I had to skip my next two morning classes because I was in tears. I called home wanting to drop out of school, or drop a class, or anything to make my life easier. I was feeling desperate, lost, and was crying hard.

My mother talked me through my options, and by lunchtime I had pulled myself back together a little. I decided to go to my afternoon class, but I just stared at the whiteboard for the whole time and didn't hear a word the teacher said. That same afternoon, I met with my political science teacher to discuss my test. Yes, it was a "B." She concurred with my mom that I was putting myself under too much stress.

That was one of the worst days of my life. Even by nighttime, when I was trying to do homework, I still was really upset and couldn't concentrate. I realized that I was reading the same sentence over and over. "Why work so hard, if I'm not getting anywhere?" I thought. "What's the point, anyway?" I was sinking again, thinking that everything was useless, and that I was worthless.

She goes on to describe how her Saturday went, which was somewhat better. The darkness had lifted a bit, and she was able to get some work done. Then came Sunday:

I decided to go to church on Sunday. The sermon was about how false witnesses try to get us when we are at our weakest, and convince us of how worthless we are. At the same time, the Lord is always there, with True Witness—messages about how much he loves us and values us. He even says, "I am the faithful and true witness" (Revelation 3:14).

This helped me realize that I had given in to false witnesses and allowed myself to believe their destructive messages. Those messages are not real, and I do not have to believe them. I can see the truth—that the false god of overachievement sets me up to believe the false message that I'm worthless. The truth is I'm **not** worthless. How could I let a "B" on one test convince me otherwise? 〞

Sometimes the truth that you need to hear may not come directly through a sermon or through sacred texts; it could come to you through others. For example, in the next journal entry, a student who plays goalie for his college ice hockey team is deeply disappointed after an overtime loss. Inner "false witnesses" have managed to convince him that he is the sole reason for his team's loss:

66 The game went into overtime, then into a shootout, and I let in the extra goal that cost us the game. Even though no one said a word to me, I was thinking that all the fans who came to watch blamed me, my team blamed me, and I blamed myself. At that moment, I honestly thought that I was the worst person on the planet. There was nothing I could do. I was quiet. I sulked. I wanted to be left alone.

After I got off the bus, I wandered around in the dark by myself for a while before going back to my dorm. Time passed. I was sitting alone in my dorm room. Then I noticed that my parents, as usual, sent me an "after the game" text. They said that they had been listening to the game online and could tell that I played a great game. They also told me about all the other good comments that strangers had made on the internet about the game.

Now, my parents are not the kind of people who fill you with fluff. If I don't have a strong game they just say that I had an off night, and that I'll do better next time. They're not overly negative, and they won't pump your tires either. Listening to what they said about the game and noticing how accurate their description was, I was astounded. It was as if they had been right there watching.

After reading the text from his parents, this student decided to break his silence and share his thoughts with them. So he called them and let them know everything: how he blew it for his team, how it was all his fault, how he let down his teammates, and how he let down his school. He talked about his shame and his disappointment. But when his parents began to speak again, they said something that shocked him. Here's how he describes that moment in his journal:

They said, "Son, don't lie to yourself. You had a great game, and you kept your team in the game. When you make fifty saves in one game, like you did, it shows that you came to play."

When they said, "Don't lie to yourself," I was shocked. After all, the commandment this week is about not lying. For some reason I remembered the section in the readings when it described David going through a dark time. The quote, as I remembered it, was something like, "Lord, you are my shield and the one who lifts up my head."

I think that this is exactly what happened to me. Deep down, I was crying out, and the Lord heard my cry. Through my parents, God was my shield and the one who lifted up my head. Their love and reassurance helped me to stop lying to myself. Tomorrow when I walk around campus, I will hold my head high. 99

The mark to aim at

You shall not bear false witness against your neighbor: tell the truth

As you speak to or about others, notice tendencies to twist, exaggerate, or shade the truth in order to defend or boost your ego. Notice also tendencies to make hasty assumptions about others, especially when those assumptions are based on limited knowledge of their external circumstances and inner lives. On a deeper level, be aware of the lies that present themselves to your mind, including destructive lies about yourself. On the deepest level, be aware of the subtlest lie of all—that people and circumstances are the cause of the negative emotions you experience. Remember that external stimuli may trigger those emotions, but they are not the cause. The cause is always something in your inner world—the false witness that flows in from "demons," "hell," "the slinking whisperer," "the enemy," your "lower nature"—whatever you prefer to call it When you notice these false witnesses arising within you, refute them with the truth. In brief, be a lie detector this week; detect not only the lies you tell others but also the lies you tell yourself. Most importantly, detect the lies that flow in from hellish influences. Then, *tell the truth*. In your journal, record your experience of practicing this commandment.

Suggestions for further reflection and practice

You shall not bear false witness against your neighbor.

The following exercises contain additional information about this commandment. Read through all of them, and then focus on one or two that spark your interest.

1 Activity: be aware of the "deadly duo"

The previous commandment, "You shall not steal," is a reminder that there is a God or Higher Power behind every loving emotion you feel, every wise thought you think, and every useful action you perform. If you fail to attribute your love, wisdom, and useful service to a source higher than yourself, you commit spiritual theft. As a result, you may develop unhealthy pride which, in turn, spawns feelings of superiority, arrogance, contempt, and excessive self-love.

On the other hand, the commandment "You shall not bear false witness against your neighbor" is a reminder that there is something going on behind every self-destructive emotion you feel, every false thought you think, and every harmful action you take. If you fail to attribute these destructive influences to "the delusions of the ego" (Hinduism and Buddhism), "satanic influences" (Judaism and Christianity), or "the slinking whisperer" (Islam), you bear false witness, not only against your neighbor, but also against yourself. This, in turn, gives rise to feelings of desperation, despair, and self-loathing. Finally, these negative feelings produce the false belief that you are worthless and life is meaningless.

As a spiritual practice then, become aware of feelings and thoughts as they arise, remembering that *you are not your feelings* and *you are not your thoughts*. Remember that there is always a temptation to be overly prideful about the good that you do (self-praise), and overly despondent about the failures you experience (self-blame). This is the "deadly duo" because it can destroy you either way. Recognizing this, meditate on this passage from the Buddha, and put it into your life: "As a solid rock is not shaken by the wind, the wise person is not moved amidst praise and blame." (Dhammapada 6:6)

227

2 Activity: notice evolutionary defensiveness (part 1)

Sometimes a lie comes so quickly that it's out of your mouth before you have a chance to stop it. Some scholars believe that the reflexive, spontaneous nature of a *defensive* lie is an evolutionary adaptation. Your ancestors needed to be constantly on guard, vigilant and defensive, lest they be attacked and killed at any moment. The ones who did not cultivate quick, defensive responses died out. On the other hand, those who became adept at defending themselves survived. This week notice how quick you may be to defend yourself with a lie—or a partial truth. Was it necessary, or was it just a vestige of an ancient, automatic, defensive reflex?

3 Activity: notice evolutionary defensiveness (part 2)

Psychologists in the field of cognitive therapy use the term "catastrophizing" to describe the tendency to exaggerate the significance or severity of an isolated event. This may be a form of evolutionary defensiveness. It's also a form of false witness. A snake hanging from a tree, ready to fill you with deadly poison, might be a harmless vine. The quiz you did poorly on does not mean it's the end of your academic career. The girl who was talking to your boyfriend this morning might not be trying to steal him from you. It's good to be aware of cognitive distortions like this, and to keep things in perspective. This week notice how quick you might be to catastrophize when something frightens or disturbs you. Once again (as in part 1), ask yourself, "Was it necessary, or might it have been a vestige of an ancient, automatic, defensive reflex?"[6]

4 Activity: make a commitment

Give yourself a mark to aim at such as, "This week I will not eat junk food; I will eat healthy food and limit sweets." Here's another example: "This week I will not be lazy; instead, I will exercise every other day for 20 minutes." Be as concrete and specific as possible, and make it a realistic aim. Write it at the top of a blank page. Then draw a line down the middle of the page. On the left side write any thoughts and lies (false witnesses) that might prevent you from honoring your commitment this week. On the right side, across from each false witness, write any true statements (true witnesses) that might help you remain true to your aim. As the week progresses, notice the stream of lies, justifications, and rationalizations that flow in to prevent you from keeping your commitment. To help ensure success, pair off with another member of the class and check in with each other during the week. Be an "accountability partner."

---

6 Hyper-vigilant defensiveness may, of course, be necessary in dangerous environments where, at any moment, we might be attacked by a wild animal or savage tribe. Rick Hanson refers to this as "the negativity bias"—an evolutionary adaption that helped humanity survive during life-threatening times. In modern civilization, however, this kind of defensiveness can take an enormous toll on one's nervous system (see *Buddha's Brain* op. cit., 23-48). We have already touched on this in chapter one when we discussed the false god of anger (page 37).

5 Activity: keep promises

If you promise to do something, do it. If you promise to be somewhere on time, be there on time. If you are unable to keep your promise, deal with it honestly. Admit it to yourself; apologize if necessary, but tell the truth about what happened without making excuses, blaming others, or defending yourself. Live in integrity, even if it's as simple as showing up for class on time.

6 Activity: make no hasty assumptions

When the judgments you make about people are based on limited information, you may be "bearing false witness" against your neighbor. If you do not know people well, it's best to avoid making assumptions about them. Instead, get to know them. Take time to hear their story. If you have a disagreement with someone, seek to understand that person's perspective. If someone says or does something to you that hurts your feelings, ask questions like, "What did you mean by that?" "Why did you say that?" "What were you thinking when you did that?" Ask in a non-accusatory way, with a sincere desire to know the truth.

7 Activity: distinguish between trigger and cause

You may have heard (or even said) statements like this: "When Professor Smith gives us those long reading assignments, it drives me crazy." In spiritual reality, Professor Smith does not drive you crazy. Neither do the long reading assignments. What drives you crazy are the thoughts and feelings that you have *about* Professor Smith and the long assignments. More specifically, what drives you crazy is believing that your feelings are an accurate picture of reality, and that the thoughts that are linked to those feelings are necessarily true.

For example, if you say, "When my boyfriend flirts with other girls, it makes me feel worthless," it does not mean that you *are* worthless. But if you accept the feeling of worthlessness as being reality, and you believe any false messages associated with it, you may end up believing that you are worthless. The truth is that the homework assignments of one of your professors, or the flirtatious habits of your significant other may *trigger* an upset state of mind, but they are not the *cause* of that upset. The true cause is always *within* you—in your inner world of thought and feeling—not in your external environment.

As you go through the week, practice distinguishing between the trigger (the external event) and the true cause of your state of mind (the thoughts and feelings that arise within you). Notice that the real battle is against the negative feelings and false thoughts ("false witnesses") that arise within you—not against the people who trigger these responses. Then use true witness—the truths that you have learned through sacred scripture—to rise above all forms of false witness.

229

"*I'm not one of those kids who has a 'college fund.' Others do, and when I think about it, covetous feelings arise. These feelings generate thoughts like, 'All the other kids can have fun, while I have to work.'*"

Rise above covetous desire ~ be content.

You shall not covet your neighbor's house.

You shall not covet your neighbor's wife, nor his manservant, nor his maidservant, nor his ox nor his donkey, nor anything that is your neighbor's.

Exodus 20:15

231

Cool Runnings

When the movie *Cool Runnings* first came out in 1993, the critical reviews were mixed. Some said that it contained some of the best sports moments in movie history; others were less enthusiastic. Today the consensus of critics on the website *Rotten Tomatoes* is that, "*Cool Runnings* rises above its formulaic sports-movie themes with charming performances, light humor, and uplifting tone."[1] It also illustrates one of the core themes of this book.

Although highly fictionalized, *Cool Runnings* is based on a true story. The time is November 1987. The place is a Jamaican town where Irv Blitzer, a former Olympic champion, is living. Several years earlier, in the 1968 Winter Olympics, Blitzer competed on the American team, winning two Olympic gold medals for his performances in the two-man and four-man bobsled competitions. Four years later, in the 1972 Olympics, he competed again and won two more gold medals. This time, however, it was discovered that he had secretly placed extra weights in the front of his sled. Caught cheating,

---

1   Accessed on October 29, 2017 @ www.rottentomatoes.com/m/1046227_cool_runnings. For an informative review by a college student at Northwestern University, see the article by Alex Nitkin in *North by Northwestern*, the daily newsmagazine of Northwestern University (February 23, 2014). Accessed on November 2, 2017 @ www.northbynorthwestern.com/story/emcool-runningsem-has-more-positive-messages-than-/

he was disqualified, stripped of his medals, and sent home in disgrace.

Blitzer did not go back to America. Instead, he took up permanent residence in Jamaica, living in self-chosen exile. As the movie begins, he's spending his days shooting pool, drinking beer, and working as a small-time bookie.

While Blitzer's days as an Olympian are over, three young Jamaican sprinters are aspiring to compete in the 1988 Summer Olympics. During a 100-meter Olympic qualifying heat, the three of them are in the lead—first, second, and third place—when suddenly one of the trio stumbles, bringing the other two men crashing down with him. The three sprinters watch as the other runners cross the finish line, leaving them sprawled on the track, their Olympic dreams dashed.

One of the trio, however, a young man named Derice Bannock, is not ready to give up on his dream of going to the Olympics. When he finds out that the disgraced American bobsledder is now living in Jamaica, he hunts him down and begs him to be his coach—in *bobsledding*! After much persuading, Blitzer, who has always believed that Jamaican sprinters could be excellent bobsledders, reluctantly agrees.

They quickly assemble a four-man team, and practice racing a makeshift bobsled-with-wheels through the picturesque Jamaican hillside. As they careen down the steep hills, the lyrics from the soundtrack capture the mood: "*Here on this mountaintop, whoa-oh, we've got some wild, wild life.*" As the team steadily improves, Blitzer becomes convinced that they can qualify for the Olympics. Eventually they raise enough money to finance the trip.

The next thing appearing on the movie screen is a palm tree that magically turns into a snow-covered pine as their plane flies from sunny Jamaica to wintry Canada. When they arrive, the temperature in Calgary, British Columbia, is minus 25 degrees Fahrenheit. It's the site for the 1988 Winter Olympics.

At first the Jamaican team is the laughing-stock of the event. *Who ever heard of a Jamaican bobsled team?!* In the eyes of the officials and some of the other Olympians, the four Jamaicans and their coach are regarded as an awkward-looking group of unqualified, wishful thinkers.

From the moment of their arrival, nothing seems to work out for the Jamaican team. There are problems with their sled, problems with their uniforms, problems in the trial runs, and problems with their attitude.

A few days before one of their qualifying races, three of the Jamaicans decide to go to a dance club. It doesn't turn out well. When a member of the East German team insults one of them, another Jamaican steps in to defend his teammate. Within a few seconds, a bar-room brawl erupts. Fists fly and bottles break as everyone dives into the action. In the end no one is hurt, but when the Jamaicans get back to their hotel, Coach Blitzer is not pleased. He tells them that they're going to have to change their attitude—or they will have no chance of winning.

This is one of the major turning points in the movie. In the very next scene, Coach Blitzer is suddenly awakened by the four Jamaican team members. It's 6:00 AM, and they are ready to begin an early morning practice, this time with a new attitude. The music pounds out a dramatic reggae beat, followed by the opening lyrics, *"Rise! Rise! Rise! Rise!"*

As the song continues, we see the four Jamaicans striding in unison, single file, across a bridge that spans a flowing river and a snow-covered field. Coach Blitzer is standing on the bridge timing them. "Not bad," he says encouragingly as they jog past him. "Pick it up, though." They continue to stride swiftly and smoothly across the bridge, their rhythmic pace perfectly matching the beat of the music. At the same time, the lyrics convey the movie's main theme:

> *Well, if you've got a problem, you've got to rise above it.*
>
> *When you face a challenge, you've got to rise above it.*
>
> *When your back's against the wall, the only way to go is up.*
>
> *Rise above it!*
>
> *Come on and rise above it!*

233

As the music plays, we see the four Jamaicans on the bobsled course practicing their starts, in the gym pushing up heavy weights with their legs, in a hockey rink learning to run on ice, and in an empty bathtub simulating bobsled turns. All the while, the music continues, accompanied by soul-stirring lyrics:

> *If those storm clouds should appear, you don't ever have to fear.*
>
> *Just rise above it! (Come on, come on.)*
>
> *I tell you once and I tell you twice,*
>
> *Big success always comes with a price.*
>
> *Come now, come now, and take my advice:*
>
> *Rise above it! Rise above it! Rise above it!*

The music is punctuated with Coach Blitzer's shouts of encouragement: *"Come on! Come on! Good! Good! You're doing fine! Go! Go! Go! That's it! That's it! That's it!"* At the same time, a deep voice on the soundtrack utters rhythmic phrases like *"Hard work," "Sacrifice,"* and *"Give it your all!"*

Toward the end of the training montage, we see the four Jamaican sprinters far below, jogging beside the frozen edge of a Canadian river, still running in rhythm, matching the cadence of the music. We, as viewers, are watching from high above, as if standing on the bridge. From that heightened perspective, the camera slowly pans across the wintry Canadian landscape, steadily lifting us high above the bridge, and above the city of Calgary. As the montage comes an end, we are given an expansive view of Calgary at night, and a final view of the entire bobsled track in lights.

For those of us who have willingly suspended disbelief, this is a moment in which the high hopes of the Jamaican team become our own. All the while, the unrelenting message continues:

> *Rise above it! You can do it!*

> *Rise above it! You can do it!*

But this is only a warm-up for coming events. On the evening before the next day's competition, Coach Blitzer comes to check on his men in their hotel rooms, to see how they're doing, and if they would like anything to eat. Derice, who is busy studying photographs of the turns on the bobsled course, is not hungry. But he has a question. Even before Derice poses his question, Coach Blitzer knows what it is going to be:

> *Coach: You want to know why I cheated, right?*

> *Derice: Yes, I do.*

> *Coach: That's a fair question. It's quite simple really. I had to win. You see, Derice, I'd made winning my whole life. And when you make winning your whole life, you have to keep on winning. No matter what. You understand that?*

> *Derice: No, I don't understand, Coach. You had two gold medals. You had it all!*

> *Coach: (Shaking his head) Derice, a gold medal is a wonderful thing. But if you're not enough without it, you'll never be enough with it.*[2]

• ● •

---

2 For a brief review of this moment see the *USA Today* web article by Luke Kerr-Dineen, August 25, 2016. Accessed on November 2, 2017 @ www.ftw.usatoday.com/2016/08/this-inspiring-speech-in-cool-runnings-is-one-of-the-best-sports-movie-moments-ever

We won't tell you how the movie ends—we don't want to spoil it for you. But we do want to point out that the Ten Commandments end with the commandment that says, "You shall not covet." It's the last and final commandment for a reason. It's talking about an anxious desire to own or possess what outward reality is not giving you at the moment. This commandment is a reminder to rest in the realization that every *spiritual* blessing is available to you in the present moment, regardless of external circumstances. A gold medal, a championship trophy, even a good grade on a test, are all wonderful things. But they should never become so important that you would cheat, deceive, or do underhanded things to get them. When the covetous desire to achieve some external goal becomes everything to you, you can quietly repeat the mantra, "I have enough. I am enough. There is no need to covet."

The commandments in world scriptures

Judaism

At the literal level, almost all the commandments speak about observable *external* behaviors. You are commanded to not bow down to idols, to not take the Lord's name in vain, to not work on the Sabbath, to honor parents, to not murder, to not commit adultery, to not steal, and to not lie. Each of these commandments, at first glance, seems to deal exclusively with the words we speak and the actions we take. They are about regulating your *external* life.

The final commandment, however, takes you deeper. It says, "You shall not covet your neighbor's house ... or anything that is your neighbor's." This is about your *internal* world, the part of you that is not observable, but which gives rise to every emotion you feel, every thought you think, and every action you take. This is the place of intention and motivation; it's the arena where your deepest, most fundamental drives are seated. It is in this deeply hidden place where "coveting" arises.

In the Hebrew scriptures the word "covet" (חָמַד *chamad*), as used in this commandment, refers to "an inordinate, ungoverned, selfish desire."[3] If you covet *anything* badly enough, you might lie, cheat, steal, commit adultery—or even murder—to obtain it. So this final commandment uncovers the underlying desire which leads to the breaking of all the other commandments. It deals with *core* issues, not surface manifestations, *causes*, not symptoms, *roots*, not branches.

Ordinarily, people understand the word "covet" to refer to anything that is desired. It also can refer to being jealous or envious of others. In the Hebrew scriptures, for example, David says that there is no need to be envious of those who appear to be getting ahead in life: "Do not fret because of evildoers, nor be envious of the workers of iniquity." Rather than worry about the wrongs of others, or envy their success, David says that you should "Trust in the Lord and do good. ... Delight yourself in the Lord." If you do this, says David, "The Lord will give you the desires of your heart" (Psalm 37:1-4).

At first glance, this seems to say that God will give you whatever you desire— the "desires of your heart." More deeply, however, it means that if you live according to the commandments, and find delight in keeping them, *right*

---

3   From *Strong's Concordance,* www.biblehub.com/hebrew/2530.htm

desires will flow into your heart—desires that are consistent with God's will.

Right desires are very different from the insatiable longings of your lower nature—the unquenchable cravings that lead to human misery. Because of this, the words "You shall not covet" mean, quite literally, *"You shall not want anxiously and desperately—so much so that you would disregard any of the commandments to get what you want."* According to King Solomon, "A heart at peace gives life to the body, but envy rots the bones" (Proverbs 14:30).

Christianity

When the words "You shall not covet" come to mind, the most common association is with envy. For example, in a famous story called "the parable of the prodigal son," Jesus speaks about a certain man who has two sons. One of the sons remains home to serve his father. The other son takes his share of the inheritance, leaves home and spends everything on a wild, immoral, self-indulgent lifestyle. Eventually, the self-indulgent son realizes that a life spent pursuing external pleasure is hollow, and decides to return to his father. Overjoyed, his father throws a lavish party celebrating the return of the prodigal son. The other son, however—the one who remained at home—is angry and jealous. He deeply resents what appears to him to be unmerited favoritism. The father, who symbolizes God in this story, reassures the faithful son, saying, "You are always with me, and *all that I have is yours*" (Luke 15:31; emphasis added).

237

In other words, Jesus is saying, "Why waste a moment coveting anything or anyone when it is God's desire to give you every spiritual blessing?" As Jesus puts it in another parable, "Come, you blessed of my Father, inherit the kingdom prepared for you from the foundation of the world" (Matthew 25:34).

Jesus, however, does not always describe coveting as a form of envy or jealousy. He also describes it as a form of grasping materialism, an unwillingness to part with one's possessions. When a rich young ruler approaches Jesus and asks what good thing he should do to inherit eternal life, Jesus tells him to not murder, to not commit adultery, to not steal, to not bear false witness, to honor father and mother, and to love his neighbor as himself. When the man replies that he has done all these things, Jesus introduces the commandment against coveting, but without naming it. "Sell what you have and give to the poor," says Jesus. The rich man cannot do it, "for he had great possessions." Because he chose to covetously cling to his possessions, he went away sorrowful (Matthew 19:16-22).

On another occasion, someone approaches Jesus and says, "Teacher, tell my brother to divide the inheritance with me." Instead, Jesus says, "Take heed and beware of covetousness, for life does not consist in the abundance of possessions" (Luke 12:15). Jesus then tells a story about a certain rich man who had a plentiful harvest. Rather than share the abundant harvest with others, the man decided to store it up for the future. In fact, he was making plans to tear down his barns and build bigger ones, imagining a life of ease, eating, drinking, and enjoying himself. Jesus ends the story by saying that God called this man a fool, as is everyone "who lays up treasure for himself" rather than being filled with God's riches (Luke 12:13-21).

According to Jesus, life is about sharing, not coveting; giving, not getting: "Give and it will be given unto you," says Jesus, "full measure, pressed down, shaken together, and overflowing will be put into your heart" (Luke 6:38). The more you love others, the more will God's love flow into you; the more you bring God's peace to others, the more will God's peace flow into you. This is an immutable law. It's a mistake to covetously hold on to heavenly blessings; they are meant to be shared. The more you share the blessings of love, joy, peace, gratitude and contentment, the more will these heavenly blessings flow into you, "full measure, pressed down, shaken together, overflowing your heart."

Islam

This same idea—that "coveting" is a form of stinginess (the opposite of generosity)—is directly addressed in the Islamic scriptures: "Let not those who covetously withhold the gifts which Allah has given them of his grace think that it is good for them. Nay, it will be worse for them. Soon the things that they covetously withheld will be tied to their necks like a twisted collar on the day of judgment" (Qur'an 3:180).

Allah, like Jesus, cautions against the illusory security of counting on wealth instead of trusting in God: "Woe to every kind of scandal-monger and backbiter, who piles up wealth and counts it over and over again, thinking that his wealth will make him last forever. By no means!" (Qur'an 104:1-3).

In Islam, the basic idea is that the wealth, resources and talents a person has are all gifts from Allah, not one's own possessions. Therefore, they should be shared with others generously: "O ye who believe, eat not up your property among yourselves in vanities, but let there be among you traffic and trade by mutual goodwill. ... And in nowise covet those things that Allah has bestowed as gifts upon you, more freely on some than on others" (Qur'an 4:29, 32).

The idea that every good thing a person has is a gift from Allah is a protection against boasting and coveting. It is also a reminder that people are given different kinds of gifts. Therefore, followers of the Islamic faith are told that they should "not despair over matters that pass you by" (Qur'an 57:23). In other words, you may not have an exceptional musical gift, athletic talent, artistic ability, or some other aptitude. If these matters seem to "pass you by," this is nothing to worry about. And it is certainly not a reason to covet what others have, for "Allah knows what is best for you" (Qur'an 2:216).

On the other hand, if you are gifted with special abilities, unique talents, or abundant resources, you should not allow this to make you proud or boastful: "Do not exult over [Allah's] favors bestowed upon you, for Allah loves not any vainglorious boaster. Such persons are covetous and influence others to be covetous as well" (Qur'an 57:23-24). In the Islamic faith, therefore, the antidote to covetousness is to be a generous giver, knowing that it is incumbent upon you to share your gifts and blessings with others.

Hinduism

In Eastern religions, covetous or selfish "desire" is seen as the chief obstacle to happiness. The antidote is to realize that everything you need is already within you. Those who understand this are no longer deluded by the vanities of the external world; instead, they dwell in contentment. In Hinduism, this state of inner peace comes about through the realization that the individual soul, the *Ātman*, is identical to *Brahman*, the invisible force that pervades the universe: "They who have found the *Ātman* are always satisfied. They have found the source of joy and fulfillment and no longer seek happiness from the external world. They have nothing to gain or lose by any action; neither people nor things can affect their security" (Bhagavad Gita 3:17-19).

The *Ātman* is our essential Self, our Higher Self. It's the part of you that sings in the shower for no other reason than that its nature is to sing; on a walk, or while gardening, or preparing a meal it may begin to hum or whistle. It is your fundamental nature, *in tune* with the universe. This is the *Ātman*, your essential core which is supremely satisfied within itself and needs nothing else to make it happy. And the key to maintaining this state of inmost happiness is to allow the *Ātman* to rule over the ego: "Thus, knowing that which is supreme, let the *Ātman* rule the ego; use your mighty arms to conquer the fierce enemy that is insatiable desire" (Bhagavad Gita 3:43).[4]

The Sanskrit word translated as "ego" in the above verse is *ahamkara*—from *aham* (self) and *kara* (pertaining to).[5] So *ahamkara* is the part of you that is all about yourself. Because it believes the illusion that it is a "separate self," self-contained, disconnected from the whole, and limited by societal definitions such as "I am a student," "I am a professor," "I am a British citizen," "I own a Cadillac," or "I am a vegetarian." Also, it is fully identified with its thoughts and feelings: "I believe in free speech," "I get angry when people insult my family," "It really upsets me when I do poorly on a test," etc.

Beyond *ahamkara* (the ego-self, or lower self)—with its narrow, constricting

239

---

4   This translation is based on a combination of Eknath Easwaran's *Bhagavad Gita for Daily Living*, Vol 1, 211 (op. cit.) and the translation given through the Bhagavad Gita Trust accessed on October 28, 2017 @ www.bhagavad-gita.org/Gita/chapter-03.html
5   This information was accessed on October 28, 2017 @ www.yogapedia.com/definition/5235/ahamkara

sense of its own separate identity and existence—is the Supreme Self (or Higher Self). This Higher or Greater Self is large, expansive, connected to everything that exists, including God.

Transcending the smaller, limited, ego-self—*without annihilating it*—is an essential aspect of Hinduism. In fact, the ego-self can be a friend of the Higher Self: "To those who have conquered the lower self, the lower self is a friend; but for him who has not realized his Higher Self, the lower self is the greatest enemy" (Bhagavad Gita 6:6). "Those who have conquered the lower self ... rise above the dualities of cold and heat, joy and sorrow, honor and dishonor. Such yogis remain peaceful and steadfast in their devotion to God" (Bhagavad Gita 6:7). Because they have risen above the covetous desires of their lower nature, they no longer grasp or covet anything. As it is written, "When the mind is established in the Higher Self and liberated from [covetous] desires ... it is like a flame in a windless place. It flickers not. ... Supreme happiness comes to the one whose mind is peaceful, whose passions are at rest, who is free from [covetous] desires, and has become one with God" (Bhagavad Gita 6:19-20; 27).[6]

In his commentary on the *Bhagavad Gita*, Swami Mukundananda puts it simply: "Freedom from coveting leads to contentment and inward peace.[7]

Buddhism

When it comes to the problem of covetous desire the Buddha is direct: "Covetousness is the worst of diseases," he says. "There is no suffering worse than selfish passion." He is also quite clear about the antidote: "Contentment is the greatest wealth. *Nirvana* is the highest happiness" (Dhammapada 15:8). The word *Nirvana* means "to blow out." In the context of Buddhist thought, it refers to the "blowing out" of every covetous desire.

The Buddha also speaks about "rooting out" covetous desire: "The covetous desires of the thoughtless grow like a creeper" (Dhammapada 334). When these covetous desires rule over you, "sorrow spreads like wild grass" (Dhammapada 24:1). If, however, you rise above covetous desire, "sorrow will fall away from you like drops of water from a lotus leaf" (Dhammapada 336). Therefore, the Buddha says, "Dig up covetous desire, root and all. Whenever you see one of these creepers growing in your mind, uproot it with wisdom" (Dhammapada 24:4-5).

The imagery is powerful, but it should not be misunderstood. Covetous desires should, of course, be extinguished—like a flame. They should be

---

6   Sarvepalli Radhahakrishnan and Charles Moore, editors. *A Source Book in Indian Philosophy* (Princeton: Princeton University Press, 1957), 124. This translation from the *Source Book* is slightly revised in the light of insights from Eknath Easwaran in the *Bhagavad Gita for Daily Living*, Vol 1, 360-361, 369.

7   Accessed on May 31, 2018 @ www.holy-bhagavad-gita.org/chapter16/verse/1-3

rooted out, like a wild, noxious weed. But not all desires are covetous. Therefore, the Buddha exhorts adherents to practice "right effort" (*chanda*). In the *Noble Eightfold Path*, for example, the sixth precept is called "Right Endeavor." In this teaching, the Buddha says that one must "struggle with all one's heart ... to stop bad qualities from arising, to renounce those which have already arisen, and ... to perfect those good qualities which have not yet arisen or are already there" (Majjhima-Nikaya, iii, 248-252).[8] It is clear that the Buddha is not against all desires—just the desires of one's lower nature. He, therefore, urges devotees to struggle with all their heart to overcome covetous desire while perfecting the desires of their Higher Nature.

• ● •

When the Buddha gave his most famous teaching, called "The Four Noble Truths," he said that "The cause of all suffering is desire" and the remedy is "to extinguish desire."[9] As we have seen, the Buddha was not talking about your higher, nobler, God-given desires, but rather the lower, baser, covetous desires that produce envy, jealousy, and the lust to possess things and control people. As it is written in the *Bhagavad Gita*: "The person who is free from egotism, violence, arrogance, and *the covetous desire to possess things or control people*, is at peace with oneself and with others" (Bhagavad Gita 18:53; emphasis added).[10] Those who discover this kind of inner peace do not need a gold medal; they are enough without one.

241

8   For the full quotation see "The Synopsis of Truth" accessed on October 28, 2017 @ www. obo.genaud.net/dhamma-vinaya/chlm/mn/mn.141.chlm.sbb.htm

9   In *Further Dialogues of the Buddha*, ii, translated by Lord Chalmers, Sacred Books of the Buddhists, vi (London: Oxford University Press, 1927), 296-299.

10 The phrase that is here translated as "control people" is translated as using "force" (Radhakrishnan and Moore, 161) and sometimes as being overly "aggressive" (Eknath Easwaran, Vol. 3, 439). Emanuel Swedenborg writes that coveting relates not only to a covetous desire to possess the goods of others, but also to a desire to *control their lives* (what they think, feel, and do)—in other words to make what belongs to others, one's own. As he puts it, to covet is to "eagerly desire to subject another to one's own authority." Today, this is called being a "controlling" person. The full quotation may be accessed at www.heavenlydoctrines.org/dtSearch.html under the search words "eagerly desire."

The commandments in the lives of college students

You shall not covet.

I heard that a new kid was going to be living in the dorm. Everyone was talking about how he was this amazing triathlon runner, and that he was so cool, and fun, and BLAH BLAH BLAH. I had not even met him, and I already hated him. I coveted the popularity he had.

Journal excerpt from a college sophomore, titled "Coveting Gets in the Way"

Contentment is the greatest wealth

Coveting begins at a young age, even before the articulation of the phrase, "I want." In the following journal entry, a student admits that, even as a child, she was filled with covetous desires:

> 66 For the first ten years of my life, I was a brat. As my parents put it, I was "spoiled rotten." We could walk into a store, and the first words out of my mouth were, "I want it." And if I didn't get what I wanted, I would throw a fit.

Over the years, things improved. Nevertheless, she had not entirely outgrown covetous desires:

> I am no longer the spoiled brat I once was, but the covetous desires are still there. For example, when I see my friends wearing nice clothes, my first thought is "I wish I had that." I seldom say, with simple sincerity and with no desire to possess what others have, "I really like your shirt," or "Nice shoes!"
>
> I know that it's not a sin to like nice things, and it's OK to wish for the newest pair of sneakers now and then; but the truth is, I have enough. Over the last ten weeks I've begun to learn the meaning of Buddha's words: "Contentment is the greatest wealth" (Dhammapada 15:8). 99

It's interesting that this student mentions "the newest pair of sneakers." In fact, "sneaker envy" comes up quite often in the context of this commandment. In the following journal entry, for example, another student describes her desperate desire to possess a pair of sneakers:

> ❝ There was this pair of KD (Keven Durant) sneakers they were about to release. Now I don't want you to think this was just any pair of sneakers. THEY WEREN'T. These sneakers defined me. They were colorful, but not weird colorful. They were *color with a purpose*. I felt like my eyes had never seen a pair of sneakers like that. They were absolutely unique. That's probably why so many people wanted them. But I didn't just want them—I NEEDED them, and I was ready to do ANYTHING to get them! ❞

Another student, whose mother refused to give her the money to buy a new pair of Retro Jordan 13s, was furious. She begged, she cried, and when that didn't work, she gave her mother the silent treatment, all to no avail. Finally, she realized what she had been doing:

> ❝ After days of thinking about this, especially because of the coveting commandment, I realized that I was in the wrong. How could I be upset with my mother because she didn't buy me a pair of sneakers? Sneakers are materialistic things that do not last forever, especially when compared with the love between a daughter and her mother. My mother has taken care of me for nineteen years of my life, so why should I be upset with her now, just because I didn't get what I wanted?

> A number of things flooded through my mind, reminding me how much my mother has always done for me, and still does. And then this thought came to me: "There are kids out there who can't even get a hot meal, and I'm upset about a pair of sneakers." I realized I had been coveting. When I realized how selfish I was being, I sent my mom a text and told her how much I appreciate everything she has done for me. I know it made her day. ❞

In the context of all these coveting stories about footwear, one more journal entry seems to be especially appropriate:

> ❝ I saw a girl walk by with a dress and stockings on with really cute wedged boots. I can't wear anything with a heel because it makes my knee bend too quick and causes me to fall. So I immediately got jealous.

> Now I know that we are working on the commandment, "Do not covet," so I promptly went to my quiet place (my car) and prayed to God. I said, "Dear God, I know I'm not supposed to get jealous over people, so please strengthen me and relieve me of these nasty, good-for-nothing feelings."

> As soon as I was done with my prayer, a thought came into my mind: "Yes, I might not be able to wear wedge boots, but I'm glad I'm able to walk." ❞

This journal entry was written by a student who had been seriously injured in a car accident. As an "above the knee" amputee, she wore a prosthetic limb. For her, it wasn't about coveting KDs, Retro Jordan 13s, or even "cute wedged boots." It was about being grateful that she could walk.

243

Rising above covetous desire, she was content with what she had—the ability to walk. She had enough.[11]

Relationships

College campuses can be wonderful places to meet someone and fall in love. But what happens when you haven't met the right person, and have no romantic prospects? In many cases, jealousy sets in—a burning desire to have what other people have, and the accompanying disappointment that goes along with this kind of covetousness. In the following journal entry, a student describes her desire to be in a relationship:

> 66 Sometimes the dorm is full of couples—one in every crevice—talking quietly and playfully—and I think, "If only I could have a romantic relationship, like everyone else seems to. Then my life would be great."

There's nothing wrong with this kind of thinking. It's perfectly fine to desire a romantic relationship. But when a healthy desire becomes a covetous longing, trouble arises:

> I even go so far as to think, "What if she didn't exist? Maybe I would be in that relationship with him instead."

She immediately recognizes that this is a selfish thought, generated by covetous desire:

> How could I think such a horrible thing? The truth is, I'm glad she exists, and I wouldn't want to disrupt the order of people's love lives for my own benefit. The level of friendships I have is perfect for me right now. I need to be content, trusting that everything will work out, in time, just fine. And I need to remember that the world does not revolve around me and my covetous desire to eliminate anyone who is in my way! 99

The desire to wish someone's boyfriend or girlfriend out of existence is not a particularly heavenly one. In fact, she describes it as a "horrible" thought. In the following journal entry, a young man gives us a glimpse of how far this kind of thinking can go:

> 66 A friend of mine and I went to a Persuasive Speaking Tournament to listen to the speakers. I knew one of the girls in the tournament and thought she was a great person. She is spunky, upbeat, and has a great sense of humor. She's fun to be around and great to talk to.

---

11 Two years later, she sent us the following email: "Remember how much I used to covet wedge boots? Well, I stopped coveting them, but guess what happened? I now have a new prosthetic foot which makes it possible for me to wear heel shoes, and I'm planning on wearing them for my first job interview! Who would have guessed!!!!?"

Her personality attracted me to her quickly, but I knew that I had to watch myself around her and keep my motivations and feelings in check. I did not want to dishonor her or myself by coveting her and wanting her for myself. I knew she was in a very healthy relationship with someone else. However, despite my best intentions, during her speech that night, the false god of covetousness came a-knocking: "She is fantastic, isn't she?" the false god whispered. "What if she were your girlfriend?"

I tried not to listen, but the voice in my head was insistent: "Does she really fit well with the other boy? What if they were to break up? You would like that wouldn't you?"

I fought hard to not give in. "Yes," I said, "She is a fantastic person. Her boyfriend is very lucky to have her."

The false messages kept flooding in. "You could have her for yourself. She could be all yours. Don't be a fool."

I refused to listen to the lies. Instead, I countered with the truth: "I am content with what I have."

The demon backed away into the shadows. 99

The idea that we should be content with what we have doesn't do away with the desire to be in a genuine relationship. In the following journal entry, a student describes her longings for marriage and family:

245

66 When my best friend announced that she was engaged to be married, I was happy for her. But I was sad at the same time. The truth is, I wanted what she had. I have always wanted to be married, and to settle down with my husband and children in a cozy home. So I have to ask myself, "Why am I being covetous of my best friend? Why can't I just be happy for her and for what I have?"

It helps to know that my desire for a lifelong companion is a God-given one, along with the desire to be a mother. I gain comfort in knowing that God instilled these desires within me; therefore, I must have faith that he will fulfill them in due time. Meanwhile, I've come to the understanding that I must be content with my current position and that it is wrong to be covetous of others. As I proceed, I will pray that God will fill my emptiness with his love, until the day that he satisfies the very desires he has given me. 99

Becoming a spiritual champion

The word "coveting" shows up quite often in the realm of athletic endeavor. It's not unusual to hear people speaking about a "much coveted" award such as the Heisman trophy in football, the Stanley Cup in hockey, or a gold medal in the Olympics. Athletes will work incredibly hard to obtain these honors, even if it means giving up everything else in a tenacious, dedicated and persistent pursuit of excellence.

Coaches will sometimes try to motivate players and teams by asking, "How badly do you *want* to win this game?" They might tell them, "You have to *want* this more than they *want* it." "You have to *want* it so bad you can taste it." "You have to *want* it like a starving person wants food, like a thirsty person *wants* water, like a drowning person *wants* air." "*Now go out there and give it everything you've got!*"

While motivational talks can be wonderful, and devotion to victory can be exhilarating, *Rise Above It* is primarily about winning *inner* battles and becoming *spiritual* champions. In this regard, consider the following journal entry from a student who had dreams of being a professional hockey player. He's talking about the thoughts and feelings that arose in him during the last game of ice hockey playoffs. The winning team would be the league champion:

> 66 As time was winding down my heart was racing, my throat was raw from yelling, and even though I was in a cold ice arena, I could feel the sweat dripping down my face. It was the last game of the playoffs, and after all our hard work it came down to this moment. Then, finally, the buzzer sounded, and gloves, helmets and sticks went flying in the air. We won the ice hockey championship! We were champions!!!

This happy young man was not on the ice. He was in the stands with the other enthusiastic fans from his college:

> As I watched my teammates swarm the ice in celebration, I was in a sea of ecstatic, celebrating fans. It truly was an amazing moment. There were no words, only high fives, hugs, and joyous screams. I even hugged my history professor! Just thinking about that moment gives me goose bumps and brings a tear of joy to my eye.

It was a sweet moment for this student, even though he was unable to play in the game. At the start of the year, he had been a key player in several initial victories. But a series of concussions had sidelined him for the remainder of the season. Even worse, the doctor had told him that he could never play hockey again. In the rush of joy immediately following the victory, he had forgotten about his injury. As he puts it in his journal entry, "It wasn't even in my consciousness."

Unfortunately, a well-meaning fan, thinking that she was offering consolation, approached him:

> In the midst of all the cheering, I was approached by my friend's mom. She knows my story and why I can't play hockey anymore. She came up to me,

right during the celebration, gave me a pat on the back, and said, "I bet you wish you were down there celebrating with the other guys."

Seriously? Up until that point I had totally forgotten about my injury and not being able to play. But as soon as she made the comment, I could sense the covetous feelings arise within me, accompanied by these thoughts: "That championship was my championship to win." "That trophy belongs to me." "I'm the one who deserved that trophy, because I was the one who got the team off to the right start this year." "Everyone should be thanking me." The more these covetous feelings and selfish thoughts flooded in, the more I saw myself sinking deeper and deeper into self-pity.

Fortunately, he remembered his aim for the week which was to rise above covetous desire:

As the covetous feelings and thoughts began to build up, I knew I had to stop what was happening within me. Instead of staying upset and coveting the experience of being on the team when they won the championship trophy, I decided to lift up my head and see things differently. Here's what I saw: I saw one of my childhood friends, the left-winger on our first line, making a childhood dream come true. I saw my new-found friends on the team achieving the unexpected. I saw a dedicated group of loyal fans being rewarded for a season of unwavering support for our team. I saw a whole community of parents, students, and teachers coming together to share this wonderful moment. I had no reason to be upset. Having risen above my covetous self, I was back on top again. 🙶🙶

His journal entry touched the entire class. We all agreed that he had won a greater championship.

Another student who had also been sidelined—not because of injuries, but because of low grades—was determined to turn things around. He would study hard, pay attention in class, and make an academic comeback. For him, it would be a brand-new beginning. He puts it like this:

🙶🙶 For me, as a player who is on academic discipline, it's hard to not covet my fellow teammates who get to play the sport I love. When coveting arises, I catch myself thinking things like, "I'm much more intelligent than they are," and "They're lucky because they take easy courses." I know that these are petty, selfish thoughts, and I don't like having them.

He then decides to rise above covetousness, and focus on the present moment:

In class we learned that we need to accept present circumstances—not covet anything—and focus on what we can do in the present moment. I like this. I can start right now. I can study hard and get back on the ice. It feels like a new beginning for me. In my mind I have a picture of the Zamboni at the ice rink, making what was cut up and choppy into something that is fresh, new, and useful again. It's about leaving what has already happened behind and letting go, because there is a new period ahead. 🙶🙶

247

Anxiety about the future

The idea of accepting present circumstances also involves letting go of the covetous need to know the future. Uncertainty about the future, especially when it involves picking a major and choosing a career, can be a source of anxiety for many college students. In a journal entry titled "The Plan," a student talks about the difficulties she experiences when facing an uncertain future:

> 66 I have always liked having a plan. Without one I feel lost. With mid-terms approaching and assignments piling up, I have been busier than normal. At times like this, I tend to have anxiety and let myself get stressed. On top of this, when I realized that it was time to reevaluate my schedule for next term, I panicked. Anxious thoughts flooded my mind: "Why am I here?" "What am I doing with my life?" "What about my future?" More and more questions poured into my head. Realizing that I might need some back-up to deal with my mounting stress, I texted a friend to see if we could meet. She, however, was out of town. I walked back to my dorm, taking deep breaths.
>
> My friend later placed an envelope in my mailbox with a quote from Jeremiah in it: "For I know the plans I have for you, says the Lord, plans to prosper you and not harm you. To give you a future filled with hope" (Jeremiah 29:11).
>
> That was a perfect message for me. I can be content, knowing that the Lord has a plan for me—to give me a future filled with hope. He also said, "Seek first the Kingdom of God and live righteously, and I will give you everything you need." So, hey, "That's my plan!" 99

In the following journal entry, a young man wrestles with a similar issue. He, too, has an anxious desire to figure out his life path:

> 66 Last night in class we talked about covetous desires and the worries they produce. The thing that worries me the most is my future. I don't know what career I want to have or even what I want my major to be. I'm a very driven and motivated person, so it's very hard for me to believe that I'm not working toward something. I feel sad and lost, and I keep thinking, "Everyone else has it figured out except for me." I know that isn't true, but that's the way I think when I'm in this state.
>
> While I acknowledge that it's tough choosing what I want to do with my life, this freedom of choice is also a gift. Most importantly, I know what really matters. In the end, it's not about WHAT I am; it's about WHO I am. So I don't need to be anxious about any of this.
>
> Here's the truth: Everything that is impermanent—including my career choices—will fade. But that which is permanent—the internal character I have formed—will last for eternity. I know what kind of person I want to be. I know what kind of husband I want to be. I know what kind of father I want to be. I know what kind of friend I want to be.

In a final paragraph, reminiscent of the rhetoric of Martin Luther King Jr., he focuses on his dream of being the best person he can be:

> I mean, I don't have it all perfect, but I know who I want to be, and I'm motivated to become that person. THIS is what matters, not the external stuff. THIS is what protects me against the covetous, anxious, sad feelings that want to know the future right now. So tonight, I feel confident. I'm not feeling sad or lost. I know what really matters. I know the path I want to walk, and the man I want to be. 🙰

Financial issues

Some students get their tuition and expenses fully paid, either by parents or through generous scholarships. But many have to supplement their educational costs, and some entirely support themselves. The extra work responsibilities can cut down on social life and have an impact on how much time can be devoted to academic studies. Sometimes a heavy workload makes it difficult or even impossible to play sports, get involved in dramatic productions, or participate in other campus activities. These can all be occasions for covetous desires to set in. One young man talks about what this is like for him:

> 🙰 This week I've been thinking about something that I've been coveting for a long time. The funny thing is, I didn't even know it was coveting until yesterday's class. It's coveting the lives of students who have all their college paid for.
>
> One of my major worries this year has been, "How am I going to pay for school?" My parents are unable to contribute anything at all. And I'm not one of those kids who has a "college fund." Others do, and when I think about it, covetous feelings arise. These feelings generate thoughts like, "All the other kids can have fun, while I have to work." "If they do work, it's just to make extra spending money, while I have to put everything I earn into monthly payments, just to stay in school." "They can split their time between school and friends and homework, while I have to concentrate on work and schoolwork. If I have any time left over, I can have a little fun, but that doesn't happen very often." 🙰

Another student describes her financial situation as her "biggest source of stress":

> 🙰 A college education is a great experience, and is unbelievably valuable to have, but it's also very expensive. My family is not able to contribute at all to my college education, and it is also very difficult for me to take out loans. So college for me consists of an enormous amount of work and talking with the school to figure out how I'm going to get everything paid for. It is probably the biggest source of stress and anxiety in my life right now.

Going deeper, she realizes that it's not college expenses that make her miserable, but rather the jealous, resentful, covetous desires that arise within her:

249

I know that jealousy and resentment toward others do me no good at all. These emotions will destroy me physically and spiritually. It would be much healthier if I focused on what I have—the opportunity to go to college, the chance to learn the value of hard work, and the privilege of getting a solid education that will prepare me for both this life and the next. I need to remember that it is not my financial situation that makes me miserable. It's the covetous desires that arise when I begin to feel sorry for myself. There is a reason the Lord says, "Do not covet." It makes you miserable! 99

Learning that the true source of human misery is not in situations and circumstances but rather in the unhealthy desires that arise within you, may be one of the most valuable lessons you learn in this course. In the next journal entry, a student who notices her tendency to constantly compare herself to others discovers the true source of her misery:

66 A friend of mine seems to have it easy. Her parents pay for her school, give her a car, and pay for her apartment. She doesn't have to work if she doesn't want to. Then I compare my life to hers. I have held a summer job since I was 14, and I juggle several jobs at school, including working in the cafeteria and being a resident assistant in the dorm. I look at my friend and think, "I have to work for everything I get, and she gets everything handed to her." I covet the life she leads.

When my friend's parents found out that she was getting bad grades in all her subjects, they said that they would no longer pay for her schooling, her car insurance or her rent. She would have to come home and get a job. To be honest, I didn't feel sorry for her. In fact, I was happy that she would get to experience the real world.

While this isn't so bad (it might be a good lesson for her), I was shocked that my covetous heart prevented me from showing her the compassion she needed. After all, she is my good friend. I felt awful when I realized that I was happy about her sad situation.

It's so clear to me now: It's not the lack of money that makes me miserable. It's the covetous desires in my heart. 99

Academic anxiety

The end of the term can be an especially anxious time. Things that have built up all term long can seem overwhelming as you gear up for the "final push." A particularly dedicated student talks about a moment when she just couldn't push herself any further:

> 66 My life is busy and hectic, but it is even more so as I approach the end of the term. In addition to my regularly assigned work, the deadlines for all my tests and papers are coming up. I have been determined to do my best, but sometimes I feel that I can't push myself any further. That's when all these worries came up: "What if missing an assignment brings my grade down? What if I can't get into law school because I don't have perfect grades? If I'm not accepted into law school, will I even get any job at all?"
>
> As my thoughts spiral downward, I begin to think I am worthless. At those times I can't breathe, and I break down crying. I know this is all because I am too anxious, but I can't let go of the thought that my worries will come true if I don't try harder. Law school is everything. I have to get in. So I barely sleep or eat until I finish all my work.
>
> Even after I finish all my assignments and submit them, I still don't feel good. It is like I have lost my motivation. I feel miserable, and it seems like there was nothing I can do about it. It is a mixture of powerlessness and depression.

251

Overwhelmed by too much to do, and not enough time to do it, she allows a steady stream of negative thoughts to take her downward into despair. As she continues her journal entry, she describes the change that comes over her when she agrees to take a drive in the country with her friend:

> My friend invited me to go into the country to enjoy the beautiful scenery. It's a pretty time of year, and it sounded like it might be a good idea. Of course, I was still worried about the homework I planned to get done that day. As we were driving, I realized that I had been missing the beautiful weather all term. When I looked around, I saw the colorful trees under the blue sky. The stunning scenery reminded me that there are so many things I can enjoy in the present moment. As I began to forget my worries, feelings of joy and gratitude arose within me. Suddenly I had an epiphany: I realized that I had been focusing so much on the future that I was sacrificing my present happiness.
>
> This is exactly what we were learning in this final commandment about holding on to everything so tightly, but I didn't really understand it until this moment. I asked myself, "Why am I always striving so hard for future happiness—a happiness that isn't even guaranteed—when I could be happy right now?"
>
> My dear friend was next to me, and we were eating delicious food while

surrounded by a picturesque landscape. I felt as if I were in heaven and that God was with me. I thanked God for giving me a great friend and allowing me to appreciate the world he so beautifully created. All my worries were gone when I remembered that God has given me everything I need to be happy, and he always will. Law school would be wonderful, but I could be happy without it. The important thing was that there was no need to worry. 🙶🙶

This student didn't need to let go of her dream to attend law school. She only needed to let go of the covetous desires that were making her life miserable. In letting go of covetous desire, she was able to enjoy her life in the present moment, experiencing the blessings of friendship and the beauty of nature.

In the academic world, so filled with quizzes, tests, papers, presentations, and exams, there are numerous occasions for anxiety, but just as many for rising above anxiety in order to experience inner peace. That's why the commandment "Do not covet" is so important. It's another way of saying, "Do not worry." And note, it's not saying, "Don't study." It's saying, "Don't worry."

Dealing with control issues

So far, we've covered a wide variety of ways that coveting manifests itself. We've described it as a deep, driving, insatiable desire that can lead you into deeper and deeper states of envy, jealousy, self-pity, resentment and despair, unless it is satisfied. Life without all the grasping, clinging and craving could be so much better. If you can remember that true happiness does not lie in the possession of *things,* or in the favorable arrangement of external *circumstances*, you can let go of covetous desires. This realization can open the way for feelings of true happiness to arise.

But we've not yet dealt with one of the subtlest forms of coveting. It is the desire to control others. While the literal teaching, "You shall not covet your neighbor's house," refers primarily to the desire to covet things and have circumstances turn out in your favor, the rest of the commandment refers to the desire to control what other people *love* (symbolized by the neighbor's "wife"), *think* (symbolized by the neighbor's "manservant"), *feel* (symbolized by the neighbor's "maidservant") and *do* (symbolized by the neighbor's "ox and donkey").

It is for this reason that the commandment against coveting is sometimes regarded as two commandments: one forbidding the excessive love of material possessions, and the other forbidding the excessive desire to control people. We have already considered the type of coveting that manifests itself as a craving to possess material objects (sneakers, trophies, money, academic achievement, etc.). We have also discussed the anxious desire to know the future as a form of covetousness, for this is the desire to have circumstances turn out in your favor.

However, as you go deeper into this commandment, you may discover that coveting also manifests itself as a desire to control others. This includes the desire to control what they love, think, feel and do. The first example comes from the journal of a student who realizes that her tendency to control others arises from her "me-shaped" view of the world:

> 66 I am very much a control freak. The truth is, I have been so since I was little. I feel an intense desire to control my environment so that everything goes the way I want, in line with my expectations and my plans. I never thought of it before, but it can be selfish to want to have things go exactly the way I want them to, and especially to want other people to believe and act exactly as I want them to.
>
> I run my own life rigidly: I always go to bed and get up at the same time; I eat the same thing for breakfast every day; I have routines for everything. When things mess up my routine, I feel anxious and scared. Because of my rigid self-control, I tend to make other people do things my way, partly because I think it's a good way, and partly just so they won't get in my way.
>
> I have never thought of myself as selfish before, but I'm beginning to realize how much I am. I tend to think of people mostly in relation to myself. How they talk to **me**. How **I** talk to them. What they do for **me**. What **I** do for them. I see the world through a "me-shaped lens" that tends to put my thoughts and my feelings at the center of everything. Often, I don't consider other people's emotions because they pale in comparison to how I see my own emotions.
>
> To stem the tide of this self-centered, me-centered approach to life, I spent the week trying to empathize with others rather than avoid them or control them. Doing this really opened my eyes to the fact that everyone is the hero of their own story. We all have our struggles, our stresses, our difficult relationships, our temptations, the list goes on.
>
> And here is the wonderful surprise: When I truly empathize with others, I feel less inclined to control them. In seeing people more deeply and more fully for the wonderful creations they are, I no longer want to change their thoughts, feelings or actions, because God did such a great job already!
>
> The Talmud says, "We do not see the world as it is; we see it as we are." I will always have my own perspective, because that's who I am. But if I widen my focus a little, I can truly stand in awe of all the amazing things other people do. I can be astounded by the greatness of God's handiwork. 99

253

A key line in the above journal entry is "when I truly empathize with others, I have less desire to control them." A beautiful insight. If you look at it the other way around, self-absorption prevents you from empathizing with others. Instead you wind up trying to control others in a myriad of ways. For example, in the following journal entry, after a local weather station announced a hurricane warning, a student talks about the various ways she tried to control her boyfriend:

66 I have been wanting to have an uninterrupted conversation with my boyfriend about the physical aspects of our relationship. My goal was to have this conversation before our next *Rise Above It* class. On Monday morning, before the hurricane really started blowing, my boyfriend and I went out to breakfast together. I considered talking to him about it then, but I didn't want to have such a personal and private conversation in a room full of people who could easily overhear us. So I decided to wait.

After breakfast they were invited to a friend's house, a situation that was not conducive to having that longed-for conversation. While they were there, the hurricane winds picked up, and the writer of this journal entry got a call from her mother telling her that it was not safe to be out in the storm, and that she should come home. She agreed. She also invited her boyfriend to come along, but he declined her offer, preferring to go back to his dorm. This was not what she wanted. As she continues her journal, she writes:

I was very upset that my boyfriend did not want to come to my house. I thought it would be the perfect opportunity to have the conversation I've been wanting to have with him. We would have quite a few hours while the storm raged outside. So I was annoyed when he said that he would not come to my house. I complained and did everything I could to get him to change his mind. I tried to make him feel sorry for me. I tried to make him feel guilty. I sulked. And later, after he still refused to come over, I grumpily texted him. By that time, I had gotten really angry.

Notice the various "control techniques" she employs: complaining, sulking, evoking pity, guilt-tripping, getting grumpy, and when all else fails, getting angry. She then has a "rise above it" moment of self-realization:

After the hurricane, I went for a walk with my brother and dad in the woods near our home. I realized that the storm that had been raging in me was no different than that hurricane. But the "raging winds" inside of me had died down. I was feeling better. I began to realize that I had been coveting my boyfriend's time and trying to control him. I know he has a ton of responsibilities, but I was only thinking about me. I sent him another text, this time apologizing for being so unpleasant and controlling. Even though we have not yet had the conversation about the physical aspects of our relationship, I am no longer anxious about it. I feel comfortable that when we do talk about it, it will be the perfect time—a time when no storms are raging. 99

In the next journal entry, a young man who is thinking about becoming a minister comes face to face with the covetous desire to control others. He begins his journal entry by describing a disagreement he was having with his girlfriend:

66 Recently, my girlfriend and I have been going through a rough patch, trying to figure out what our future looks like. We want to stay together, but she wants to move back to England after graduation, and I want to stay in

America to start studying for the ministry. She has told me that she hates the idea of being a "minister's wife," and that this would be a real problem for her if we were to get to that stage in our relationship.

When this came up, my automatic reaction was to get offended. I tried to tell her how wrong her attitude was, how she shouldn't be thinking that way, blah, blah, blah. Basically, I was controlling her, telling her what she should think and what she should feel. I told her that she should care more about our relationship than what occupation I might end up in.

Although it all sounded good at the time, I can see how controlling I was being. I totally disregarded her hopes and dreams, focusing only on what I wanted. I was caring about me and my wants, not her and her life. I was focusing on our relationship, to be sure, but only focusing on my side of it. It was about my needs, not hers. That's not a relationship.

To sum up: I can see that I've been selfish, disrespectful, inconsiderate, and above all, controlling. The end of the Lord's Prayer reminds me to avoid all attempts to control others. For Thine is the kingdom, Thine is the power, and Thine is the glory, forever. In other words, God is in control—not me. 99

"Sharing"—the antidote to coveting

During our last few weeks together, and especially while we are studying this final commandment, you are invited to reflect on your spiritual development during the course. The idea is to encourage you to look at the "Big Picture," reflecting on your spiritual development in terms of both understanding and practice.

In the following end-of-course self-assessment, a student reflects on his state of mind at the beginning of the course, and some of the changes he noticed along the way:

66 When I first started this class, I was very skeptical about whether it would do me any good on a personal or spiritual level. I had many doubts about my ability and willingness to work on myself spiritually. One of the reasons for this was that I had reached a point in my life where I had become very cynical about life. I was one of those "Who cares? Nothing matters anyway" kind of people. I didn't think much about spiritual matters, and my religious practice had become more about going through the motions than heartfelt devotion.

Because of this, it was hard to seriously consider using the Ten Commandments as a method of introspection. I just wasn't up for the challenge, and I wasn't interested in confronting my "inner demons." I thought it was going to be a waste of time, and that I would have to bluff my way through.

Interestingly, something happened that brought about an attitude shift for this student. It wasn't anything he read in the text or anything his instructors said in class. Rather, it was something he observed among his classmates. As he continues his self-assessment, he writes:

> Even so, one of the things that helped me develop a willingness to accept the challenge was hearing the other students share their experiences in the course. To my surprise, other students were struggling with the same things I was afraid to confront. I could also see that by admitting their flaws, they were making progress. I guess "coveting" (in a *good* sense) kicked in. I, too, wanted to make progress.

He knew this would mean not only taking spiritual work seriously, but also being willing to participate in class discussions—something he ordinarily tried to avoid. He writes:

> I usually detest any kind of group work in classes. I much prefer sticking to myself. But I soon learned the value of hearing other people's stories, ideas, and concerns on a personal level. The encouragement I gained from merely hearing somebody relate to my story (or my relating to theirs) and realizing that I am not the only one dealing with certain uncomfortable issues in my life, was invaluable. As I talked about these issues directly, and heard the insights of my fellow students, I was able to come to my own conclusions as to what my position should be on specific issues.

He ends with a tribute to his classmates:

> The readings, the exercises, the class discussions, and especially the insights of my classmates have strengthened my faith in what I always knew was true. 🙢

Henry David Thoreau once said, "There are a thousand hacking at the branches of evil to one who is striking at the root."[12] Over and over, the students who have preceded you have testified that the assigned readings, the journal reflections, the group work, and the journal entries from both current and previous students, have helped them to "strike at the root" of their issues. In the following end-of-course self-assessment, a student reflects on how important it was for him not only to hear from his classmates each week, but also to read about the experiences of students who had taken the course before him. It helped him "get to the root" of his problems:

> 🙢 The insightful journal entries that we got to read from past students were very useful. It is enlightening to know that I'm not alone in my struggles and that sometimes people are having a harder time than I am. Some of the entries really struck me in ways that couldn't happen in a typical textbook. Being able to do the weekly journal work, and share it with classmates, was also very beneficial. It helped me get to the root of my problems, because now (maybe

---

12 Henry David Thoreau, *Walden, or Life in the Woods* (Boston: Houghton Mifflin, 1854), Volume 1, 120.

for the first time) I was looking at them in the light of the commandments. That alone is an invaluable skill—one that I hope to continue using for the rest of my life. 🙶

Another student linked his self-assessment to the commandment against coveting:

🙶 As the weeks went by, I found myself continually coming out of selfish states of mind and into more loving ones. Then came the final week—the week when we learned about coveting. This was the climactic ending of the course for me. I suddenly realized how selfish and covetous it is to know all these wonderful things but not share them with others. This may have been what Jesus meant when he said, "Take heed and beware of covetousness, for a person's life does not consist in the abundance of possessions." (Luke 12:15)

It struck me that my "abundance of possessions" is everything I've learned in this course, but that just knowing about the commandments is not enough. It's important to share with others the insights I've gained and the happiness I've discovered. This brings to mind my favorite quote, which I will use as the ending for my self-assessment. It comes from the movie, *Into the Wild*, and it sums up what I feel will be my greatest takeaway from this course: "Happiness is only real when shared." 🙶

257

The mark to aim at

You shall not covet

There are two parts to this commandment. In the first part, the mark to aim at is to *distinguish between healthy desires and covetous cravings*. This includes both the covetous desire to possess *things* as well as the covetous desire to have *circumstances* turn out the way you want. As you do so, distinguish between the healthy desires of your Higher Nature and the unhealthy cravings of your lower nature. In the second part of this commandment, the mark to aim at is to notice covetous desires to control what *people* love, think, and do. A sign that a healthy desire has crossed the line into an intense craving is the tendency to become upset, angry, depressed, or miserable if your desires are frustrated or thwarted in some way. Learn to distinguish between things that really matter and things you can hold lightly. Even if it's something that "really matters," learn to accept all circumstances graciously, knowing that the refinement of your soul is more important than the achievement of your dreams. Remember: covetous desire is the root of everything else, so *strike the root*! In your journal, record your experience of practicing this commandment.

Suggestions for further reflection and practice

You shall not covet.

The following exercises contain additional information about this commandment. Read through all of them, and then focus on one or two that spark your interest.

1 Journal reflection: my heart was set on …

Think of a time in your life when your heart was set on something. You were desperate to attain it—jubilant if you did, deeply disappointed if you didn't. Maybe it was about getting a new bike, or trying out for a team, or getting a part in a play, or wanting someone to love you. Whatever it was, think about it again in the light of this commandment. To what extent was it an excessive longing of your lower nature (the "old you"), and to what extent was it a healthy desire of your Higher Nature (the "new you")? If you didn't obtain the object of your desire, what was your reaction?

259

2 Journal reflection: where is your treasure?

The following quotations talk about the treasures we set our heart on, treasures we intensely desire. The first quotation is from Jesus:

> *Do not lay up for yourselves treasures on earth, where moth and rust destroy, and where thieves break in and steal; but lay up for yourselves treasures in heaven, where neither moth nor rust destroys, and where thieves do not break in and steal. For where your treasure is, there your heart will be also.* (Matthew 6:19-21)

The second is from the Buddha:

> *The wise person acts righteously, creating for oneself a treasure that no one can steal, and that cannot rust away.* (Khuddakapatha 8:9)

In the context of the commandment against coveting, think about a "treasure" that you might be setting your heart on—in other words, something you might be passionate about. To what extent is it either a heavenly desire (arising from your Higher Nature) or a hellish craving (arising from your lower nature)? To what extent is it a treasure that cannot rust or be stolen?

3 Activity: rise above jealousy

It can be hard to accept your circumstances, especially when other people seem to be getting a better deal than you. You may need to earn money to finance your education, while other students might be fully supported. You may not have a boyfriend or girlfriend, while other students seem to be in wonderful relationships. You may not have exceptional athletic, academic, or artistic abilities, while other students seem to excel in one or more of these areas. Whatever the case might be for you, notice feelings of envy or jealousy creeping in, and rise above them. Shift your focus from what you don't have to what you do have.

4 Activity: enjoy the moment

We "covet" when we can't let go of the past, and when we cling to expectations about the future. Holding on to the past and speculating about the future takes away the opportunity to enjoy the present moment. While eating dinner in the cafeteria, talking to a friend, walking across campus, or just sitting in class, remain fully present. Observe your surroundings, enjoy your conversations, empathize with others, and allow yourself to listen and learn without being distracted by random thoughts. If your mind wanders into the past or begins to anticipate the future, gently bring it back to the present moment. When you're eating, eat; when you're studying, study; when you're working, work; and when you're having fun, have fun! Enjoy the present moment without covetously clinging to the past or anxiously anticipating the future.

5 Activity: let go of the old story; embrace the new

This activity is similar to prompt #4 but goes a little deeper. When you covet, you hold on tightly and have difficulty letting go. For example, you may tend to hold on to "old stories" you've been telling yourself. In this chapter, a hockey player who was on academic probation was holding on to an old story about his situation—that he had poor grades because he took hard courses. He then decided to tell himself a "new story." In the new story, he would buckle down, study hard, get good grades, and get back on the ice again. He compared the new story to the Zamboni coming out to clear the ice. The chipped and broken ice would be made smooth again, and there would be a brand new beginning. This image motivated him to let go of the old story so that he could embrace a new one. Try it for yourself. Practice *letting go* of an old story. Tell yourself a new story, sing a new song, and notice how letting go of stories that do not serve you well opens the way to better stories and greater joy in your life.

6 Activity: let go, and let God

In the Christian scriptures, Jesus concludes his model prayer with the words, "For Thine is the kingdom and the power and the glory, forever" (Matthew 6:13). Try using this as a meditation. As you do so, let go of every anxious desire to possess things, or control people, or have circumstances turn out the way you want. If you believe in God, let this be an opportunity to fully trust that there is a divine power in the universe that can bring good out of everything. If you don't believe in God, this is a good chance to practice the willing suspension of disbelief. Try believing that there is a power in the universe who has everything under control, even if it doesn't look that way. As they say, "Let go and let God."[13]

7 Activity: practice the art of allowing

"You are the author of your own life, and the hero of your own journey," said a previous course participant. "No one else can write the script for you." In the spirit of this journal entry, allow others to be the heroes of their own journey. While it's wonderful to encourage, and offer support, there is a vast difference between offering help and desiring to control another person's life. People need the opportunity to make their own choices, face their own consequences, learn their own lessons, and be the hero of their own journey. We call this "the art of allowing." This week practice the art of allowing. Lend a hand if necessary, offer your perspective if you think it might be helpful, but let go of any covetous desire to control what others feel, believe, or do. Let others write their own script and be the hero of their own journey.

8 Meditation: learn to say "I have enough"

Sacred scripture promises that everything we need for true happiness is already within—or immediately available. But this cannot be experienced until we rise above covetous desire. In the light of this promise, select one the following teachings as a meditation as you stay focused on the idea that everything you need for true happiness is available to you right now, in this present moment:

Judaism: "The Lord is my shepherd, I shall not want." (Psalm 23:1)

Christianity: "The kingdom of God is within you." (Luke 17:21)

Islam: "Those who put their trust in Allah have enough." (Qur'an 65:3)

Hinduism: "The Lord dwells in the hearts of all creatures." (Bhagavad Gita 18:61)

Buddhism: "Abiding joy will be yours when all selfish desire ends." (Dhammapada 20:16)

You can also use the words "I have enough" or "Peace comes from within" as a mantra. Keep in mind, throughout your meditation, that every spiritual blessing you could ever want or desire—happiness, joy, peace—is immediately available to you. The Buddha puts it beautifully when he says, "Wisdom has stilled their minds; their thoughts, words, and deeds are filled with peace" (Dhammapada 7:7).

---

13 Joyce Meyer titles one of her books, *Good Morning, This is God! I Will Be Handling All Your Problems Today. I Will Not Need Your Help -- So Have a Good Day. I Love You!* (New York: Time Warner, 1981) Front cover.

9 **Activity:** picture this

In the Hebrew scriptures, David writes, "In a time of trouble, the Lord shall set me high upon a rock" (Psalm 27:4-5). The following exercise is designed to help you get to that high rock so that you might gain a more comprehensive view of a situation that has been disturbing you. It may help you "rise above" covetous desire. The exercise works best if someone asks you the questions and guides you though the visualizations. However, you can also do the exercise on your own.

9.1 What happened?

Begin by talking about (or writing about) a disturbing situation that still bothers you (even if occasionally)—either a recent one, or a past event. If it still bothers you (even a little) when you bring it to mind, it is not over yet. In other words, you have not yet completely "risen above it."

Briefly describe the disturbing situation. What was said? What was done? Just the facts.

9.2 What were your thoughts and feelings?

Briefly describe your thoughts and feelings about the situation. Which thoughts were dominant? Which feelings were strongest?

9.3 In what way did a normal healthy desire turn into a covetous one?

Look again at the thoughts and feelings that arose, seeing them not as *your* thoughts and feelings but rather as thoughts and feelings generated by covetous desires. Identify specific areas in which a normal, healthy desire—*when threatened, injured, disturbed, or thwarted*—turned into a covetous one. These areas might include any of the following:

Desires related to self-esteem
(a desire to be respected; a desire to belong)

While these are normal, healthy desires, they can become covetous ones when threatened or thwarted in some way. The truth is, your self-esteem should not depend on whether or not others respect you or include you. That's up to them. Brooding about it does no good; nor does desperately wanting it to be different. That's when a healthy social instinct becomes an unhealthy covetous desire. If not satisfied, the covetous desire can generate feelings of being insulted, snubbed, ignored, left out, discounted and overlooked. These feelings, in turn, can generate self-deprecating thoughts such as, "I'm a loser," "I'm socially inept," and "Nobody likes me." These negative feelings and destructive thoughts are often supported by the illusory belief, *"In order to be happy, I must be respected and included."*

Desires related to ambition
(a desire to accomplish things; a desire to achieve)

A sweet, gentle bride wants to have a beautiful wedding (a good desire). But when she finds out that the bridesmaid dresses are the wrong color, and someone forgot to order the cake, she turns into Bridezilla. You have a big test tomorrow and want to do well (a good desire). But when your roommate keeps playing those annoying video games, you get irritated. Good desires in this area can turn into covetous ones that generate response symptoms such as irritation, annoyance, frustration, exasperation, resentment, and anger. These feelings, in turn, can generate thoughts such as: "I can never get anything done around here," and "I can't stand all these interruptions." Thwarted ambition, and the accompanying feelings of frustration, are often supported by the illusory belief, "*In order to be happy, I need to accomplish my goals.*"

Desires related to sharing one's viewpoint
(a desire to make one's own ideas known)

The desire to share your opinion or viewpoint is commendable, especially when it could benefit someone else. But when this desire becomes covetous, trouble arises. When this happens, there is little tolerance for disagreement, a fierce need to be right, and either anger or hurt feelings when one's viewpoint is not accepted. When covetous desires arise in this area, they can manifest as disapproval, condescension, and contempt, giving rise to thoughts such as: "My way is much easier," "Those idiots are too stupid to understand what I am trying to say," and "If they weren't so selfish and pig-headed, they would see it my way." On the other hand, the covetous desire to have your viewpoint accepted could also lead to feeling slighted and rejected, followed by false thoughts such as, "My opinion doesn't matter anyway" and "Nobody cares about what I say." These arrogant or self-denigrating thoughts and feelings are often supported by the illusory belief, "*In order to be happy, I need people to feel, think, and behave in certain ways.*"

263

9.4 What role, if any, did you play in the disturbing situation?

This is where you get to say, "Even though I blamed external circumstances for my upset, I acknowledge that *I chose to get upset.* I am responsible for my upset state. No one else is to blame." Some questions to ask yourself in this area include, "What, if anything, did I do or say to bring this about?" "What covetous desires arose in me, and how did I feed them?" "Did these covetous desires lead me to say or do anything that may have led to others being resentful or upset with me?" "Did these covetous desires produce ill-will towards the person or circumstance?" "Are these covetous desires still responsible for any lingering resentments that I might be holding onto?" If you can admit that you *chose* to get upset, you are ready for the next step.

9.5 Are you ready to acknowledge your need for God (or a Higher Power)?

If you said "Yes" to this last question (that you *chose* to get upset), it means that you are no longer satisfied with temporary fixes, momentary distractions, and superficial cures; you want a remedy that is deep, thorough and permanent. Here is a visualization that may help get you there. It works best if someone reads it to you while you keep your eyes closed:

Imagine that you are gradually being lifted up, higher and higher. (Pause.) Now think back to some of the many truths and insights that have come to you along the way in this course. Or maybe it's a truth that you have always believed. For example, it could be about God's love and care for you, or about your sacred significance as an individual, or about the joy available to you when you let go of anxious desires. Whatever that truth may be, imagine that this truth is lifting you higher and higher. (Pause.)

Next, realize that God works through truth. God pours love, peace, joy, and strength into you through truth. Allow the truth you have chosen to be a vessel for the gifts God wants to pour into you. As you reflect on the truth or insight of your choice, allow this higher wisdom to still your mind. Take a moment to feel this happening. Keep repeating your truth as a mantra while you visualize the qualities associated with your mantra gently flowing in and filling you. (Pause.)

Notice how these qualities lift you higher and higher. (Pause.)

With your eyes still closed, imagine that you have been lifted to a very high, comfortable place, perhaps high up on a beautiful mountain, with a wonderful view. Picture yourself standing or sitting there. (Pause)

As you look around, enjoying the view, you can hear birds and you can smell flowers. It is a lovely day and you are perfectly safe. Down below, in the valley, you see a village with streets and homes and people about the business of their daily lives. Listen for any sounds you might hear, perhaps a church bell ringing in the distance. (Pause)

Now imagine that a part of you is down there as well, but the person "down below" is not the "Real You." The "Real You" is up here on the mountain. This is the "Higher You," the one that is seldom upset, loves life, and loves people. The "lower you" is down there in the valley. Looking more closely, you notice that this "lower you" is concerned and upset about something, perhaps a current disturbance. Go ahead and bring that disturbance to mind now, but view it from above. (Pause.)

From your higher vantage point, seeing the bigger picture, and filled with the qualities associated with your mantra, reflect on what happened. Notice any new insights that might be arising in this state of higher consciousness. (Pause.)

Choose the highest thoughts that arise (or flow in) and dwell on them. (Pause.)

Notice if this helps you to see and feel differently about the situation. (Pause.)

When you feel ready, gently open your eyes, and then, if you are willing, share your experience.

9.6 Take action!

This course has invited you to lift your mind and your whole being toward the mountaintop state. It has invited you to see the big picture. In this "rise above it" state, far above covetous desire, you are free to be the person God intended you to be.

You can now go back down the mountain and enter the village. As you do so, remember how you felt on the mountaintop and what you learned in this course. Then bring those mountaintop thoughts and feelings into your life as you love and serve others. That person down in the valley is no longer your lower self. That person is now who you truly are, the person God intended you to be. It's the Real You. Congratulations!

One thing have I desired of the Lord, that will I seek:

that I may dwell in the house of the Lord …

for in the time of trouble, he shall set me high upon a rock."

Psalm 27:4

265

*To me a summit is a symbol
that with the force of our
minds and our bodies and
our souls, and with the power
of these two small hands, we
can transform our lives into
something miraculous.*

Erik Weihenmayer
The first blind person to reach
the summit of Mt Everest.

Epilogue

I will pour out my Spirit on all people.
Your sons and daughters will prophesy.
Your old men will dream dreams.
Your young men will see visions.

Joel 2:28

A vision from above

As we concluded the previous chapter, we suggested a final exercise in which you imagined yourself on a mountaintop, looking down upon the scene below. As you looked down, you saw yourself struggling with some issue in your life. From that higher perspective you were able to see "the bigger picture", the picture which includes not only your worldly aspirations, but also your vision of the kind of person you hope to be. Then we asked you to go back down the mountain, with your "vision from above" in mind, and live your life according to this higher vision.

The value of having a clear vision for our lives was brought home to us when we attended a lecture given by a 39-year-old mountain climber named Erik Weihenmayer. He spoke about what it takes to climb Mt. Everest, the tallest mountain peak in the world. For him, it began with a simple vision: he saw himself climbing the mountain and reaching its summit. Friends and acquaintances told him that he could never do it.

What made this presentation remarkable is that Erik Weihenmayer is blind. When people told him that he would not be able to summit Mt. Everest, he refused to listen. He believed that with a clear vision in mind, with careful planning, with faith, and with the right team of people to assist him, he could do it. During the lecture, he admitted that an attempt to climb Mt. Everest would be very difficult, especially for a blind person. It would be a condition of extreme adversity. But he raised an important question for the audience to consider. He asked us, "Will adversity crush you, or will it be the source of your flourishing?"

For Erik Weihenmayer, the vision of himself climbing Mt. Everest was an exciting and empowering one. It would help him to turn a tragedy, the loss of his sight when he was thirteen, into a triumph. And he would do it not only for himself but also as an inspiration for others. He said, "I wanted to square off with adversity. I wanted to walk into the very midst of it. I wanted to show that we could use adversity to compel us forward."

After he had lost his sight, Erik Weihenmayer could have chosen to give up on life, see himself as a victim, and find little incentive to go on. Instead he decided to rise above his setback and find new ways to contribute to the world around him. Speaking directly to the audience, he said, "This is not the time to be swept to the sidelines. Pick a dream and then use your strengths to achieve it." He said that we should not allow ourselves to be limited by the low expectations of others, or by the people who say it can't be done. If we do, those low expectations become the boundaries that we set for ourselves. Instead, we should "rise to the level of our own potential." And he added, "I figured that if my potential fell short of the summit, then so be it. That's a far more honest path than being talked out of something before I started."[1]

Although Erik had a vision of conquering Everest, he also knew that he wouldn't be able to do it by himself. So he assembled a team of people who shared his vision, a team of people who believed he could do it. "Having a vision is stronger than a goal," he said. "The vision comes first. It's like having a compass that guides you through the bright times, but also through the dark times. Next comes the gathering of a supportive team. Then you develop a plan for accomplishing your goal."[2]

That's exactly what Erik and his team did. They generated a detailed plan that was carefully thought out. It included things like attaching bells to the garment of the teammate who preceded Erik so that he could climb in the direction of the sounds. But Erik would need more than signals from his ears to guide him over the treacherous, icy terrain. He would also need to rely on signals from his hands and feet. And, throughout the ascent, Erik would have to place complete trust in his teammates.

On May 25, 2001, after an arduous, two-and-a-half-month climb, Erik Weihenmayer and his nineteen-person team made it to the top of Mt. Everest. It was 10:00 AM in Nepal. As he reached the summit of Mt. Everest, Erik was thinking, *I can't believe I'm here*. He was remembering that when he first went blind, he had a hard time even finding his way to the bathroom. Now, twenty years later, he had found his way to the top of the world's tallest mountain. In an interview with Jay Leno,

---

1   In an interview with Oprah Winfrey, at minute marker 8:12, Erik Weihenmayer says, "Being a blind climber is like being a Jamaican bobsledder. The words don't connect right away in people's minds." "Erik Weihenmayer on Oprah," accessed on November 22, 2017 @ www.youtube.com/watch?v=GKIGXHzbyPY

2   This information is from the notes we took at the Erik Weihenmayer lecture given at the Mitchell Performing Arts Center, Bryn Athyn, Pennsylvania, November 2, 2007.

when he was asked how it felt to summit Everest, Erik said, quite modestly, "It felt like I'd come a long way."[3]

Erik Weihenmayer had indeed come a long way. He had become the first blind mountain climber in history to make it to the top of Mt. Everest. Eventually he summitted the seven highest mountain peaks in the world. He had risen above a seemingly insurmountable physical challenge. More importantly, his inner vision, determination and faith made it possible to rise above a mental and spiritual challenge as well. Here's how he put it:

> A lot of people say they summit mountains for the beautiful view. … But I think a summit isn't even a place. To me a summit is a symbol that with the force of our minds and our bodies and our souls, and with the power of these two small hands, we can transform our lives into something miraculous. And when we join our hands to those around us, we can do even better than transforming our own lives. We can transform the very face of the earth.[4]

• • •

What's your "Mt. Everest"?

As you conclude this course, we invite you to reflect on one "Mt. Everest" in your own life, some personal challenge that you would like to surmount. Perhaps it's forgiving someone who has wronged you, or apologizing to someone you've hurt, or being more patient with those around you, or having greater trust in God, or rising above the urge to procrastinate, the desire to criticize, or the tendency to blame. Maybe it's simply a resolve to come from love, no matter what happens.

Choose your own Mt. Everest.

Whatever your personal Mt. Everest may be, envision yourself reaching the summit of that mountain. As Erik Weihenmayer puts it, "I have to envision myself standing on the summit, or I'm not going to make it."[5] Then, with the help of God, the help of your friends, and a whole lot of effort on your part, you can turn that vision into a reality. After all, God says, "I will pour out my Spirit on all people" (Joel 2:28; Acts 2:17).

In other words, you can do it. **You can rise above it!**

---

3   This information is from the YouTube video, "Erik Weihenmeyer and Jay Leno." See minute marker 6:46-7:41. Accessed February 18, 2018 @ www.youtube.com/watch?v=16Xy6Qh3mCA

4   This information is from the YouTube video "Erik Weihenmayer." Accessed on November 22, 2017 @ www.youtube.com/watch?v=QrSLb7hWSMc&feature=youtu.be

5   "Erik Weihenmayer and Oprah." This is at the minute marker 7:44. Accessed on November 22, 2017 @ www.youtube.com/watch?v=GKlGXHzbyPY

Appendix

How to write journal entries, weekly reports, and the end-of-course self-assessment

1 Journal entries

College is a time for learning how to think deeply and express yourself clearly, in both written and oral form. In this course you will create journal entries and written reports that demonstrate your ability to observe yourself, especially your inner world of thought and feeling, in the light of universal truth.

A well-written journal entry is usually about 200 words long, just enough to record a course-related experience you've had, and what you learned from it. Two or three well-written journal entries per week are required. A journal entry is not a sound bite, or a text message, or a tweet. It's a thoughtful spiritual reflection. It also includes the date, time, and place of the experience, as well as the commandment that you're using for self-examination and reflection. Here are two examples:

Wednesday, September 7, 2016, 10:30 AM.

Just before Wednesday chapel.

You shall not take the Lord's name in vain.

I was early to chapel, and was sitting in a chair, just listening to the music, when I decided to pray. I was sitting alone, so I bowed my head and prayed. I prayed to God for help with my shortcomings, to give me Strength and Patience (two of the Lord's "names") in trying encounters, and I thanked him for all the blessings in my life. As soon as I was done, I looked up, and who was coming to sit by me, but the last person I wanted to sit near me. This is a guy with whom I have "a history," and he always makes me feel uncomfortable. As he sat down near me, I felt myself shutting down (taking the Lord's name in vain). But then something strange happened. I smiled, a genuine smile, acknowledging the coincidence of the situation. I had just asked the Lord for Strength and Patience, and here I was with an opportunity to use these gifts. I did. As I recognized my demons (false gods, negative attitudes) they went away. (180 words)

Saturday, April 16, 2016, 7:30 AM.

Riding my bike to the Farmers' Market to help out.

Remember the Sabbath day to keep it holy.

Random thoughts were flowing through my mind as I pedaled along. "My boss from my summer job still hasn't paid me what he owes me." "My senior paper is due pretty soon and I have hardly gotten started." "Blah, blah, blah." As the gears in my head buzzed along with the gears of my bike, I took a moment to look outside of my own head. Just then, almost like an answer to an unspoken prayer, the sun peaked above the tree line, illuminating a field of ferns sparkling in the morning sunlight. I was humbled by this sudden, subtle, beauty, and remembered the words, "Behold, I stand at the door and knock. If anyone hears my voice, and opens the door, I will come in." In that moment I realized that the Lord is always with me, always there offering me peace, quelling the storms of my spirit. It was a moment of Sabbath rest. (156 words)

2 Weekly reports

Once a week, one of your journal entries is expanded into a written report. These reports are usually two typewritten pages (400-600 words, double spaced, Times New Roman). They must be well-written and long enough to fully describe (1) the context of the situation (*who, what, when, and where*) (2) the thoughts and feelings you experienced, (3) any breakthroughs or realizations you had, and (4) what you learned about yourself.

Throughout the week, any number of situations may arise in which you will have an opportunity to apply that week's commandment to your life. The more personally aware you are, the more situations you will see. You can write about any of your experiences.

Please use editorial discretion.

In other words, you are free to edit your own work, choosing what you want to share within the learning community and what you want to keep private. Honor the distinction between what is "personal", talking about your inner world of thought and feeling (which is encouraged), and what is "private", disclosing information that you would rather keep to yourself. Your grade for each weekly report is based on your demonstration of *self-awareness*, your ability to examine yourself honestly in the light of universal spiritual principles, not on how much you are willing to disclose about your private life.

Weekly reports are evaluated based on the following criteria:

- Academic understanding: Understanding of spiritual principles, including the effective use of scripture in your report.

- Self-awareness: Ability to apply spiritual principles to life situations, including a recent experience of how you applied (or forgot to apply) the week's commandment to your life.

- Written form: Attention to grammar, spelling, sentence structure, paragraphing, organization, and style.

On the following pages you will find a rubric for weekly reports, followed by two examples of weekly reports written by students who took this course in previous years. The names of the students are fictitious, but the reports are real.

Rubric for weekly reports

Name: _____   Date due: _____

SECONDARY AREA OF ASSESSMENT (FORM)	Satisfactory	Improve
Font and line spacing: Use Times New Roman, 12-point font, double-spaced (except for heading, title, and epigraph, which are single-spaced).		
Heading: Begin with a single-spaced heading (name, course number, report number, date and time of submission, word count). See #1 on next page.		
Title and Epigraph (scriptural or doctrinal quote): Begin the report with a creative title in bold. Under the title, artistically center a single-spaced quote in italics. No quotation marks. Include the source. See #2 on next page.		
Grammar and style: Proof-read. Correct spelling errors, comma splices, run-ons and fragments. Write in an interesting style (paragraph effectively; use quotations for dialogue; and use italics to indicate internal thought). See #3 on next page.		
Length: Write at least 400 words and try to stay within the 600-word limit. Two-page limit—not three.		
Time of submission: Submit your report before 9:00 AM on Wednesday*.		

PRIMARY AREA OF ASSESSMENT (CONTENT)	Excellent	Satisfactory	Improve
Explain what aspect of the commandment you're focusing on: Summarize, in your own words, what this commandment is about, both at the literal and spiritual levels. Be sure to include quotations from scripture and doctrine in your report—especially the epigraph you used under the title. See #4			
Set the scene ("outer world"): Use specific details to describe the context of the situation, including any necessary background information to help us better imagine your situation. Carefully explain who, what, when and where. See #5.			
Observe your thoughts and feelings ("inner world"): Describe the thoughts and feelings that arose within you. The focus is on your inner world, and your inner response to a specific situation—not so much on the actions of others. See #6			
Describe your "moment of truth": Describe a recent incident where you experienced a "moment of truth" or an important realization about yourself. Be sure to relate it to the readings. In other words, what did you learn about yourself? See #7			

*10-point grade deduction for reports received after 9:00 AM on Wednesday
*20-point grade deduction for reports received after 9:00 AM on Thursday
*A grade of "0" is given for reports not received within seven days.

Adjusted Grade for Late Submission: _____   **GRADE:** _____

95-100 = far exceeds requirements (very rarely given)
90-95 = above requirements (occasionally given)
80-85 = meets requirements (most commonly given)
70-75 = minimal pass (occasionally given)
50-65 = shows little ability or effort (very rarely given)

Seven steps for writing a weekly report
···

Use Times New Roman; 12-point font; 400-600 words

1 **Begin with a single-spaced heading that contains key information.**
   Here is an example:

   > **Name**: John Smith
   > **Course**: Religion 272
   > **Report #1**: You shall have no other gods before me
   > **Submitted**: December 4, 2017 @ 12:30 PM
   > **Words**: 557

2 **Choose a creative title and place a scriptural or doctrinal epigraph under it.**

   Here's an example of a creative title and epigraph. Both are artistically centered:

   Pressing Pause

   *Let the wise person give up the lesser happiness,
   so that the greater happiness might be attained.*
   —Dhammapada 21:1

3 **Use appropriate grammar and write in an interesting style.**

   Proof-read. Correct spelling errors, comma splices, run-ons, and fragments. Use effective paragraphing. Use quotations for dialogue and *italics* to indicate internal thought. (See #6 below.)

4 **Explain what aspect of the commandment you're focusing on.**

   Include a summary, in your own words, of what this commandment is about, on both the literal and spiritual levels. This could include something from the introductory story, or the teachings from world religions, or a journal entry from one of the previous students. What sparked your interest? Be sure to include quotations from scripture and doctrine in the body of the report, especially the epigraph you used under the title.

5 **Set the scene (outer world).**

   What happened? Give us the context of the situation. Describe *who* (if anyone) was with you, *what* occurred, *when* it took place, and *where* it was happening. Supply background information that will help us better understand what was happening in your outer world.

6   **Describe the thoughts and feelings that you were experiencing (inner world).**

Use *italics* to describe your inner world of thought and feeling while the external things were happening. Focus on what was happening within you , not so much on the actions of others, or the immediate circumstance. For example, a student who was trying to overcome the false god of making hasty assumptions about others wrote, "I was sitting in church thinking, *Wow, he looks grumpy* and *Why would she wear an outfit like that to church?* Then the thought came, *You don't know the whole story* and *Don't bear false witness against your neighbor.*"

7   **Describe your "moment of truth"** (i.e. "takeaway," "epiphany," "turning point," "sudden awareness," "flash of self-realization").

How did living in the light of a commandment help you see yourself in a new way? *What did you learn about yourself?*

Name:	Mary Peterson
Course:	Religion 272
Report #1:	You shall have no other gods before me.
Submitted:	12/6/17 at 12:19 AM
Words:	631

Needing Netflix

I am the Lord your God
who brought you out of the land of Egypt,
out of the house of bondage.
—Exodus 20:2

In examining myself and the false gods in my life, I have discovered one of my leading false gods, Netflix. This false god rules over me mercilessly. Watching shows has become my way to de-stress, my way to procrastinate, and my way to have fun. I love stories, and always have, and watching television shows is the easiest and fastest way to see a story unfold. Netflix in and of itself is not a bad thing, but bowing down to it definitely is. Netflix seems to be a master in my life and I know that I need to turn to the Lord to help guide me out of this "house of bondage" (Exodus 20:2).

Just this past week I was particularly busy with important deadlines, but even so, I found this only slightly diminished my Netflix habit. While my busy schedule made it much more difficult for me to watch my shows, I heard myself thinking *I just want to watch a show.* I had tons to do, but my false god kept calling with the thought, *I just want to watch a show.*

Usually I manage my need to worship Netflix by multitasking, watching Netflix while doing other things. In fact, this has become so habitual that I automatically feel the need to watch something as soon as I pause for a snack or sit down for a meal. Eating has become a trigger to watch a show. I tell myself, *Oh, I have to make time to eat anyway, so I might as well watch something.*

Here's the worst part: I often even get irritated with my parents when we have family dinners together, because I would much rather eat in front of my computer screen watching something. My desire to watch television is so strong that I will watch shows that I really don't like, just because I feel the need to watch something.

Before taking this class, I had never seen loving Netflix as a problem. I never realized how all-consuming this false god has been in my life. For example, whenever I had a break from school, whether for a weekend or for a vacation, I would plant myself in front of the television and watch Netflix all break. I told myself, *I work so hard. I deserve this.* Even though my parents tried to guide me away from my false god by asking me to help around the house, or to sit down with them for a family dinner, I would usually ignore them, preferring to feed my need for Netflix.

Whenever my parents spoke unfavorably about my false god (my love) it irritated me. But this is all going to change. Just the other day I was set on going to my room and watching television, and even started heading there while my mom was talking to me. I paused to see what she had to say, and tried to see if I could hurry the conversation along so I could get to my show. It then became clear to me that my mom simply wanted to spend time with me and was feeling a little lonely that day. This realization made me remember what I had learned in class, and I saw how my false god not only takes me away from the people in my life that really matter, but also takes me away from the true God. I then spent the hour I had meant to spend on television talking with my mom and did not watch anything that evening. It felt like I had taken my first step "out of the house of bondage."

Name: Sam Harrison
Course: Religion 272
Report #1: You shall have no other gods before me.
Submitted: 9/2/16 at 9:30 AM
Words: 605

Asking for Help
This the Buddha knows ...
how consciousness arises and perishes.
—Majjhima Nikaya

Personally, I think people should be completely comfortable asking others for help. It's an essential part of being human. Everybody should be looking to help one another in the different aspects of their lives, whether it be mental, physical, or spiritual.

Even though I know this, it's often hard for me to ask for help. I find it relatively easy to offer others help, yet I will hesitate when asking for my own aid. It's not that I have a fear of asking for help in particular; instead, it is the fear that the person I ask for help will hold that favor over me as if they expect something in return, or maybe they will simply be annoyed with me. In any case, I don't like to look weak or needy.

Just this week I had a situation that took me several days to "rise above." It may seem very simple to other people, even petty, but for me it was a huge struggle. It's about asking for money. The whole process of enrolling and living at college has been a big financial strain on both me and my family. On top of that the time came to buy books and materials for class. It meant that I would have to send a message home asking for additional money. In my mind I'm thinking, *That's my mom, of course she will help me.* But it's not that easy when that thought is in a constant tug-of-war with the other side that is saying, *Why do I have to be such a pest, so needy, and what can I even give back to her?*

After this past Tuesday's class, I began to put labels on what exactly was making it so hard to ask for help. After a lot of self-examination (paying attention to the arising and perishing of thought), I've concluded that it is my ego, or "lower self," that is making asking seem difficult. Every day I went not asking my mom for help, I was simply giving in to that false god lurking in the back of my mind. My higher nature knew she wouldn't mind. But my lower nature kept holding me back. In the midst of my struggle, I saw "it" clearly. I said to myself, *There **it** is again, that thing that keeps me from asking for help.*

I finally rose above "**it**" (my lower self), swallowed my false pride (disguised as "not wanting to bother anyone") and gave my mom a call. The relief of finally overcoming this false god was great. I realized that "it" was all in my head. I had spent three days allowing "it" to stress me out when deep down I knew it would be fine. By carefully observing "how consciousness arises and perishes" as the Buddha teaches, I was able to identify and name my false god: *foolish pride arising from ego.* I realized that there is a big difference between being a pest and having the courage to ask for help.

Of course, there was no question about it. Mom gave me the money I needed and a little extra besides. How good it feels to "rise above it."

279

3 End-of-course self-assessment

The end-of-course self-assessment is a two-to-three-page report. It is similar to weekly reports in structure, except that it is 600-800 words in length. This is an opportunity to review your journal entries and weekly reports, reflecting on recurring themes and patterns to see what you have learned about yourself during the course, and how you have grown. Feel free to quote from your journal entries and reports. The end-of-course self-assessment should include the following:

3.1 A creative title with a scriptural or doctrinal epigraph under it

Let the title and epigraph carry the main point of your self-assessment. It should pique your reader's interest.

3.2 Appropriate grammar and interesting style

Proof-read your self-assessment. Correct spelling errors; avoid comma splices, run-ons and fragments; use effective paragraphing. Also, use quotation marks for dialogue, and use *italics* to indicate internal thought.

3.3 An introduction

Describe where you were, spiritually, at the start of the course, and introduce the reader to what is to come.

3.4 Turning points

Describe any new insights about yourself, especially the gradual (or sudden) development of awareness as you observed yourself in the light of higher truth. Include key moments when you became aware of a habit or pattern that was not serving you or was hurting others. Be sure to note and reflect on recurring themes and patterns in your journal entries and reports. You can quote from what you've already written. Or you can write about it anew from what is now a higher, more spiritually developed, end-of-course perspective.

3.5 A conclusion

Where are you now as compared to where you were at the beginning of the course? What are some of the messages from scripture that have spoken to you? What insights about yourself will you take with you into the future? How do you intend to keep developing spiritually beyond this course? If you wish, you can conclude with a final quotation that wraps up this learning experience for you and serves as a foundation for your future.

Acknowledgements

Special thanks to our friend and colleague, Mark "the Pen" Pendleton, who poured his heart and soul into helping us edit this book. No words can adequately express our appreciation for his tireless efforts, grammatical savvy, perceptive insights, and friendly "back and forth" in helping us bring this book to completion.

Bob Jungé, Marian Nelson, Greg Baker, Dale Morris, and Richard Morris provided much appreciated doctrinal, editorial, and technical help while we worked through the many drafts of the manuscript, as did Laura Shelley compiling the indices. George Dole provided an "insider's look" at the day Roger Bannister broke the four-minute mile. Ann Graber helped us to accurately tell the story of Viktor Frankl. Leon James helped us understand the connection between "associative memory" and emotional "triggers." And Peter Rhodes helped us understand the spiritual art of rising above ego concerns. In fact, it is largely because of Peter's influence that we chose to conclude each chapter with a specific "aim," which is the title of one of his books.

As we researched the teachings of the major world religions, the writings of Eknath Easwaran, Rick Hanson, and Paul Carus provided valuable insights into Eastern thought; the writings of Shaikh Muhammad Raheem Bawa Muhaiyaddeen illuminated the inner meaning of Islamic texts; and the writings of Emanuel Swedenborg revealed the deeper meaning of the commandments in both Judaism and Christianity.

Our teacher at the Hindu temple, Balaji Krishnapuram, helped us understand things in the *Bhagavad Gita* that would have otherwise been inaccessible to us. Beyond that, he introduced us to the enlightened teachings of his own teacher, Swami Paramathananda.

To all these people we say, "Thank you for your love, wisdom and continual encouragement. We deeply appreciate the part you have played in the creation of this book."

There are many others, too numerous to name, who have provided valuable help in bringing this book to completion. They too, whether here on earth or in heavenly realms, have inspired us with love and guided us with wisdom. To all of you, whether seen nor unseen, we say, "You have blessed us in countless ways. Thank you for being part of our 'community of saints.'"

Thanks, most of all, to the many students who have taken this course and contributed to this book. May your honest words serve to encourage all those who read them; may your courageous efforts to rise into the light of higher truth and the warmth of greater love inspire future generations of students; and may you continue to *rise above it* in all your endeavors.

With gratitude, *Ray and Star Silverman*

Selected bibliography

Books, Articles, and Addresses

Astin, Alexander, Helen Astin, and Jennifer Lindholm. *Cultivating the Spirit: How College Can Enhance Students' Inner Lives*. San Francisco: Jossey-Bass, 2011.

Bawa Muhaiyaddeen, M.R. *Islam and World Peace: Explanations of a Sufi*. Philadelphia: The Fellowship Press, 2004.

_____. *The 99 Beautiful Names of Allah*. Philadelphia: The Fellowship Press, 2004.

Carus, Paul. *Amitâbha: A Story of Buddhist Theology*. Chicago: Open Court Publishing, 1906.

de Saint-Exupery, Antoine. *The Little Prince*. Translated by Katherine Woods. New York: Harcourt, Brace & World, 1943.

Dostoyevsky, Fyodor. *Crime and Punishment*. Translated by David McDuff. New York: Penguin Books, 1991.

Easwaran, Eknath. *The Bhagavad Gita for Daily Living* (Volumes 1-3). Petaluma, California: Nilgiri Press, 1979.

_____. *The Constant Companion: Inspiration for Daily Living from the Thousand Names of the Lord*. Tomales, CA: Nilgiri Press, 2001.

Emerson, Ralph Waldo. "The American Scholar." In *Selections from Ralph Waldo* Emerson. edited by Stephen E. Whicher. Boston: Houghton Mifflin, 1957.

Frankl, Viktor. *Man's Search for Meaning*. New York: Washington Square Press, 1984.

_____. *Man's Search for Ultimate Meaning*. Cambridge, MA: Perseus Publishing, 2000.

Frye, Northrop. *The Educated Imagination*. Bloomington: Indiana University Press, 1964.

Further Dialogues of the Buddha. Translated by Lord Chalmers. London: Oxford University Press, 1927.

Hanson, Rick. *Buddha's Brain: The Practical Neuroscience of Happiness, Love and Wisdom*. Oakland CA: New Harbinger Publications, 2009.

Harpur, Tom. "Psychiatrist links violence to philosophy of 'naked ape.'" *The Toronto Star*. February 12, 1973.

Hedges, Chris. *Losing Moses on the Freeway: The 10 Commandments in America*. New York: Free Press, 2005.

Herold, Andre Ferdinand. *The Life of the Buddha*. New York: Scholar's Choice, 2015.

Klingberg, Haddon. *When Life Calls Out to Us: The Love and Lifework of Viktor and Elly Frankl*. New York: Doubleday, 2001.

Loftus, Elizabeth. *Witness for the Defense: The Accused, the Eyewitness, and the Expert Who Puts Memory on Trial*. New York: St. Martin's Press, 1991.

Mack, Maynard. "The World of Hamlet." *The Yale Review* 41 (1952): 523.

Mahathera, Narada. *The Buddha and His Teachings*. Mumbai: Jaico Publishing House, 2006.

283

Meyer, Joyce. *Good Morning, This is God! I Will Be Handling All Your Problems Today. I Will Not Need Your Help, So Have a Good Day. I Love You!* New York: Time Warner, 1981.

Nicoll, Maurice. *The Mark*. London: Watkins and Dulverton, 1981.

Palmer, Parker, and Arthur Zajonc. *The Heart of Higher Education: A Call to Renewal*. San Francisco: Jossey-Bass, 2010.

Pokorny, Julius. *Indogermanisches Etymologisches Woerterbuch*. Bern und Muenchen: Francke Verlag, 1959.

Robert Browning, "Andrea del Sarto," First published in 1855. In *Robert Browning: Selected Poems*, with an introduction and notes by Daniel Karlin. London: Penguin Books, 1989.

Sarvepalli Radhahakrishnan and Charles Moore, editors. *A Source Book in Indian Philosophy*. Princeton: Princeton University Press, 1957.

Shakespeare, William. *The Tragedy of Romeo and Juliet*. In *Shakespeare: The Complete Works*. Edited by G.B. Harrison. New York: Harcourt, Brace, and World, 1952.

Shaw, Charlotte F., editor. *The Wisdom of Bernard Shaw*. New York: Bretano's, 1913.

Silverman, Ray, and Star Silverman. *Rise Above It: Spiritual Development through the Ten Commandments*. Philadelphia: Touchstone Seminars, 2005.

Smith, Huston. *The World's Religions*. New York: HarperCollins, 1986.

Swedenborg, Emanuel. *Arcana Coelestia*. Originally published in Latin. 12 volumes. London 1749-1756. Translated by J.F. Potts. New York: Swedenborg Foundation, 1969.

Telushkin, Rabbi Joseph. "Words that Hurt, Words that Heal: How to Choose Words Wisely and Well." *Imprimis* (Hillsdale College, Hillsdale, Michigan) Vol. 24, no. 1 (January 1996): 1

The Dhammapada. Introduced and translated by Eknath Easwaran (Petaluma CA: Nilgiri Press, 2007),

The Holy Qur'an: Text, Translation and Commentary by 'Abdullah Yusuf 'Ali. Brentwood Maryland: Amana Corporation, 1989.

The Holy Bible: Containing the Old and New Testaments. Nashville: Thomas Nelson. 1982.

Thoreau, Henry David. *Walden, or Life in the Woods*. Boston: Houghton Mifflin, 1854.

Van Epp, John. *How to Avoid Falling in Love with a Jerk*. New York: McGraw Hill, 2007.

Weihenmayer, Erik. Lecture given at the Mitchell Performing Arts Center, Bryn Athyn, Pennsylvania, November 2, 2007.

Internet Sites and YouTube Videos

Bormann, Jill. "Mantram Repetition for Relaxation." Accessed on November 17, 2017 @ www.jillbormann.com/9.html

Chataway, Chris. "Obituary: Franz Stampfl." *The Independent* (April 5, 1995). Accessed on November 6, 2017 @ www.independent.co.uk/news/people/obituary-franz-stampfl-1614402.htmlhis

"City of the Ten Thousand Buddhas." Commentary on the Flower Adornment Sutra. Accessed on November 13, 2017 @ www.cttbusa.org/fas40/fas40_9.asp

"Class of 1987 Heralds New Era at Columbia." Columbia University Online Newsletter. Accessed on December 26, 2017 @ www.college.columbia.edu/about/coeducation/classof1987

Coelho, Mabio. "10 Commandments or Ten Promises." Department of Theology, Centro Universitário Adventista de São Paulo. Accessed on October 11, 2017 @ www.researchgate.net/publication/273130579_10_Commandments_or_10_Promises

Coffey, Wayne. "Bias Ten Years after His Death: His Mother Delivers a Message." *New York Daily News* (June 17, 1996). Accessed on November 25, 2017 @ www.nydailynews.com/archives/sports/bias-ten-years-len-death-mother-delivers-message-article-1.723715

Dorough, Bob. "Erik Weihenmayer on Oprah," (August 31, 2012). Accessed on November 22, 2017 @ www.youtube.com/watch?v=GKlGXHzbyPY

"Dr. Lonise Bias on the Rock Newman Show." Accessed on November 23, 2017 @ www.youtube.com/watch?v=Xje5arcsDvU

"Dr. Lonise Bias." Accessed on November 23, 2017 @ www.youtube.com/watch?v=MrjMXdLWdJ8&t=328s

Guy, Molly. "7 Tech Free Things to Do on the National Day of Unplugging" (March 7, 2017). Accessed October 6, 2017 @ www.vogue.com/article/national-day-unplugging-digital-detox-tips

Hammond, Claudia. "Is it bad to bottle up your anger?" (July 30, 2014). Accessed on July 9, 2017 @ www.bbc.com/future/story/20140729-is-it-bad-to-bottle-up-anger?ocid=ww.social.link.email

"Heavenly Doctrines.org." A search engine for accessing words and phrases in Emanuel Swedenborg's theological works. Accessed on November 23, 2017 @ www.heavenlydoctrines.org/dtSearch.html

The Holy Bhagavad Gita. Translation and commentary by Swami Mukundananda. Accessed on January 2, 2018 @ www.holy-bhagavad-gita.org/chapter/6/verse/19

IM The Online Guru. "Breaking a Belief System … First Four Minute Mile Roger Bannister 1954" (April 7, 2015). Accessed on October 11, 2017 @ www.youtube.com/watch?v=qAXL3waljqo.

"Islam Awakened." A website listing several generally accepted translations of the Qur'an. Accessed on November 13, 2017 @ www.islamawakened.com/quran/4/36/

"Jnana Yoga: Knowledge of the Ultimate Truth". Accessed on October 22, 2017 @ www.dubjockey.co.uk/bag2.html

Keller, Helen. Address to the American Association to Promote the Teaching of Speech to the Deaf (Mt. Airy, PA, July 8, 1896). Accessed on June 4, 2018 @ www.en.wikiquote.org/wiki/Helen_Keller

Kerr-Dineen, Luke. "This inspiring speech in *Cool Runnings* is one of the best sports movie moments ever." *USA Today* web article (August 25, 2016). Accessed on November 2, 2017 @ www.ftw.usatoday.com/2016/08/this-inspiring-speech-in-cool-runnings-is-one-of-the-best-sports-movie-moments-ever

King, Jr., Martin Luther. "What is Your Life's Blueprint?" A speech given on October 26, 1967. Accessed on July 9, 2017 @ www.old.seattletimes.com/special/mlk/king/words/blueprint.html

Larsson, Peter. "Track and Field All-Time Performances" (October 25, 2017). Accessed on November 7, 2017 @ www.alltime-athletics.com/m_mileok.htm

Leading Authorities. "Erik Weihenmayer." (June 2, 2008). Accessed on November 22, 2017 @ www.youtube.com/watch?v=QrSLb7hWSMc&feature=youtu.be

Lindsay Goobersoly, "The Top 50 Colleges with Stressed Out Student Bodies" (May 9, 2016). Accessed on October 22, 2017 @ www.universityprimetime.com/top-50-colleges-with-the-most-stressed-out-student-bodies/

Loftus, Elizabeth. "How reliable is your memory?" TED talk. Accessed on October 22, 2017 @ www.youtube.com/watch?v=PB2Oegl6wvI&t=223s

Majjhima-Nikaya, sermon 2, p.135. Accessed on June 18, 2017 @ www.sacred-texts.com/bud/bits/bits013.htm

"Marshmallow Experiment - Instant Gratification." (April 29, 2010). Accessed on October 13, 2017 @ www.youtube.com/watch?v=Yo4WF3cSd9Q

McCuan, Jess, and Carlos Folgar. "The Science Behind Internet Addiction." *Quid* (January 1, 2017). Accessed on July 10, 2017 @ www.quid.com/feed/the-latest-science-behind-internet-addiction

Nitkin, Alex. "*Cool Runnings has more positive messages than any sports movie you›ve ever seen.*" *North by Northwestern*, the daily newsmagazine of Northwestern University (February 23, 2014). Accessed on November 2, 2017 @ www.northbynorthwestern.com/story/emcool-runningsem-has-more-positive-messages-than-/

Online Etymology Dictionary. Accessed on November 27, 2017 @ www.etymonline.com/word/mantra

Potenza, Marc. "Expert Opinion: Internet Addiction." *Yale News* (November 2015). Accessed on July 10, 2017 @ www.news.yale.edu/videos/expert-opinion-internet-addiction

Rajneesh, Shree (Osho). "The Thief." Accessed on July 5, 2017 @ www.spiritual-short-stories.com/spiritual-short-story-77-the-thief/

Robinson, Roger. "Four Minute Everest: The Story and the Myth," *Runner's World* (May 1, 2004). Accessed on November 6, 2017 @ www.runnersworld.com/running-times-info/four-minute-everest-the-story-and-the-myth?amp

Rotten Tomatoes. "Cool Runnings 1993." Accessed on October 29, 2017 @ www.rottentomatoes.com/m/1046227_cool_runnings.

Ryan, Kate. "Len Bias' mom: 'Love is my motivation.'" Accessed on November 25, 2017 @ www.wtop.com/prince-georges-county/2016/10/len-bias-mom-love-motivation/amp/

"The Nineteenth Greater Sin: False Testimony." Accessed on July 11, 2017 @ www.al-islam.org/greater-sins-volume-2-ayatullah-sayyid-abdul-husayn-dastghaib-shirazi/nineteenth-greater-sin-false

"The Spiritual Significance of Jihad." Accessed on October 10, 2017 @ www.al-islam.org/al-serat/vol-9-no-1/spiritual-significance-jihad-seyyed-hossein-nasr/spiritual-significance-jihad.

Touch the top. "Jay Leno interviews Erik Weihenmayer." (June 7, 2012). Accessed on February 18, 2018 @ www.youtube.com/watch?v=16Xy6Qh3mCA

Wass, Mike. "Sheppard Talk Breakthrough Hit 'Geronimo,' Cracking America & Their Next Single." *Idolator* Interview (November 14, 2014). Accessed on November 12, 2017 @ www.idolator.com/7570487/sheppard-geronimo-cracking-america-next-single-interview

Weinreb, Michael. "The Day Innocence Died." Accessed on November 25, 2017 @ www.espn.com/espn/eticket/story?page=bias

Wood, Ryan. "Geronimo Allison living up to his name." *Packers News* (August 17, 2016). Accessed November 17, 2017 @ www.packersnews.com/story/sports/nfl/packers/2016/08/17/geronimo-allison-living-up-his-name/88890842/

Yecto. "Search for Meaning." (September 20, 2007). Accessed on November 11, 2017 @ www.youtube.com/watch?v=fD1512_XJEw

Index

K

N

O

P

Plagiarism as stealing, 186–88, 202
Pornography, addiction to, 157–58, 159–60
Possessions. *See* Material possessions and needs (materialism)
Possibility thinking, power of, 122
"Post-it" notes. *See* Sticky notes, use of
Potenza, Marc, 36n18
Praise, accepting, 195–96
Prayer, 64, 68, 151
    asking God's assistance in prayers, 63–64, 80–81, 82–83, 243
    ending for in Hindu prayers, 77
    "house of prayer" as a symbol, 179
    how to pray, 51
    prayer vs. using Lord's name in vain, 67
    use of mantras, 83, 83n6
    as a weapon in God's arsenal, 62
    when prayer is difficult, 166, 167
    See also Lord's Prayer; *Shema Yisrael*
Premeditated murder. *See* Murder, distinguishing gradations and types
Present moment, being in, 27, 235, 247
    enjoying the moment, 36, 84, 251–52, 260
    happiness is already within, 261
Pride, 78, 181, 197, 279
    excessive pride, 194, 202
    healthy pride, 195
    self-praise, 227
    unhealthy, 227
Procrastination, 218–19, 269, 276
    as a false god, 32–33, 37, 213
Promiscuous sex, 153, 155, 160
Promised Land, 23, 75, 103
Promises
    keeping promises, 229
    Ten Commandments as promises, 45, 135–36
Pure Land (Buddhism), 103

Q

Qualities, Divine. *See* Divine qualities
Qur'an, 12, 24–26, 52, 53, 85, 101, 150, 179, 210, 222
    Arabic meaning: "continuous recitation, 24–25
    citations from. *See* Citation Index, Qur'an
    as the holy book given by Allah to Muhammad, 25
    use of term "stealth," 178
    See also Islam; Muhammad

R

Rape, false accusations of, 205–207
Raskolnikov, Rodion (fictional character), 171–75
Rastafarian, 59

Rationalization, to justify behavior, 217, 218, 219, 228
Ratzach (Hebrew meaning: "murder"), 127, 141
Reason, false reliance on, 174
Reasonable cause, 124n10
Reboot (organization), 72
Reconciliation rather than revenge, 124
Reconnecting with God, through the Sabbath, 74, 78, 81, 85, 109
Reflection and practice
    related to honoring marriage and not committing adultery, 165–68
    related to honoring parents and seeing the best in others, 115–17
    related to identifying false gods in your life, 43–45
    related to keeping the Sabbath holy and letting the Divine work, 91–93
    related to not committing murder/spiritual murder but rather be life-giving, 141–43
    related to not coveting, 259–65
    related to not lying or bearing false witness, 227–29
    related to not stealing but being a credit-giver, 201–203
    related to not taking God's name in vain, 67–69
    use of within chapters, 15
Relationships
    basis for good relationships, 147, 147n3
    coveting and jealousy in, 244–45, 253, 260
    and do-overs, 68
    as false gods, 36, 38
    and forgiveness, 165
    with God, 56, 154, 168
    with others, 82, 85, 140, 156, 157–58, 191
        with parents, 105, 106, 107, 109, 111, 115, 162, 163
        sexual relationships, 149n4, 153, 154–55, 158–59, 164, 254–55
Religion
    etymology of word, 74
    teaching in college, 7–8, 8n1, 9, 10–11
    See also names of major world religions (i.e., Judaism, Christianity, Islam, Hinduism, and Buddhism)
Religious services, as a source of spiritual renewal, 91
    See also Sabbath day
Remorse, genuine, 174
Reputation, ruining someone's, 126, 127, 132, 140, 141
    See also Spiritual murder
"Re-seeing" parents, 110–11, 115–16
Retaliation, law of, 123, 124, 209, 276
Riches, spiritual. *See* Wealth
"Right effort" (*chanda*) and "Right endeavor," 241
    See also Noble Eightfold Path
"Right Speech," 212

T

Citation index

Note

In order to provide the most accurate, readable, and useful translation of a particular scriptural passage, we have used a variety of scholarly sources, sometimes blending the best aspects of available translations. Passages from the Hebrew and Greek scriptures (Judaism and Christianity) are primarily based on the *New King James Version* of the Bible (NKJV). However, we have also made ample use of the website "Bible Gateway" which offers over sixty different translations of Bible verses. Similarly, passages from the Arabic scriptures (Islam) are primarily based on the *The Holy Qur'an* (translated by 'Abdullah Yūsef 'Ali), but we have also used the website, "Islam Awakened" which provides over forty acceptable translations of the *Qur'an*. For translations of the Sanskrit scriptures (Hinduism and Buddhism), we primarily relied on the scholarship of Sri Eknath Easwaran (translator of the *Bhagavad Gita* and the *Dhammapada*). We also used *A Sourcebook in Indian Philosophy* (edited by Sarvepalli Radhakrishnan and Charles Moore). Just as the various religions help to illuminate the many aspects of the same gem, the various translations of a passage help to reveal the deeper meaning of the scriptures. As it is written, "In your light, we see light" (Psalm 36:9).

B

P

Q

56776732R00175

Made in the USA
Middletown, DE
24 July 2019